O
COME
YE
BACK
TO
IRELAND

O
COME
YE
BACK
TO
IRELAND

Our First Year In County Clare

Niall Williams
&
Christine Breen

Pen and ink drawings by Christine Breen

Portions of "Inniskeen Road: July Evening" and "Spraying the Potatoes" from *The Collected Poems* by Patrick Kavanagh, copyright © 1964 by Patrick Kavanagh, quoted by kind permission of Devin-Adair Publications. A portion of Chapter Three appeared in somewhat different form in *Ireland of the Welcomes* magazine.

Published in the United States of America by
Soho Press, Inc.
1 Union Square
New York, NY 10003

Library of Congress Cataloging-in-Publication Data
Williams, Niall, 1958–
    O come ye back to Ireland.

    1. Clare—Social life and customs. 2. Farm life—
Ireland—Clare. 3. Williams, Niall, 1958–
4. Breen, Christine, 1954–   . I. Breen, Christine,
1954–   . II. Title.
DA990.C59W55 1987   941.9'3   87–12420
ISBN 0-939149-22-2

Manufactured in the United States of America
1ST PAPERBACK EDITION

*This book is dedicated to all those who
believed in us,
to all those whose dreams we carried with us,
to all our neighbors and friends in Kilmihil,
and to Sabra.*

Authors'
Note

This book was written by two people. Few episodes belonged exclusively to either of us—whether in the living or the writing. Sections were drawn from both our journals and from many long, enjoyable conversations as we sat alone before the turf fire on dark winter evenings. Each of our pens has had a part in the work and it is hoped that this book bears witness to that.

CHAPTER ONE

Driving on the wrong side of the road, Christine managed better and better as we passed through each town on the last stage of our journey from New York City to Kiltumper Cottage. From Naas through Kildare and the green richness of the Curragh. Monasterevin, Portlaoise, Mountrath, Roscrea, Nenagh and Limerick. The rain began to fall as we crossed the Shannon and entered West Clare. The road to Ennis became narrower and wetter; past Ennis, the rain poured. We were dispirited. When we finally drove into Kilmihil, the nearest village to our future home, we entered a landscape of gray rain. A place all closed unto itself. Our car bumped along the potholed road and it seemed that we had left the village of Kilmihil even as we entered it. Was that *it?* There was not a single person on the street, and whatever shops there were looked closed. We had come

1

three thousand miles from one of the largest cities in the world to this—a village that had gone to sleep on a rainy Wednesday afternoon. Our first impressions were not pleasant ones, but having made our choice we journeyed ahead and hoped for the best.

Kilmihil is a village of two main roads. It is also a parish encompassing nearly four hundred families. Kiltumper is a townland. (Within the parish there are approximately fifty townlands.) Townlands vary in size; our townland of Kiltumper consists of about three hundred acres. Nine families live within it. Most are the families of farmers.

From Kilmihil to Kiltumper was a long two miles. After a sharp dip in the road to the left the road drops down into a *botharin* (Irish for a tiny little road), then continues down past our cottage. But our first stop was at our new neighbors, Mary Breen and her brother-in-law, Joe Breen. (Mary, a widow, sold the farm to Chris's father. When Mary moved to her new home, Joe, who had always lived with his brother and Mary, naturally moved with her.) No sooner had the car stopped than Mary came out in the lashing rain to greet us. Huddled in the wet, she grasped our city hands and warmly said, "Welcome to Kiltumper, Crissy and Niall. I hope you'll be happy here."

We nodded and smiled, but at that rainy moment outside Mary's new bungalow on the road to Kiltumper Cottage, neither of us could imagine ever being happy there.

Tea, scones and Mary's brown bread by the warm turf fire made us welcome. She and Joe gazed at us with as much disbelief as we felt. So, we were really there. The four of us stared out over the view of rainswept fields and cowering cattle while drinking strong sweet mugs of tea. It seemed forever before Mary put down the last mug and said, "Now," (Mary pronounced it with two syllables) "will we go back to the house?"

"We will."

And so bundled into the car, we drove slowly off along the road on the last lap of the journey. A winding narrow road the width of one car, it was strange and new to us as it rose bumpily around three bends.

"These are yer fields," said Mary waving her hand to the land to the right of us. The fields and meadows were bounded by hedgerows of whitethorn, blackthorn, and gorse—called furze here—just breaking into yellow fruity blossom. As we passed them they seemed daunting and a major undertaking to maintain. Within minutes we had swept past the little green iron gate of the cottage's front path and the great bushes of privet and wild rose and fuchsia that grew around it. Briefly, we glimpsed the gray house before driving into the *street* (as driveways are called) bordered on both sides by two-hundred-year-old stone *cabins* (sheds) where hens, chickens, turkeys, pigs, cows and calves might be kept.

Our anticipation and hesitation were tremendous but we restrained exclamations and comments because we were in company. Mary stopped at the back door before entering and said, "Welcome and God bless all here." Then suddenly we were inside Kiltumper Cottage in the middle of a very white kitchen.

It was extraordinarily small. We were astounded, although neither of us could say so. In the two years since we had last seen it, our imaginations had drawn it much, much larger. The floors were, of course, poured concrete, flaking and musty and dusty. The whole place smelled damp. The hearth, huge and black, filled the entire opposite wall, a gigantic maw. Mary was looking keenly at us. What did we think?

"I hope ye like it, Crissy."

"Oh, I do, it's lovely," Chris responded with as much enthusiasm as her distraught spirit could gather, which seemed to soothe Mary's anxiety, allowing her to point out the cottage's claim to loveliness: the freshly painted white walls. (We were later to discover that the locals called it the White House.)

It was certainly bright. Brighter even than we had imagined. The windows that we had remembered as small in fact extended almost from floor to ceiling, making the rooms strikingly cheerful and open. They face south; beyond, though invisible, lies the Shannon River. A hill rises greenly from a valley about one hundred yards from the front door and as we walked from room to room it was to this southern view that we found ourselves drawn.

The door frames are barely six feet high. For days I went in peril of cracking my head. There wasn't any furniture except an old sugan chair—a wooden chair made by hand without using nails. The seat of woven straw is called *sugan*, although in modern times the sugan has been replaced by colored cord. It was the very same chair that Chris had sat upon inside the hearth fifteen years ago, when she made her first visit to the cottage. The other furniture we had previously envisioned buying now seemed totally out of place. The whole interior had to be rethought, for it was after all a cottage, and over two hundred years old. There were no big rooms among these five. We chided ourselves for having romanticized it.

What did we think? What could we say? It was less and more than we'd anticipated. The walls are two and a half feet thick, but wind gusted from a thousand drafty cracks, under doors and through window frames. We told Mary that we loved it even as we felt a sinking foolishness. After all, this was it. We were here now.

We had not left New York to come to live in the West of Ireland without much agonizing over the decision.

"Tell me how it's going to be there, Niall," had

been Christine's favorite question as our departure became imminent. She asked it of me late at night or early in the morning.

"It will be grand," I would reply with ardor. "We will have time and beauty. We will make the house a home of books and music, of painting and flowers, of homemade bread and hot scones, of pullets and piglets, carrots and turnips, and the thick, sweet scent of turf fires. We will get up early in the morning with strong brewed cups of tea, and go to work in the garden, feed the animals and tend to the house. We will use the fine changing light of afternoon for more tea and work, writing and painting until later at nightfall, we will drive circular, coastal roads to the sea. To Doolin to hear music and see the majestic, mood-heavy tumble of the world's greatest ocean.

"We will have a party at the house shortly after we get there and invite everyone around and get to know them all—the parish priest of St. Michael's, the publicans, the fiddlers of Kilmihil. What stories we will hear, the folklore of Clare and the tall night tales of such musical, magical places as Kilfenora, Corofin and Kilnamona. And tales, too, of the place itself, where the house was built, and where up under the back fields the great giant himself—Kiltumper—is buried."

It was with these hopes and plans that we assuaged the anxiety which came and went as we prepared to set out. We, Niall and Chris, an aspiring young couple working in Manhattan, with good jobs and lofty expectations, had resolved to quit everything to go and live on a farm in the wild West of Ireland. And we would be going to Ireland to make our "fame and fortune" when Irish emigration was at its highest in years.

It might not seem so strange that I should be returning to Ireland since that is where I was born, in an affluent section of Dublin called Stillorgan. But

Dublin is almost two hundred miles and a world away from the rugged farming country of West Clare where we were headed. And Chris was practically a native New Yorker, reared in easy circumstances in Westchester County, and unaccustomed to many of the ways of Ireland, much less those of the rural West. Yet, after much hesitation, and with many lingering misgivings, we had decided to do it. Over the Christmas holidays we had given ourselves one hundred days in which to take leave of one life and begin another. The big day was to be March 28, 1985.

We had met at University College Dublin (UCD). Americans think of Trinity College in Dublin when they think of an Irish university but, in fact, UCD is Ireland's national university. Chris had come to study for a Master's degree in Anglo-Irish literature and drama. I wanted to be a writer and was enrolled in UCD's Master's degree program in American and English literature. Our courtship started the moment we sat next to each other in the cafeteria. I was eating chips (an Irish version of French fries) and Chris, yogurt and an apple. Two years later we were married in New York.

Chris had first visited Ireland when she was seventeen. She had gone with her father and grandmother to visit the birthplace of her deceased grandfather. A cousin, John Breen, and his wife Mary were still living there in Kiltumper Cottage and farming the land. On subsequent visits to Ireland, Chris had always been drawn back to the cottage.

The first time I ever heard of the place was at Eastertime that year in which we had met at UCD. Johnny Breen had died, and Chris, the visiting cousin from America, went to the village of Kilmihil for the funeral. In retrospect, it seems to me that from that first sad tiding of sudden death, all that followed led, inevitably, to our present resolve to go and live in Kiltumper. But it took us five years to realize it. Mary

6

Breen had to decide to put the farm up for sale; then Chris's father had to decide to buy it. Now the cottage stood empty, the fifty acres of grassland which came with it leased until the end of this year to a local farmer. And it had called to us.

We were settled in New York, our feet on the first rung of the proverbial ladder. We fitted the young, upwardly mobile picture; we were eager for a better life. Chris was employed at a professional journal and I worked at a mass market publishing house where I wrote advertising copy and a romance newsletter under the pen name, Sarah Reynolds. But ever since the possibility of going to live at Kiltumper dawned on us, our days had been checkered with arguments for and against the idea. We each had a lot to think about as neither of us had ever lived on a farm. We went to visit the place together twice and twice we felt certain that we could never live there. It struck us as so utterly different from anywhere we had ever been, so remote, so very rural. Each time we shook our heads, and returned to New York.

Why then did we change our minds and commit ourselves to the West of Ireland? Because when we walked up the streets of Manhattan too many people pushed too hard to cross the street or squeezed too hard to get into too few subways? Because on a beautiful summerlit day there was no time to catch anything but the tiniest part of it in the dying evening? Because the dullness of corporate days flecked our lives not with the great pressures and pleasures of high executivedom but with the tiny, mundane weariness of insignificant duties? Because the winters in New York are too cold and the summers too hot? Because we couldn't imagine working and living and raising the family we hoped to have in New York? Because, and probably most of all, on certain days that Irish *feeling* came and, as the train sped us from the city to our apartment in a suburb, the light, dying against the windows, was replaced by the remembered image of the cottage and the fields, the bright nights of August gleaming past ten o'clock, and fuchsia redly blooming like crazy, high as the hedgerows. And there would suddenly be the sense of a place far from the rushing streets, a place remote from the extravagant, urgent business of today, an old place growing older in the rain. There were a thousand reasons not to go, but one that irresistibly beckoned.

We had to dismantle our old life. We moved from our apartment in a Victorian house in Mt. Kisco, sold our furniture and put our new car up for sale. Everything we were not taking with us—our entire past life—had to fit into ten cardboard boxes which Chris's sister had agreed to store for us in a closet. She was also kind enough to take temporary charge of our books and wedding china. We threw most of our old clothes out and donated the rest to charity.

The cost of flying to Ireland and buying a car there would not leave us with much money to buy furniture or rugs or other necessities. Were we seeing the pitfalls too late? We battled with figures, trying to make a budget. And finally, when the equation was nearly—but not quite—balanced, the greater sum seemed to have an unaccountable dash of romance, that easy Irishry that shrugs its shoulders at the practical world and goes on down the road in the blue evening whistling a tune.

At last, the day came when we gave our notice and quit our jobs. We were buoyant and giddy with freedom and stepped out like swimmers before the incoming tide, full of energy and hope. As numerous people stopped by my office, I told as many versions of Kiltumper as there were questions. But by five o'clock my enthusiasm had worn thin. After all, in the hush of the stories and the laughter, the same stubborn fact remained; *we* were the ones who were actually going to do it. As I went to the elevator I was the loneliest man in the building. I was already out, already in another world in the eyes of every executive. When a senior vice-president got into the elevator he smiled knowingly at me.

"So," he said, "I hear you're off to live in Scotland."

Suddenly our plans receded into unimportance as Chris's grandmother O'Connell died after a long, courageous struggle with cancer and our last days assumed a new shape, grief. We had a wake and funeral and our minds were full of Nonni O'Connell.

Her mother was a MacGillacuddy, one of Ireland's ancient, noble families from Kerry, who gave their name to the country's highest mountains —the MacGillacuddy Reeks.

During the spring-warm day of her funeral, Chris and I vowed: This summer we will visit the heights of the MacGillacuddy Reeks and, on the green hilltops, say a prayer for Nonni.

The next day we boarded the airplane landing, finally, in Dublin. And now we were here, here in Kiltumper, the place where we had resolved to make our home. But before we could actually move in to the cottage much had to be done. Fortunately, Mary Breen had offered to put us up until that day.

After viewing our future home, we drove Mary up to Dooley's, her sister Breda's house, to visit their aging mother Nora. At Dooley's, there was a low turf fire built on the floor. With generous welcome, more tea, more scones and more brown bread were offered. Having eaten a half-hour before, we were not hungry.

"Will ye have a cup of tea?" urged Breda.

"No, thanks, we won't."

"You won't?" Breda said with surprise. But from a chair in one corner of the semi-dark room, Michael Dooley suddenly spoke.

"You will have a cup of tea in my house." It was an urging of his will, hospitality that was not to be refused.

"We will so," I said, and smiled as Breda poured.

We were welcomed by Mary's mother, Nora, who, at 84, was ailing and was in a bed in the next room which we visited. With kerchief about her white head and her large bony hands laying out on the blankets before her, she welcomed us with a nod and a smile.

"Yer down in the house of Jack O' the Grove," she said to us.

"Who?"

"Jack O' the Grove. Yer in the Grove."

"He would have been Crissie's great-grandfather," explained Mary.

It was the fifth anniversary of Johnny Breen's death we were startled to learn. Had we known, we would have delayed our arrival a couple of days. But just so are things in Ireland. Coincidences, patterns, and omens all blown together in the wind and the rain. After supper, then, we drove to the Church.

Religious practice in America is relatively open; we had come to an intensely Catholic country. And nothing is more religiously intense in Ireland than Holy Week. Mass on Spy Wednesday was at eight. At half-past seven with Mary and Joe alongside we were in the lovely, creamy yellow and pink church of St. Michael's. A mass was being offered for Johnny's anniversary. No sooner were we in the church than there began the long prayer of the rosary. Mary began a Hail Mary; halfway through she paused and another woman took up the prayer and completed it. She began the next, and another woman, somewhere further away in the pews, finished that. And so it built, one lone voice rushing through the half prayer, and a chorus ending it. Soon the church was humming, the prayers rising to a crescendo with

10

astonishing, spellbinding power. Chris and I were swept up into the rhythm of the rosary. The force of belief is immense and the monotone voice of two hundred people in unbidden prayer in the country church brought us, more than any other single thing, into Ireland.

The place was packed. There were seven in a pew, kneeling shoulder to shoulder. Before the priest came to the altar another woman hurried up the aisle. There was no room for her, but she stopped abruptly before our pew, genuflected and, simply as you like, bumped her way in! And *then* there came the last of the latecomers. All along the church women bumped into place, pushing into the pews till the church actually seemed to bulge outward and the whole place was like a bellows of prayer, rising and falling with Hail Marys and the thunderous murmur of faith.

While it was still bright we returned from church. (In Ireland, the clocks had already been changed for summer time). Chris and I decided to go over to the cottage by ourselves before dark. We still hadn't told each other what we felt, having been surrounded since we had arrived by well-wishers and welcomers. We left a trail of people talking about us—the visitors, the Yanks.

Twilight is the best time. Blue skies prevail and the clouds and the day die in the West with a beautiful flourish of light. The fields are a fabulous rich green and it seems like another day entirely, nothing to do with the dull wet morning. Chris turned to me with a smile as we reached the peak of the hilly road with an overview of the pastures in the valley. There was a look between us: it was for *this* we had come.

And so to Kiltumper Cottage for the second time. We were more prepared. Our imaginations had started anew to redefine our new home. Chris went in ahead of me and looked at each room with an eye to interior design; she saw a table here, and a telephone alongside, a chair over there by the window so that we could sit and look across the meadows toward the coast and the deep green waters that, eventually, lapped the shores of Long Island.

In the brilliant light of evening the windows were an even greater delight. There was nothing to block the light, the beams were undeflected by buildings. I was standing by one of the windows when Chris yelled from the parlor and ran to me.

"Niall, there's somebody in there!"

Crouched, fearing that someone had been living in the empty house, I went toward the room we had decided would be our bedroom.

"Who's there! Come out!"

The door was closed and my call startled a fury of activity into being as if someone was hurriedly putting away a scattering of papers. No one came forth. I put one hand on the doorknob. Chris was standing just behind me, peering forward.

Suddenly we swung open the door, ready to jump or be jumped by the intruder. And there he was: an enormous shiny black jackdaw! Swaggering busily about in the all-white room he tried to ignore us in his search for the way out. Another omen, we thought. A black bird in a white room on the fifth anniversary of Johnny Breen's death. Timidly, in different directions, the three of us moved about: the bird leaping and strutting with characteristic jerky strides, toward the window; I going over to it with open hands; and Chris charging from the room to the front garden. At last I managed to open the window, and at last he managed to get free. When he went, it seemed like the departure of something more than a bird. It was *our* new home now. The next day we would begin to fix it.

The following day was mottled with rain clouds and disappointed our waking hopes. But the sense of our waiting chores back at the cottage got us up and out despite the weather. There were things to be done. Our bed was expected to arrive from England any day and we wanted to have the bedroom ready to receive it. And the garden had to be dug. We had arrived in the very heart of busy springtime and every day lost meant a smaller, later harvest. And so, after morning tea and brown bread and fresh farm eggs, we went back to the cottage to begin.

But *where* were we to begin? Once we entered the cottage we sat in the deep windowsill of the bathroom (which used to be a bedroom when the bathroom was just outside the back door). It was as if we were at the heart of a maze. We were overwhelmed by the enormity of the tasks ahead. Mary had given us a bottle of milk and a spoonful of loose tea, and so, unable to decide what to do, we did what all Irish men and women do: we had tea.

Suddenly the sun appeared and not for the first or last time we felt it uplifting us and changing everything. It seemed like a holiday. With borrowed shovel I went out into the garden to tackle the weeds while Chris tried to light our first turf fire in the Stanley oven.

Out in the garden I dug with energy. Like most city people when first faced with a shoveling job I went at it with great gusto. I concentrated on the actual task and the more energy I threw into it, the faster it went. I had no sense of pace. That is something the earth itself teaches you, for when you look at any countryman digging a field you will notice that he seems to do it with remarkable slowness and ease. But of course the secret is really the pacing and the rhythm of the land. Knowing nothing of such things, I threw myself into it. With a cavalier romantic spirit I thought I'd impress Chris with my first hour's digging. But, it was harder work than I had done in months. The weeds were deeply settled and didn't come away in easy shovelfuls. They needed repeated

13

pulling and hacking, and within the first boastful hour I raised a neat line of blisters all along the inside of my hand. This, then, was the beginning of it, I said to myself. The sun was beaming broadly and the garden was beautifully sheltered on all sides. Smoke puffed pleasantly from the chimney as Chris waved successfully from the kitchen window; I felt like a king.

CHRIS'S JOURNAL

I am impatient to get started. There is so much that needs doing, not to mention fixing! All the floors need coverings, but we can't afford that! There's dust everywhere! And drafts everywhere! The cabins are full of stuff and dead, dry animal manure. The garden is absolutely ruined. Not a bare spot of earth to sow a seed anywhere. Are we crazy? Only the rhubarb patch has survived. We must have some of the biggest, healthiest rhubarb I have ever seen. I recall my father remembering that his father had a love of stewed rhubarb: a link back to Kiltumper perhaps?

That first day working in the cottage we imagined it would be only a week before we were settled in the house. And even that week seemed to be a long time to wait.

As showers came and went across the afternoon sky the day had a dozen different weathers, each one as fickle and brief as the one before. Rain of course is a familiar visitor here and no one pays it much mind. (That is, of course, until the rain becomes a constant companion.) While I was digging in the garden,

Joe Breen—Chris's cousin, Mary's brother-in-law—looked through the green iron gate. Rain softly pelleted from the gray sky.

"How's it going?" he asked of me.

"It's going fine, Joe," I shouted back to him as I was about to run inside before the downpour that seemed to threaten us.

"Fine day," he continued in what seemed to be dead seriousness. I was talking with him simply out of courtesy. Rain was bucketing down and we had no coats.

"Will you come in, Joe?" I asked him at last as he tossed away the butt of his cigarette.

"I will so," he answered. "It's getting heavy now." He was only waiting for an invitation.

Half an hour later the sky was clear and blue again. The garden was full of birdsong. Chris marched me out and told me where to dig. She actually saw some pattern to the wilderness and went about the weeds like a treasure-seeker, head down and poking about. Within an hour she had rescued wild strawberries, perpetual onions, and a few other stalwart perennials. All picked carefully from their waywardness and now saved to be transplanted into place once I had gotten the soil ready.

She is the brains behind this, I thought. How would I know what to rescue from whatever was growing? No. I prepared the ground. A kind of reverse sexism, a pattern that would in the months ahead seem complementary to our relationship.

We made our first steps in the house and garden. It seemed a lot and a very little. Would we ever be moved in and the garden growing and the typewriter keys clicking softly against the fall of night? Would Chris ever stand by the great front window with her easel up, brush stroking across the canvas? For a moment, I caught a glimpse of those days.

Tell me how it's going to be there, Niall. But the

blisters stung, black with dirt, and the spade hit nothing but rocks.

Good Friday was a beautiful day, warm and bright and cloudless. In the sunlight the yellow blossoms of the furze dazzled us with color. The roads were lined with them, big wild bushes toppling over stone walls and invading good grassland. We were delighted and inspired, and that morning worked with high hearts digging out the new garden. There's no feeling quite as satisfying as the sense of triumph in seeing a garden begin to come alive. As we tore out the couch, or scutch grass, and other perennial weeds, and lifted off a layer of stones we could see it happening: the brown bed of earth becoming ours.

Again we lit the fire in the Stanley range to dry out the dampness of five neglected years. The Stanley is the heart of our home. It has replaced the open hearth as the center of many kitchens—the room where the living is really done. It has two dampers and lighting it is no small trick. It takes a while to get used to its operation. Like any solid-fuel cooker, it must be fed continually if it is to reach the temperature at which it will not only heat iron skillets for cooking but also the boiler tank upon which we depend for hot water. At the cottage we had a small "rick" (stack) of turf, fuel to keep our fires burning until summer.

Everything ceased on Good Friday afternoon. And from every house people set out on bicycle, tractor, foot and car to the village. Every car was full of neighbors. By the time we drove in along the potholed road the village streets were packed. A line of farmers stood along the path outside the church, and before three o'clock Kilmihil itself came to a complete halt. You could hear the wind blow lonely out along the country roads. There were no sounds of tractors or of men working then, and the crossroads were blocked with triple-parked cars and vans. No one would travel those roads for an hour, for no decent person would be anywhere but in church!

In St. Michael's, the pews were packed as tightly as a football stadium. The Hail Marys had already begun by the time we squeezed in and the pretty church was again asway with prayer. We were sitting on the outside. But not for long! Within moments the crush was on and a short, stout woman elbowed us in. A minute later, Chris was in the middle of a bulging, murmurous row of big, devout Clarewomen. It seemed as if nothing anywhere in the world outside was happening. Everything had come to this: a packed little church of prayers on a warm Good Friday in the West of Ireland.

In Manhattan Chris had asserted that we would use no chemicals of any kind in the garden. Least of all weedkillers. *We* were to be the weedkillers, but by the time we stood amidst the tangles of weeds in Kiltumper we felt doomed. Spring was about to overtake us, and for the two of us to dig the entire garden and lift out the deep-rooted weeds would take months. We *needed* something.

"Where would we get weedkiller?" I asked Mary Breen.

"Down at Eamonn's," came the replay.

"Who's he and where is he?"

"He's the chemist in the village," she informed me. Chemist, I knew, meant drugstore owner.

We went to his little shop. A bell rang when we opened the door, and from behind a narrow plastic-striped curtain came a genial, round-faced man with smiling blue eyes. He looked like he had just been told a joke. We had the sense he would burst out laughing in a moment.

He knew at once who we must be, for the rumors had certainly preceded us. Yet he said nothing, and waited until we introduced ourselves.

"Hello," I said. I'm Niall Williams and this is my wife, Chris. We're moving into the old house back up in Kiltumper. Mary Breen sent us down to you because we need weedkiller."

"You have a lot of weeds," he said with a grin. Leaving us to consider this statement he disappeared into the room from which he had earlier emerged and returned with a plastic bottle marked "poison" with skull and crossbones pictured on the label in a black warning.

"That will do it for you," he said smartly.

"How will we apply it?" asked Chris. He looked at her with bright blue eyes and said, "You'll need a knapsack sprayer."

"But we don't have one," she said.

"Oh, you don't indeed, but you'll need one anyway. It's dangerous poison." He pointed to the label.

"Well, where would we get one?" asked Chris, pursuing the thing with American thoroughness.

The little chemist paused a moment, that brief happy instant in which the laughter rolled around inside his head. He weighed carefully his sought-for opinion.

"Well, now, I'll tell you what you do. You ask Mary Breen if yer man who lives just a few roads over from you doesn't have a sprayer. I'm certain he'll be glad to do it for you. It'll just take him ten minutes."

"Will he really do it for us?" asked Chris, delighted by this further demonstration of the warm and generous welcome the local people were prepared to give us.

"Oh, he'll take care of your weeds all right. He's a great man for the weeds."

With that we left his shop with a great sense of gratitude and good fortune.

Back at Mary's, we shared our news with her. We gave her the description of the man who the chemist had said would help us. Mary burst out laughing: a breathless happy giggle spilled from her and she couldn't even speak.

"Him?" she said. "*Him*, indeed. Sure *he*'s the last man to kill any weeds, Crissie. Everyone knows *he*'s famous for having weeds all over his own house!"

She giggled again thinking of it. And we were again welcomed to Kilmihil.

CHAPTER TWO

We drove to Dublin for Easter to be with my parents. A journey of one hundred and eighty miles, but the distance itself hardly measures the difference between east and west, between "culchie" (country fella') and "jackeen" (Dublin fella'), between country and capital. We had only been in Kiltumper for four days, but by the time we reached my parents' house we felt as if we had arrived in *another* country. We were back in more familiar surroundings. There were thicker carpets on the floors, color television with BBC programs, central heating, albeit timed so that it went off during mid-day, and restaurants, bookshops and movie theaters.

Easter in Ireland has always been a nostalgic, emotional time. For besides the religious climax of the church year, there is the dual national remembrance of the Easter Rising of 1916. In my boyhood, the Easter Parade was as much a highlight and thrill as opening chocolate Easter eggs and breaking the Lenten fast. The parade as it came down O'Connell Street—the largest street in Dublin's City Center— was mostly composed of the military: soldiers and artillery and jeeps, everything a schoolboy loves. And then there were the old men, survivors, contemporaries of the Rising who walked beneath banners of commemoration.

It says much for the present political climate in Ireland, with the Northern conflict sixteen years old, that there is no longer any military Easter parade. Emotional associations between the Easter Rising and the outlawed Irish Republican Army are strong, and continuing the parade would only invite turmoil and clash.

Easter Sunday was swept by windy rain. It was the kind of weather for which Ireland is known. Nowhere else does the sky gather so grayly and the clouds seem so ominously threatening. And when the rain falls ceaselessly on a Sunday afternoon there is nowhere gloomier. We sat all day and evening by a warm coal fire but as the rain lashed down, our minds were chilled with thoughts of Kiltumper on such a day. For this, too, was Ireland. Undeniably damp, gray, cold, and thoroughly, utterly miserable. Chris was frozen and sat with her cold toes on the radiator.

Back to Kiltumper on Easter Monday for our second start. Before we saw Dublin again we would be settled in the West, moved in and living in the cottage with garden, paintings and stories well underway.

Our bed, the bed that Chris had picked out over many lunch hours in Manhattan, had arrived in Ireland from England at the end of March. But there its journey halted, for in Ireland everything goes slowly. First, there was VAT (Value Added Tax on luxury items) to be paid, which was a staggering twenty-five percent. We were crushed, our budget was crushed. But the bed wouldn't move from Dublin until the tax was paid. Then, to get the bed brought to Kiltumper, there would be another charge. It was going to be the most expensive bed in the country.

Stranded, without a stick of furniture in the cottage (beside the sugan chair) we were hopeful that once the tax was paid at least the bed would come speedily. Fast Sea and Air should surely be able to deliver it in a day or two. Meanwhile we were guests at Mary Breen's, we were "the visitors" to the people in the village, and we were desperate to get settled.

We had faced a similar situation when we tried to buy a car in Dublin before setting out for the West. After our flight from New York we had stopped over at my parents' to get over our jet lag and to find ourselves an auto. We heard about a 1979 model 504 Peugeot. Someone in Dublin wryly told us that all farmers had them, which they don't, of course, as we later learned: most West Clare farmers drive Fords. (What little they know in Dublin!) The purchase price turned out to be more than the two thousand pounds Chris had budgeted for, but a good used Toyota, which we had been hoping to find, seemed scarce and we felt we couldn't wait—we had to get to Clare. The Peugeot seemed perfect. On that very Sunday afternoon, it was brought up to Kilmacud for us to see. In a flurry of excitement after the Sunday mid-day dinner, my father, Jack, put on his tweed hat, Mam took off her apron, and out we went for our first spin in the new car. It looked wonderful all right, and the four of us sitting expectantly looked lovely too, but . . . the blasted car wouldn't start. No hand turning the key could ignite the engine. We all tried. And we sat in a stupor until at last, rain lashing down, we ran into the house. "Well, it's a fine-looking car, really," my mother said, "and it's a small thing, really, that it won't start."

Once that "small obstacle" was overcome, our next major step was to procure insurance. We asked mother (Philo, short for Philomena) how much insurance would cost and, pausing first, she deftly answered, "A fortune!" It was a typical Irish answer, nice and vague.

Jack was next to be asked. Deliberating sadly, in deep perplexity he said, "Chris may not be able to get insurance."

"Why wouldn't she?" I asked. "She's been driving fourteen years."

"Well, when I called the PMPA, Ireland's leading insurance company, they said they wouldn't insure an *alien*." The past four years in America *I* had been the alien; suddenly the coin was flipped. Chris became distraught and defensive.

"Well, that's what *they* said anyway," said Jack. "I just don't know. They consider she's been driving fourteen years on the *wrong* side of the road."

Chris could hardly contain her frustration between this and the next fact—that we would have to pay a government road tax on the car based not on the year or make but on the engine size. We felt a surge of helplessness. We might have been in India or Greece, the rules seemed so impenetrable. It wouldn't have mattered as much about Chris not getting insurance if *I* could have gotten it. However, I didn't even have a driver's license. It's not unusual in Irish cities for young men and women not to be able to drive. First of all, access to a car is limited because they are so expensive and most families only have one, which is used nearly exclusively by the parents. Second, insurance for first-time drivers is exorbitant.

It seemed to us that insuring and buying a car in Ireland would debar us before we even got started. But, we fortunately learned that in Ireland all rules can be bent if not broken; with American forthrightness Chris called a friend of her uncle's who she knew had something to do with insurance. She didn't realize that he was the chairman of the board of one of Dublin's most prestigious insurance companies. On Sunday he was roused from his table to hear Chris beseeching him to help. He remembered her, of course agreed to help us, and added, "Welcome to Ireland."

They said it couldn't be done. In Ireland you cannot expect to open a bank account, get a checkbook, buy a car, insure your car and drive off before the day is dark. We were thinking too fast, too New York-ish! Yet, insurance came through, the bank account was opened and the check for two thousand two hundred pounds cashed without our having to wait for the funds to clear.

We could only hope that once more we would find that where there's a will, there's a way to get action. But matters were not being helped by the Irish telephone system in the West. Kiltumper, Kilmihil and even Kilrush were all still without direct dial telephones. Indeed, many houses had no telephone, and those that did often reserved it for the rare, long-distance call to relatives in England or America. And so, to call Dublin, we first had to ring round the winder and get the operator down in the village. This was not always easy. As the operator himself told us, "Operators must sleep, too." Kilmihil would then crank up Kilrush and bestir them to send our call; Kilrush, in turn, would crank up Ennis. From there the line to Dublin would hum and buzz for minutes until the call went through. All this underlined our isolation here. Even Dublin seemed a vague, faraway place. Consequently, we focused our attention inward and occupied ourselves with the chores of house and garden.

On the timeless gray days of that second week, we put in our potatoes, plopping them in furrows of fresh cow manure. Chris began seed trays of broccoli, zucchini, lettuce, chives, thyme and zinnias. The weeds had withered all around the edges. (We had compromised by using the chemical weedkiller but restricting its application to the borders of the garden where the nettles and knapweed were heaviest.) Soon the wet, black earth of the garden was exposed.

Evenings came slowly. Despite numerous calls to Dublin our bed still hadn't arrived. And there was nothing to be done but wait and return to our temporary home, tired, weary and anxious. Anxious to unpack our cases. Anxious to unpack our lives.

One day, Mary's bright blue eyes over the rim of her teacup were excited. She asked, "Have you heard the cuckoo?"

Neither of us knew what to answer, and our immediate thought was of a clock and not of a bird. I think I hardly even knew that there was such a real bird as the cuckoo.

"No, Mary, we haven't."

"Michael Donnellan (her brother) heard him this day on the bog," she said happily. "He's often the first to hear him." It was a boast we didn't yet appreciate, and as Mary recited the rhyme for us we got only an inkling of the cult of the cuckoo.

> The cuckoo comes in April
> He sings his song in May
> In the middle of June,
> he whistles his tune and
> In July he flies away.

The song of the cuckoo is a harbinger of the warm weather, a friendly portent of the summer to come. Against the knot of our impatience and frustrations it seemed another Irish omen. Yet we had not heard or seen him. We wondered if the robin was singing his tune in Westchester.

Without the money to do everything, or the tolerance to do nothing, we threw our energies into righting the more urgent wrongs. I came in from the field one day and found Chris working eye-level on the floor fixing the back door, bridging the broken wood where creatures might have made an entry to visit our pantry. She swept the concrete floor ten times a day, but the brush seemed to lift layer upon layer of the crumbling cement itself and soon the kitchen would be clouded with dust. Drafty windows were stuffed with newspaper. There was no room for American-style cleanliness here. We had to make do and adapt.

Our stone cottage. From the distance of photographs, or the memories of brief visits, it seemed the most idyllic place. Yes, we *had* idealized it. We *had* forgotten details: crumbling masonry of the stone cabins, flaking plaster that peels away from the plaster-covered stone walls of the house, rotting wood of the windows and doors. The odd slanting angles. The door doesn't meet the jamb and the wind whistles and howls. The misfit and the stuck and the broken. And the spiders. Oh, the spiders! Will we always be plagued by spiders with long legs spinning their webs in the corners, every corner?

And it's cold. Forget the days of T-shirts and bare feet. Even inside I'm wearing several layers of clothing. There's no hot water until I build up the fire. There will be none to wake up to. Taking a bath in the evening will no longer be a luxury but a chore. One healthy-sized bath will use the whole tank. It's like being on a permanent camp-out!

In Clare, all roads lead to Ennis. And to Ennis we drove to buy our floor coverings. Compared with our village, Ennis seemed like an extraordinarily busy, hectic place. Its streets are narrow and winding, and traffic snakes through them with a slow curious pace perfect for tourists. The tiny, old shops are packed tightly, and the whole town gives an impression of closeness and bustle. The shoppers ogle offerings with a cautious eye, for in the West of Ireland most shopping still consists of an assortment of glances, nods, headshakes, sighs and walking about the thing in question.

We were novices to all this. We walked into a shop advertising carpets, vinyls and furniture, and strolled about unattended. There was no sign of salesmen or customers. No prices were marked anywhere. It was only when we turned toward the door to leave that the salesman appeared. He was young, with the same clear eyes that Chris had noticed on many Claremen.

"Right so?" he said, and rubbed the palms of his hands softly together.

"We'd like to see the vinyls," we said. "We have a bare cement floor."

"Fine so," he said. "There's this." He pointed with his foot to one among a number of rolls. Again there were no prices. He seemed intensely preoccupied with some other mental perplexity, and, while we stood there staring at the roll he had pointed out, he moved to one side as if in a dream. Perhaps he was dreaming about his dinner as it was nearly half-past twelve. In watching him, we nearly forgot ourselves until Chris finally ventured, "Well, what about this?"

He came from his trance in a flash, looked at the

one she had pointed to and cautiously nodded. "There's that, too, all right," he said and instantly resumed his contemplation. At Chris's elbowing the vulgar task fell to me, and with apologetic and hushed voice, I asked, "How much is it?"

He seemed taken aback, quite literally, by our pointed query. It occurred to us that maybe people didn't usually buy on the first look and he must not have expected *us* to pursue the sale. As he stepped back, we followed.

"That one, is it?"

"Yes," said Chris, pressing him for an answer.

"Well, that one is . . . let me see now." By this time we had backtracked to the cash register. He was reading from some invisible book of figures.

"How large is the room?" he asked, and I showed him the dimensions, and again he calculated in his head, gauging as well our ability to pay.

"Forty pounds," he said at last.

"Will you put it in for that, too?"

"I will. But we can't send anyone until, let me see. . . ." His fingers roamed through the log-book.

"Wednesday next," he said, turning over a blank page. We groaned at once. He looked at us with surprise, for in Ireland, such service would actually be quite fast.

"We are waiting to move in," I explained to him. "It's my wife's birthday on Friday and we were hoping to be in by then." He looked from one to the other of us, then down again to the book.

"It'll be Friday so," he said, and penciling us in, turned upon me his best blue, conspiratorial smile.

We concluded our business by further buying a nine-by-twelve foam-backed, inexpensive carpet for the bedroom. The other rooms would have to wait.

We were sitting at breakfast at Mary's on Thursday morning.

"Do you know what I've thought of, Crissie?" she said. "Michael Dooley said that it was time ye applied to the forestry department for the burning of yer bog."

"What's that, Mary?"

"They come to burn yer bog."

"Why do they?"

"Because of the heather that's on it."

"Oh, I see," said Chris, not seeing at all. "Who are *they* anyway?"

As it turned out, *we* wanted *them* to burn the heather off our bog because heather holds water, which makes cutting and drying turf even more difficult than it already is. If we were to "open our own bank of turf" (which we would have to do), our bog, overgrown with beautiful wiry heather, had to be stripped bare. Unless the Department of Forestry came to oversee the burning, it would have to be stripped by hand. Then, the top "bar" of turf would be bad and the business of getting the bank opened at all would be all the more difficult. The Department of Forestry in Ireland carries out these burnings because they are concerned for the numerous new forests they have planted on the otherwise unfertile boglands of the West, and they are mindful of the birds that nest between April 15 and August 15. All this we learned over breakfast, and at once I went out into Mary's hall to phone the operator to get the department on the line.

A voice at once bright and stern said, "Department of Forestry."

"Hello, I'd like to make an application to have someone burn my bog."

"Who are you?" he thundered. "And where do

you live? And why do you want to burn the bog?"

I gave him hurried answers as I was interrogated.

"I see," he said. He paused. "Well, you're too late!"

"I'm too late? I was just told about this an hour ago! I only arrived a week ago, and besides I was told the deadline was April 15."

"That's the deadline all right," he said. "But applications have to be in a week before that. Your chances are nil now, I'd say." Leaving me stunned and silent for the moment, he asked, "Is the bog near the forest?"

I had no real idea and I guessed. "Yes, very near."

"Oh, that's terrible dangerous altogether," he chirruped with a mellifluous Clare accent, managing to sound solemn and musical at once.

"Well, I suppose you *could* fill in an application," he said at last. "Your chances would be nil now as I said, but you could fill one in like. I suppose you could."

"I suppose that's the best I can do then."

"Yes, it is that."

"Where do I get an application?"

"P. J. Brown in Kilmaley. You know Kilmaley?"

"No."

"You know Moran's Pub?"

"No."

"Well, it's just a bit up from Moran's. You can't miss it."

"Well, thanks very much."

That evening was overcast: a pale pasty sky overhung the hills as we drove north on a road we had never traveled. We were out on business, on our way with few directions, to see a man about burning a bog. Quickly the road wound out of Kiltumper and became a single long, gray line rising and falling into an utterly empty horizon. A minute's drive and we were in the most desolate beautiful place in the world. Blanket-like bog spread away on either side of us. Miles of it, light brown stuff with even, black seams where banks had been cut; they looked like scars in the body of Ireland. Then there was the road: the image of all roads, the eternal naked ribbon, absolutely deserted, absolutely straight, and utterly lonely as it went on forever across that windy, beautiful place. We drove in a trance on the roof of the world. There was no sign of human life anywhere. No houses, no chimney smoke, no cars coming or going, only the great soft expanse of the bog, immutable and silent.

The road had us rapt and wordless. Suddenly to the left appeared the silvery, mysterious waters of an upland lake, Lough Na Mine, the lake of the Mermaid. Cold and isolated, we thought it had a kind of separate, still beauty of its own. Nothing moved upon its bog-colored surface except refractions of light. The Department of Forestry had planted the surrounding land with pines and spruces. A misty rain hung above the lake conjuring up the mermaid. We were hushed. This was the wildness of the West, the unpredictable and sudden moment of startling and other-worldly beauty. As we drove on, it was almost like madness to us. A vision. And I wondered: What had it been to these local people to live all their lives on the verge of such a place? As the evening sky grew darker and the rain fell, unsettling stories of Irish schizophrenics and lunatic madmen wandering the bogs came to my mind. We sped onward. The lake went behind the trees and was gone.

We found the department's envoy in the pouring rain just at twilight. He looked like Kris Kringle and came to his door with a round red face and smiles and welcome. His several dogs roamed about the yard and as Chris stayed in the car I went in to do our business. In the West, regardless of women's movements and the like, women are still largely excluded from matters of business *outside* the home. In the home it is a very different story. There remains a fierce shyness in all matters between men and women who are strangers to one another in rural Ireland. Inside the dim, unlit kitchen, where two more dogs sat by his chair, P. J. untied knots of red tape while loosening his trouser belt for his oncoming dinner.

"Don't mind that fellow in Ennis," he chortled. "I'm the man who'll burn yer bog for ye. Never mind 'bout any deadline. Wait'll I get the papers."

The papers came with his potatoes and a thick slab of boiled bacon. Sometimes his wife appeared and immediately disappeared. I signed where he told me: the Official Application for the Burning of the Bogland of Kiltumper.

"Leave the date blank," he added.

So I did.

Another thing to wait for.

CHAPTER
THREE

Are ye going on the cuaird tonight?
When we first arrived in Kiltumper we knew nothing of the *cuaird* and when first invited had no idea of the full meaning of the word. We were new to the western landscape of field, hedgerow and silence, and found ourselves missing the variety of entertainment we had grown so used to. Looking out on the approaching night there was no movie theatre close by to escape to, no string of restaurants along a well-lit street—only the distant lights of separate houses on a hill and a sense of great stillness. So we decided to go on the *cuaird* that night with Mary and Joe. Venturing with lamp in hand, we were led along the botharins with a sense of great expectation. It was seven o'clock and the evening mists rolled across Hayes' Hill. Down our road men and women finished up the day's chores and got ready for the *cuaird*. Hens were locked

up for the night, the range was loaded with turf, the nightlamp and the warm overcoat or bicycle were made ready. As darkness narrowed the townland into a tight little community of kitchen-lit windows and turf smoke, there was a bustle of activity and the *cuaird* began to take shape.

The word *cuaird* derives from the Irish *cuairt,* the old Gaelic word for visiting. It is among the oldest living traditions of the West. The sound of it—a sound at once songlike and pleasurable—reminds me of other old-fashioned words, of courtesy, courtliness and courtship, all of which, I believe, are in some way related to the cuaird. But cuaird means more than visit, and more, too, than any one of the English words it resembles. It's a way, a habit of being in a small community that has been passed down for so long that no one is quite certain when it started.

No word had been sent ahead, no appointment made, for none was necessary. Inside the back door of nearly every house is a chair, often a sugan, empty and waiting for the nighttime visitor. No explanation is required: You simply come in the door, sit down and pull a chair to the fire—for the cuaird *is* the night's entertainment. It's a scene set for conversation, for story-telling and laughter, for tall talk of fairies or ghosts, as well as for cattle prices or the weather. As we sat to our welcome in a neighbor's house we were introduced and, even though Mary had brought a half-dozen fresh eggs to our hostess, we came to understand that the *real* gift a visitor brings is news. How are your chimneys pulling? How are ye managing? Everyone wanted to know, and all of a sudden we realized that we possessed a world of news, a whole host of ordinary subjects waiting to be shared. Here, on the cuaird, you can broach any subject, share any joke, any problem, and know that you will always have an attentive, and often helpful, audience.

As we sat in the parlor at Dooley's warmed by a

great glowing turf fire, Nora was brought out to join us. She had welcomed people to her house for sixty years and we had heard warm tales in the village of men and women coming down across the mountain to her kitchen to hear her play the concertina and to dance the winter night away. We thought she was the embodiment of the cuaird. Her great bony hands shook ours and she smiled at us. Welcome, welcome. Did we like music? We did. Did we dance the sets? We didn't. Well, we must. A concertina was brought from a cupboard. She hadn't played in two years with the arthritis in her fingers, she complained, and she might not be able to get a tune. But all the company urged her, and, unsnapping the fasteners of the concertina, she began to play and that parlor in the middle of the west Clare countryside was suddenly concert hall and dance hall. The cuaird had come alive.

We stepped to the floor for our first lesson. Chairs were moved back, voices lilted the tune, and with a little stiff awkwardness we began to step a Clare set. Everyone smiled and laughed as we lost the air and came asunder. There was more music and more dancing and laughter. The dark was forgotten, the rain unheard, the wind that tunneled along the black and winding roads blew unnoticed, for the cuaird was on, the kettle was boiling above the turf fire, and the tart was being brought from the oven.

A new meaning to a familiar word: *Feather dusting*. The cottage is inches deep in dust. Mary presented me with a gift of a semi-fresh, white-feathered goose wing.

"There, Crissie, there's a grand brush for ye now."

I tried it out immediately, secretly and alone. It worked marvelously well. But who from my Westchester days of only a month ago would ever believe the sight of me, bent down over the hearth and sweeping up the finest of dust with an old greying, feathered goose wing? I guess its use for small jobs could be compared with the battery-operated Dust Buster we used to have in New York.

Thursday, April eleventh: another day of lashing rain. And still our bed had not arrived. I called Fast Sea and Air (ironic name!) and heard weak excuses: it was Eastertime, customs had it, it was a bad time of the year. At long remove, over a static-laden telephone line, my anger was impotent. The bed had been in the country two weeks and was still no nearer to Kiltumper. Chris was shattered by the news of further delay, and wanted to cancel the order, get our money back, threaten action, write to Gay Byrne, Ireland's Phil Donahue. It was hopeless. We needed the bed and had no means of getting it. It was promised for the following Tuesday. After all, we would not be moved in by Chris's birthday. More gloom, disappointment and rain.

In the afternoon we drove to the Garda station, the police force in the village, to hand over our notification of Intent to Burn Bogland. But surprisingly to us, at mid-afternoon the Garda station was closed. We had planned later to drive to Kilrush, a fairly large town by Irish country standards, ten miles to the west of us. But our good intentions were forestalled again when we learned, just as we were about to go, that Thursday was a half-day in Kilrush. The entire town was closed for the afternoon.

So much for plans for the most efficient use of

time we had become predisposed to by our urban existences.

April twelfth was Chris's birthday, and the world's worst day. Sheets of rain streamed from a dark sky and wind flew fiercely at all living things. Mary, however, slow to condemn the weather, said, "If there's enough blue in the sky to make a sailor's jacket the day will be fine." And so, sitting late over breakfast with several cups of tea, we watched the sky like lookouts for any clearing. And still the rain rained.

Against the disappointment of being unable to move into the cottage, I had booked us into the Old Ground Hotel in Ennis for the night. An extravagance, but I judged we needed it. Chris especially, for the comforts of Kiltumper fall far short of anything vaguely American. In some of our neighbors' homes bathwater comes brown and uninviting from the taps. Many rooms are damp and dark, and after years in America the small details of hygiene and comfort are sorely missed. There are no cottony soft toilet tissue rolls here, no handy paper napkins, no supersoft fluffy towels.

Against our expectations, the van delivering the vinyl for the kitchen and the carpet for the bedroom *did* arrive in the morning as promised. Once the floor was laid the house immediately seemed friendlier and more intimate. We *were* making our mark on Kiltumper Cottage.

The sky, naturally, cleared. Doesn't it always? asked Mary. Heartened and hopeful and ready for a treat, we drove to Ennis. The Old Ground Hotel was originally a private mansion built in the early eighteenth century. It has over forty rooms, and sitting in the very heart of the lively town it looks grand and elegant. The outer gray stone walls speak of age and history, and inside the furnishings and paintings match this mood. Everything is a piece of Irish history, Irish culture. Poems by Yeats hang framed in the hall and a great turf fire in the foyer is encircled by large soft chairs.

From our new perspective of Kiltumper, the Old Ground was a palace. The moment we entered our room, Chris charged into the bathroom, turned on the taps and ran herself an immense hot bubblebath. Later, laughing, she ran to the bed. White cotton towels, cotton sheets, and color television! And direct-dial telephones! It hardly mattered that the television only had the two channels, or that the wallpaper was peeling a little in the corners, or that the brown-flowered carpet (identical to the wallpaper) was somewhat worn. For in the wilds of rural Kiltumper, Chris and I had put behind us our American perspectives. We were in heaven. I mean, there were even a kettle and teapot awaiting us in the room! Dinner was superb. The dining room was high-ceilinged and lighted with chandeliers. The menu was French and the food exquisite. And over cups of dark brewed coffee—our first *real* coffee in Ireland—the manageress presented Chris with a box of Cadbury's chocolates in honor of her birthday. There we were, foundlings in the West of Ireland, impatient, frustrated and still lonely. And at just that moment the surprise of chocolates endeared the place to us and made us welcome. We felt like peasants become lords. For all the time we were there—and we stayed until the very minute before noon checkout and bathed three times in sensual luxuriance—we were conscious of the staggering contrast between Kiltumper and the Old Ground. It seemed we had traveled a world away in just thirty minutes. Kiltumper Cottage and the Old Ground date from roughly the same period, but between the echoes of vanished aristocrats, whose portraits line the stone stairway of the hotel, and the bellowings of beasts in the field behind our bedroom, lies the entire history of Ireland. Gentry, farmers and gombeenmen. Our brief stay reminded us over and over of the complex and embittered past, of the Anglo-Irish and the Gaelic peasantry. The great gilt-framed portraits that hang on the hotel's walls contrast with the walls of country cottages we visit, covered very differently with simple pictures of Jesus, Mary and Joseph.

"Mary, what's that *white* bush that's in bloom now? *White*thorn?"

"No," replied Mary, "that's the *black*thorn tree, Crissie."

We were finally all set to move in. The bed was in Limerick and had been promised to be delivered in the afternoon. In the spirit of things Chris cut some of our abundant rhubarb and tied the sticks in small bundles. Then, we were off to the village in the big blue Peugeot to market. We walked into one of the several small shops that has a little of everything, leaving the rhubarb outside.

"I see you don't have any rhubarb," I said.

"No," said the shopkeeper hesitantly, "it's early yet for that."

Chris smiled at me. We were going to pull it off—our first time bartering and we were nervous with the thrill of it. "How would you like some of Kiltumper's best?"

The deal was done. The shopkeeper was delighted to be able to offer her customers early rhubarb for the Sunday dinner and Chris ran out to the car to bring in the clean red sticks. Like merchants we counted them out and tied them again. One pound forty-five pence was our price, and it seemed good as a fortune to us as it bought milk, butter and biscuits. We had picked the rhubarb only an hour earlier, and there it suddenly was on the grocer's shelf. As we drove away we were both thinking that we would come back tomorrow to see if it were sold. Wherefore goes our rhubarb? Who sits down to it today?

Back in the garden we looked at every growing thing in a new light. Everything that rises greenly above the soil is intimately a part of our life here. We were newly conscious of cycles, rhythms and patterns. There is a wonderful sense of closeness between earth and human. All old clichés perhaps, but to the person who actually grows the thing and cares for it through good and bad this in an undeniable truth. And that afternoon in the sunshine it filled Chris and me with deep satisfaction. It seemed a fitting prologue to the imminent arrival of the bed and our first night in the cottage. We had the fire in the stove burning warmly, and all eyes were on the road from the east waiting for the van. All our friends in the village were waiting, too. Mary from her kitchen window down the road was waiting for it. Pauline, next along the road, was waiting, too. In the front green garden, where we stood with ears pricked for any sound, nothing came or went. Time ran on and still nothing came, and a familiar sinking feeling crept into our hearts. Everyone had an opinion: It could be delivered as late as eight in the evening. It could be held up somewhere back up the road. It could be broken down. It could be lost. But of course it was not lost, just delayed once again. It did not come that day. Nor had we any news of it, and letting the fire burn low and returning to Mary's for the night, we were downhearted.

"You can get nothing done in this country." Chris said angrily. "Nothing. They've had our bed three weeks. They're only in Limerick, an hour away now. It's so bloody Irish, so incompetent! AAAH!"

The curses continued. Mary, fretting and unhappy for us, drew us off to Dooley's for tea. There Chris voiced her fury and Michael Dooley sat silver-haired by the turf fire listening while she ranted. Once she had finished he looked over to her with his lovely, lively blue eyes and said, "Crissie, have ye heard the cuckoo?"

And when it was good, it was very, very good. At last the bed arrived. The long delay has filled us both with hesitation and doubt, but once I had unpacked and assembled the unpainted blonde ash headboard and frame, it fit perfectly with the mood of our farmhouse cottage. Once the quilts and pillows that we had carried across the Atlantic were arranged on the mattress, the scene looked picture-perfect, just like the Conran's catalog. All day I thought of it, proof that we were now inhabitants. We left Mary's, blessed with holy water from the local blessed well, and drove back up the road to our cottage in a high pitch of excitement. So there we finally were. We had no television, our radio was broken. There was not a sound, and earlier, writing in my journal, I had felt the unsettling sensation of the loudness of my pen as it scraped softly upon the paper.

The stove was burning over five hundred degrees. A hot-water bottle readied the chilly sheets. Hot milk preceded, and when we finally laid down our heads, the room with the three-foot thick walls was absolutely still and quiet. It felt like a cave, but with one long window to the sky of deepest blue patterned with infinitesimal stars. Gusts of wind rustled in the bedroom's old chimney, and with our heads beside it, we vaguely thought of birds or bats descending in the night. The ceiling above us, Chris said, seemed to breathe and sigh and she heard soft shuffling sounds somewhere in the rafters. The sense of disturbing ancestral ghosts snuggled us closer together. Don't go to sleep until I'm asleep, she said to me. And so, alert and listening to every sound, from the thrashing branches of the sycamore trees to the distant bellowing roar of some bull, we lay in the dark, waiting, waiting, waiting for the silent visitor of sleep on our first night in Kiltumper Cottage.

CHAPTER FOUR

We were awakened at dawn by the roaring of an angry cow. Betsy, that great brown and white beast in the back field, wanted to be milked. Her calf wanted to be fed. And so, in a dialogue of bellowing, Betsy blundered her way through the makeshift fence and raced by our bedroom wall, roaring at the seven-bar gate that lay between her and the calf in the shed below.

For almost an hour, behind the thick bedroom walls, we tried to ignore the hullabaloo. Betsy was not our cow, and we were expecting the farmer who owned her to arrive at any moment. Or at least we hoped so. At last, as the bellowing was gathering to a murderous intensity, Chris urged us from the bed to see what the cow had gotten into amid the many obstacles in the backyard. "She might have been caught against something," Chris said. "Come on!"

After all, as novice farmers, we had a certain responsibility to her.

Outside, in the early dawn light, Kiltumper was utterly still but alive with thrilling, tremulous birdsong. Coming from the dark, cozy cave of our bedroom to the uninhabited stillness of morning, I opened the door with a little apprehension, for by now the ululation was louder, more urgent than ever, and it made us cringe to hear the plaintive answering cries of the newborn calf from inside the cabin.

Of course, neither of us knew the first thing about cows. As we opened the door Betsy galloped past in a clatter of muck and anger and we quickly stepped back inside. Cows are *very* big, and between the chorus of bellowing and the stomping brute force of her angry charge, Betsy seemed fierce to us. What were we to do? In the country we had already seen herds of twenty cows being driven quite easily by boys of no more than seven years old. All you needed was a stick and a few yelps. But what were *we* to do with her? The calf was making a great commotion for its mother. Still, against the obvious—that the cow must be brought to the calf to suck—stood our joint ignorance. Perhaps we would be doing wrong, perhaps she was not supposed to be brought to the calf yet. We had no confidence in our patchy knowledge of the thing, and decided that we must drive the cow back inside the field, secure the gate and wait until the farmer came.

So, armed with sticks, we went outside again into the morning. The plan was simple. I would drive the cow back from the gate toward the gap where Chris would be waiting, and as the cow came toward her all she had to do, I said, was to wave her arms, shout and guide the animal through the gap. I would be coming directly behind her to shut the gate as soon as we had Betsy in. All right?

So much for plans. We had underestimated the

44

stubbornness of the mother's determination to be with her calf. As I came up carefully behind her, Betsy seemed to sense at once that the plan was not to her liking. Do cows feel guilt, I wondered? Did she know that it had been wrong to crash her way through the gap? Did she know I had never stood that close to a cow in all my life? She made a little back kick to warn me that she did. I tapped her behind with the stick, like a gentleman. "Come on, now, get h'up!" I said in fluent droverese. She turned her head a fraction, showed me two great watery eyes of derision, and roared so loudly that I jumped back.

"What's happening?" yelled Chris from her post at the gap around the corner. "Is she coming?"

"Yes, just a minute!"

I tapped this time a little harder, then I gave her a proper thwack. The watery eyes looked around with a melancholy expression, as if to ask if we really had to go through with this. I thwacked again and Betsy bolted away from the gate. I had turned her, there was nothing to it. Hurrying along behind her with the stick I called to Chris to be ready. But I needn't have. At the top of the "street" the cow turned west instead of east and galloped off toward the empty hay barn and away from the gap.

A morning chase was on. With my stick waving, with a series of insistent yelps, I ran after Betsy while my wife laughed from the gap, and the calf renewed its crying from below in the cabin. It was a morning farce. Thank God no one could see us, but it sure beat sitting at a desk. Finding any way she could to avoid the entrance to the field, the cow thundered around and finally managed to clamber up against the wall that dropped several feet to the road outside. I was terrified she would jump, for surely she would break both front legs, and our first morning in the cottage would go down in infamy and disaster. I hid the stick behind my back. But how do you call a cow back? "Here, Betsy, Betsy" wasn't working.

She answered to nothing, but stood there waiting on the very edge of the wall as if determined that death or the fulfillment of her wish was the only resolution. I surrendered. I walked away from her and waited out of sight at the top of the street. And, of course, at once she came, sashaying almost, with victory. At the corner I waved the stick and gave my loudest roar. In terror and surprise she turned toward Chris and the gap beyond. I gave her behind a belt with the stick and she was off and running!

But so, too, was Chris. The sight of the angry charging cow coming toward her along the narrow passage between the hedge and the house was too much. Dropping the stick, Chris bolted for the house, and Betsy thundered by.

"You've made her too mad," she complained. "I couldn't stop her now."

It was true. The false surrender and surprise had maddened the poor cow even more, and as she eyed us at the back door, she tramped past once more, her great balloon of udders swaying hugely with every step.

It took us two more tries to get her right. Once more she turned and thundered along the passage, plopping dung where she should have veered in the gap. Once more we ended back inside the house in dismay. We were lucky that none of our neighbors were about that early hour of the morning, for what a sight we would have been, struggling to outsmart Betsy in the backyard. The final time, Chris left her stick in the house and instead took a short wooden ladder for protection. If she held it horizontally, she argued, maybe the cow would think it was a wall and simply turn into the field.

How can you argue with such reasoning? I didn't, it was too ridiculous. But, of course, it worked perfectly. Chris stood her ground and within a minute Betsy was back in her field. The gap secured, we hurried inside to the sound of the farmer's tractor coming up the road to bring the mother to her calf!

Back in the empty stone cottage, that morning we had a marvelous sense of independence. We were alone here, but not lonely, and we were free. It was Thursday, but what matter, all days except Sundays were to become the same to us. No morning train nor cluttered desk awaited us. Patches of morning cloud uncovered a blue sky and looking from our kitchen window over green fields, we were glad to be in Clare.

I imagine that to anyone who has undergone the discipline of a long commute, the tight scheduling and timetabling of office life, the sudden structureless freedom of Irish country life might seem—as it did to us—at once wonderful and terrifying. It was difficult not to laugh with holiday humor. Chris saw the danger first. We must impose our own order on the green days, she argued, or the heady spring and early summer would strangle our dreams like those blasted weeds in the garden.

And so with little delay we went to work in the garden. Before long Mary and Joe arrived, "to see the bed, Crissie" and to help us set the potatoes. For anyone with even a scattered knowledge of Irish history, it is impossible to set potatoes in Irish soil without a shiver of remembrance of the famine of 1847 and the fear of blight, a fungal disease that comes over the crop in any wet, foggy summer, destroying all the potatoes within days. The tragedy of the famine so many years ago has soaked into folk memory. The land and the people remember, and many horrific tales are told of starvation and bodies on the roadside.

Nowadays, there are means of combating blight— none of them infallible, however—and the shadow of a failed crop still looms over every sowing. The seriousness of this cannot be overlooked. Our neighbors all attempt to grow a year's supply of potatoes. Potatoes remain part of every Irish meal in the West: pasta, pizza and rice remain a novelty in this part of the world, although this is slowly changing because of Ireland's membership in the European Economic Community (EEC).

In the garden that morning, Mary advised while Joe helped me dig the furrows. The men went back and forth with barrows of fresh cow dung and the women began halving the British Queen seed potatoes. Then, following the advice of our neighbors, we sat the bright white half-potatoes down on the brown cushion of manure and covered them over with a mound of earth. It was slow work, but it contained an implicit element of faith, a bonding of man and land, and not a few murmurings to the heavens.

"God bless the growth," said Mary when it was done, and for a while the four of us stood on there in the sunshine, leaning on our spades and looking on the tidy brown drills with satisfaction. How neat they were. Our potatoes were in; our garden had begun.

Alone again that afternoon we tried some Americanized gardening. Chris had brought Burpee seeds from New York, and like a secret weapon we took them out when no one was about. In a small, fresh seedbed in the windless grove, Chris set broccoli and spinach, bibb lettuce and chervil, and directly into the open garden went long rows of more spinach, carrots, onions and our favorite vegetable—sugarsnap peas. Bucket upon bucket of water was carried out to them from the bathroom tub tap, and we imagined them rising above that tilled earth into the oncoming summer for a marvelous harvest.

Other plants were already growing in the garden. Although wild and misshapen, they were vigorously alive, and there to stay. Gooseberries, blackberries, black currants and raspberries lined the eastern ivy-covered stone wall, and in those first rushed days of April Chris doctored them all. Strawberry plants had sent their little wire-strong runners out everywhere and small plants appeared in unusual places. These, too, she retrieved from the wilderness, rebuilding a patch for them, and reshaping, day by day, the garden of her forebears.

That evening, the work done, we set out on the road that runs past the cottage and leads west to the sea at Doonbeg, twelve miles away, to end our first full day as country dwellers. It was the kind of day we had long imagined for ourselves. In our fancy we would drive to the sea, strip off, and swim into the Atlantic's invigorating waters. Well, not quite. For although the evening road led to the golden sunset and an ever-increasing sliver of calm ocean, we knew where dreams must end: the ocean in April would be freezing! We stayed on the shore and waved to New York.

Drizzle was falling. Chris was attending to four steaming pots on the turf-fired range in preparation for our first Sunday dinner guests. We had acquired an old wooden table which we resurrected from an abandoned house, painted, and treated for wood-worm. We had taken a worn-out armchair from my parents' house in Dublin, and along with the sugan chair, now had a total of two more or less comfortable chairs. Mary and Joe, dressed in their Sunday best, came with their own chairs. The food was to be tradi-tional Irish: beef, potatoes, carrots, peas and brown bread. The rain came on as they arrived, carried in their chairs and sat down.

"God bless all here," Mary said, as she still says each time she enters our house.

It was our first large meal in the cottage, and that we chose to share it with them was warmly appreci-

ated by Joe and Mary who knew that good neighbor-
liness was being offered. Together we sat around in
the lulling, nearly hypnotic weather. There was no
sense of time; the world passed us by.

"Would ye like to go to the Bannermen tonight?"
asked Mary at last.

"The Bannermen? Do they play Irish traditional
music?"

"Yes, and they'd be at Daly's tonight."

Pipes, fiddles and a bodhran (a goatskin-covered
Irish hand drum, shaped like a tambourine) sounded
immediately in our imaginations and we agreed to go.
Clare is famous for Irish music and we were delighted
at the prospect of hearing some. And so, in the early
evening, carrying the good humor of the Sunday dinner, we all set out for Daly's lounge bar in the village.

The Bannermen were not what we expected, but
really wonderful. Chairs were placed all along the
walls, creating a dance floor. A small stage was set up
in the corner. As we sat down we noticed that the
place was full of women. Niall was practically the only
man there. The other men of the parish were in the
pub side, drinking. But we had little time to dwell on
the beginnings of what could have been an embarrass-
ing situation because the music started almost at once.
We saw what they meant by Irish "traditional music".
The Bannermen did not, in fact, play traditional music
as I understood it. Instead they played popular "Olde
Time Waltzes". The Bannermen were dressed in what
can only be described as the Irish version of an

American cowboy outfit, complete with string ties and wide belt buckles. Their music was pleasant to listen to and as soon as it began women stepped out to dance. They formed in circles of sixes and eights and held hands together high. At a nod, the dance began, and circles of women shuffled into motion. It was an amazing sight in the crowded, dark room with middle-aged women tiptoeing and tapping their feet in traditional set-dancing. It was beautiful and heart-warming. Smiles abounded and men eventually gathered in the doorway from the pub to watch.

Despite the bright faces, there was no real sign of emotion, no yelps or whistles like the kind often heard at a traditional music session. Rather, the set-dancing was quietly performed; dance as dance, the pleasure of steps to music. It was innocent and lovely. We soon lost our sense of feeling out of place and out of tune. The rainy evening shaped about the little pub and as the familiar, similar tunes and airs repeated, the set-dancing induced a mesmeric trance, a stay against the fall of night. On and on they played. Men came through the doorway and watched with pints in hands as their wives stepped and swung in constant motion, going round and round in delight like so many carousel ponies.

The next day it was time for us to start "farming", time to use the one acre and three cabins, all that were ours until the following March when the lease on our fifty acres of grassland expired. We turned to "the book," John Seymour's *The Complete Book of Self-Sufficiency*. There the mysteries of hens, ducks, chickens, goats and other farm animals are explained in layman's terms. But there is a world of difference between book knowledge and the real thing. We read of hen houses and feeding stuffs, of possible pitfalls and the symptoms of disease. We talked avidly, and naïvely, of goats and the milking of them, of making cheese and yogurt. But first, most necessary and easiest of all, we wanted some humble farmhouse hens for the laying of our breakfast eggs.

We began by cleaning the hen cabin. Chris informed me that if we were going to keep animals, we were also going to insure that their living conditions were . . . how shall I say, more than comfortable? Monday morning, therefore, saw the two of us out in the rain with two pails of limewash and a hand scraper to clean the floors of what seemed to be a hundred years of muck. No hens had been there for five years, and the small stone confine was now the home of dangling spiders who fell in dry dusty tangles to the floor as Chris brushed furiously past. Would our hens-to-be appreciate this, I wondered? Chris was adamant that they would.

Neither of us, of course, had known anything about the biology or anatomy of poultry. Hens, chickens, who laid, who didn't, how many eggs did a hen lay? But between Mary and "the book" we assimilated enough so as not to embarrass ourselves as we set off to Kilmihil to buy four point-of-lay pullets, that is, nine-month-old hens who are about "to come into their laying."

Nothing is ever right the first time; Chris's cautious nature was proved right again. There were no pullets to be had that day or in the immediate future; they were all sold. We drove home and past our clean, white, empty hen house with an accustomed feeling of disappointment. Now our hens would have to come from further afield, and having scoured the ad page of the *Clare Champion*, we came upon an ad: one-year-old hens for sale. One pound each. Ballynacally Farm.

One-year-old hens: they might not be laying, they couldn't be very healthy, as they would have been confined in the battery, but they were our only hope if we were to have hens that spring. The very next morning, we set out for Ballynacally Farm.

It was a glorious sunny day. The road wound about green hills and across a river, until at last we came to the poultry farm. In the mid-morning it seemed deserted. We parked the car and announced our arrival with a hoot of the horn. Nobody came. We went to find somebody, but as we prowled about there seemed a strange, eerie quality to the silence. We walked about the great warehouse-like building with caution when suddenly it struck us. What had originally seemed to be the faintest whistling in the far-off wind grew louder and louder as our ears recognized the hum for what it was—the noise of a thousand clucking hens. Turning to the sliding iron door of the building, we opened it slowly and saw the most extraordinary sight. The place looked like a hen factory. There, before us, thousands of hens screeched, jumped and poked their heads out from their tiny individual jail-like cages. They had just enough room to reach a food tray. Their eggs fell to another tray behind them. The smells, the sounds, the manic fury of their captured bodies petrified us. It was Hitchcockian and horrible. The fact that these birds had probably never seen daylight, never pecked grass, never walked more than two steps, seemed immeasurably cruel. Their confinement was unbearable to watch. We rushed outside to the beautiful blue day, gasping and silent. Our throats felt parched, feathers tickled our nostrils. We barely had time to talk when a masked and gloved man appeared from a small shed. Did we want hens?

We did, and hesitantly followed him back into the hatchery again and stood while he arbitrarily pulled four squawking birds from their cages. He held them upside down, tied their legs together, and stuffed them into our waiting box. We had read that good hens had rich reddish combs. These had pinkish ones, but so, too, had all the rest, and to our inexpert eyes they seemed healthy enough. What did we know? On top of everything, a hen can be notoriously unpredictable in the matter of laying; that is, it is possible to have a happy-looking animal that quite simply won't lay for you. And so, paying out our four pounds into a gloved palm, we hurried to the car and set off for home. We felt mixed emotions in silence, for while four hens had been liberated, behind us lay three thousand more for whom no sunshine would come that day.

Drive the bumpy, winding roads of West Clare in a hurry with your first four hens in the trunk, and soon enough you will know what potholes there are in Ireland. Chris's eyes were glued to the rearview mirror, as if she half-expected to see the birds hop out in dismay somewhere along the way. By the time the car was turning into our farm, we felt certain these hens would never lay.

We were wrong, of course. When Chris opened the trunk to move the box of hens to the relatively enormous freedom of the newly whitened cabin, one of them had already laid an egg. An omen? Nervously, we handed them into their new home, and stood watching as they tried out their legs in small, stumbling steps. The slightest movement terrified them. For an hour we stood around and watched. It was is if they were some new species and not common hens at all. They were our first animals to care for and we felt immensely responsible. Within a day they showed signs of adapting to their newly given freedom; they dared to step outside their cabin as long as Chris was standing near. They discovered the use of their feet, and began to scratch about in the grass. Within a week, they went much further afield by themselves and eggs—large, brown eggs—began turning up in the strangest places below the fuchsia hedge at the back of the cottage.

Problems, remedies and advice. We had smoke in our chimneys; we had paid for the installation of a telephone three months prior to our arrival in Ireland

and it was still not installed; we had borrowed a black-and-white television only to find it uselessly misted and without an image when we turned it on. The smoke was certainly the worst problem. Chimneys are the most characterful and independent part of old houses. They have a mind of their own, it could be said. A house may be sturdy but its chimney may be crumbling, and likewise, an old ruin may still breathe with an excellent chimney. They have their own reputations, too, as we soon discovered. Our main chimney, the open-hearth fireplace in the kitchen, had an excellent name. It had drawn beautifully with the occasional puff of smoke escaping into the room. But at that time it had had a large opening to the sky, through which, poetically speaking, it was possible to see the stars, but through which, practically speaking, there fell great showers of hail-stones, rain, and soot. And so, in an attempt to keep the open hearth and the grill on the floor and yet avoid getting the elements indoors, a flu pipe had been installed inside the chimney's cavity, considerably narrowing the opening to the sky. Ever since our first days in Clare, any fire set on the floor would cause the room to fill with turf smoke, albeit sweetly scented, just as if a ghost upon the roof gaily blew our efforts back at us. We were inconsolably dismayed as time after time we built a fire only to be forced to escape from the room, carrying the smoking sods out the front door with us. In the way of the West, we took our disappointment to our neighbors one evening on the cuaird. Many of the homes about us had, at one time, similar open-hearth fireplaces with the long swinging crane to hold a pot and kettle above the flames. However, most of these have disappeared and the "French fireplace," as it is known here, has taken its place. The hearth itself has been bricked in and the corners of the great fireplace closed off and made into closets. The grill remains on the floor but the opening to the chimney has been reduced to two-and-a-half-by-one feet. To Chris and me the old hearth is an ancient part of the country and we were desperate to preserve it and have it "pulling."

On the cuaird then, we sought advice and solutions.

"It's easy enough to destroy a chimney," said Michael Dooley. "There used to be a grand draw on that chimney of yers, one time."

Chris, with her usual American inquisitiveness, asked Michael what he would do if the chimney were his. "I'd brick it up, to be sure. J. J. Keane had a chimney one time with the open hearth like yers and he put in a French fireplace and . . . now he can set down a fire and every bit of smoke will draw up the chimney."

"But what would you do if you didn't *want* to brick it in?" There was a long pause at this point because Michael had already told us what *he* would do. There *was* only one solution, in his mind.

"Woll, tho only man who could right a bad chimney would be a stone mason," he finally offered.

Chris thought she was onto something now. "Great, is there one in Kilmihil?"

Again he paused before answering, blue eyes shining into the fire before us. "Well, I don't know of one of them left anywhere."

Chris had not wanted to have a television. She remembered too well the easy addiction it had become when long delays in the city sent us home weary and too useless for anything but watching television. I was less worried about addiction than I was about the eventual dark evenings of the Irish winter. We would need one then, I thought, for we were to be without all the usual fallbacks of movies, concerts, dining out and other forms of urban entertainment. And our viewing would, of necessity, be limited with only two channels and six hours a night of programming available. A second-hand television had been offered to us. And after much discussion, and on the proviso from Chris that it would not cost us anything, we took it. We took it, but it proved useless. We turned it on and it responded, but we had no picture.

One evening, J. J. Keane arrived at our back door. We had met him only briefly. A warm, genial man of sixty-odd years, he had a reputation for ingenuity. When he arrived that evening at our house, he sat for coffee for over an hour without letting on that there was another reason beside his welcome for his visit. He told anecdotes, spoke of gardens and bogs and of other visits long ago to the house of Jack O' the Grove. All this was by way of courtesy and friendliness, and then, the three of us having warmed to each other, he leaned forward in the chair and said, "You're having trouble with a television?"

I carried it out from the back room and he sat to fiddle with it, but the misted screen would not yield a picture. At last, J. J. sat back in his chair. He put his hands on his knees and looked at the thing before him, saying, "An aerial would do it."

I glanced at Chris. An aerial—money! No television. "I see," I said to J. J., and went to switch it off.

"But no need to buy one," he added. "I can rig one up for ye in a few days." Days later he returned as promised and with him he brought a long, slender piece of wood, a roll of copper wire and a hammer and some nails. "Here's yer aerial," he told us with a grin.

And so it was, and is still. An hour of trying it out, of moving the precious aerial around the attic to shouts of *"there, you nearly have it . . . no, it's gone . . . wait, wait, don't move, there, yes there,"* and finally our television worked. It was one of those moments when we genuinely experienced the hospitality and warmth of the West. A neighbor had come to help with no other intention than to make us feel welcome, and that night as we said goodbye to

J. J. Keane and watched him drive his old battered but well-running blue Ford happily into the night, we believed ourselves to be among good people.

Telephones are not so easily provided, we found out. Our telephone, which had been paid for in December, was still not installed by May first. I was told at the post office that a man in Kilrush, the nearest large town, was the man to answer my inquiry. He was a supervisor for Telecom Eirinn, the new phone company, and on a gray morning in May I found him alone in his office in the deserted Telecom building, eating his sandwiches.

Upon him, with Chris's reinforced American sense of outrage, we poured our ire. Where was our telephone? They had cashed the check, hadn't they? So where was it?

Unruffled, Mr. Supervisor moved to his ledger. "Well, let me just take a look." Pages were flicked past his weary gaze. Most of the pages appeared to be blank. "Ah yes," he said, "I see," and with that he quickly shut the book. "Well, we'll be right onto it then."

What was one to do with a man like that?

"When?" demanded Chris.

"What's today? Tuesday? Well, let me see, they'll hardly be out by the end of the week. They might come Friday." He ruminated on this for a moment, and I believe he hoped that while he did we might just go away. We didn't, and so at last he turned back to us.

"Well, depending on how the other jobs go, how about Monday, would that be all right?"

What could we say? It was almost another week away, but in Ireland that was soon enough.

"It all depends, you see," he said. "There's only one digger for the whole county to put in the telephone poles."

And with that and very ambivalent feelings, we

left him. Was it a victory? Had we hurried him on, or had he simply given us a load of blarney to send us on our way and him back to his sandwiches.

Ten days later we were still no nearer to having a telephone.

CHAPTER FIVE

The ways of the West. As our first weeks unraveled, we began to live in the way of the people
around us. We wanted to become familiar with as
many of the old customs and manners as possible and
practical. Many of the traditional ways are dying out.
For example, there are not as many *seanachais* (storytellers) as there once were; tractors have replaced
horses and donkeys; farms are becoming increasingly
mechanized. Nonetheless, the ways that do survive
their modern alternatives are essential to life here.
And, it could be said, that it was two of these time-
honored traditions that became our first rites of
introduction into life in Kiltumper: cutting the turf
and baking brown bread. In more than half the homes
about us, a cake of brown bread is baked every other
day; and in May every neighboring farm sends an
able-bodied man to the bog to cut turf. Quite often

down in the village or out on the cuaird we heard the praises of Mary's brown bread, of Breda's scones or of Michael Dooley's skillful artistry with the slan. Likewise, there were those who humbly admitted that they simply couldn't do it, or didn't have the time to do it, and chose instead bakery brown bread and machine-cut turf. They didn't have the touch for bread; as Mary explained to Chris one evening; brown bread is "in the hands," and some simply didn't have it.

In the hands, too, or, more exactly, in the arms and shoulders, lies the skill of the turfcutter. Before I ever went to the bog I had heard much about it. I knew that, like brown bread bakers, there were those who did and those who didn't cut turf, and that the turfcutter was the quietly sung hero of the West. For it was he who could handle the tricky, one-wing-sided slan spade, he who worked alone in the mystical landscape of the bog and in one week could cut enough fuel for one entire year, with some to spare or sell. The names of Michael Dooley and Michael Donnellan were spoken in admiration when it came to talking about cutting turf. (Luckily, for us, they had each offered to give us a day as their welcome to us.) I doubted my own ability to master the slan quickly enough for our year's turf, but also wondered if it was really as difficult as they said.

I need not have worried. Standing alone in the back meadow with an old slan of Johnny Breen's, I swung and practiced it like golf, digging invisible sods from an imaginary bog. But the whole action of the slan is backhanded and awkward at first, as each sod is thrown from right to left up onto the bank. As I tried to become used to it, I found myself thinking again and again of that mystical skill. Could I cut turf? Did I have *it?*

The red-haired man from the Department of the Forestry never came to burn our bog. He was overruled by his man in Ennis, and so, before any of our turf could be cut, the bank had to be stripped of a top foot of heather and roots. It was an arduous task. The bank, four feet wide and over fifty feet long, was thick and wiry with heather, the hardiness of which resisted any efforts to simply dig it out. Instead I was told to go at it with a "slasher" or billhook, and a hay knife with a T-bar handle. In this way, I cleared the bank, exposing the flat, silky brown earth of good turf.

Deserted as the bog was, it still held in undying memory the *meithels* of men working in teams with big wooden barrows, or the donkey and dray, the dinners on the bog, the bottles of lukewarm tea or poteen and thickly buttered brown bread. Among the bog's most curious surprises are the great, weathered, ashen-colored trunks of trees—the bog deal—that lie scattered among the banks. They surface after centuries out of the depths of the bog and now lie exposed like startling pieces of old shipwrecks thrown up on the soft, dark shore. Peat acts as an excellent preserver. Barrels of butter have been known to surface in the bogwater after decades and still remain fresh, a chilling reminder of the cool underworld where memories are long kept alive. But trees? Where did they come from? There was no sign of even a single tree anywhere on the horizon. How such great trees, giant oaks as these trunks intimated, could ever have once forested the spongy bogland is a mystery.

Those first days spent stripping the bank were our first real taste of being on the bog. And what a wild, weird place it is. An unbelievable hush pervades. The wind whistles, long and slow, over the lonely brown and purple waste and in that wiry and weathered world the birds make their song among the living and the dying heather. Sphagnum, lichen, petrified bog deal and feathery purple moor grass are the emblems of the landscape—a place full of secrets and past lives.

Mary told me that the bog deal would make for very good firing. And when I asked her where it all came from she said, "Years ago, Crissie, I often heard it said that it was a forest here back before the time of the Flood."

She was referring to Noah's flood.

Telephone poles had been laid out along our road. Could the phone be far behind? We dreamed of that, our connection to the world. Meanwhile we waited nervously for the day when our turf would be ready to cut. We were waiting for dry weather. It began to seem like we would be waiting for months. Each morning was *scamalach* (cloudy), and rain fell by noon just as our hand-washed clothes were put on the line between two sycamore trees. In the meanwhile, Chris tried, for the third time, to outsmart the jackdaws, who had already robbed us of three sowings of sugarsnap peas. Today, she intrigued our curious neighbors by building an elaborate tent of garden netting over the seedlings. American know-how. Or so we hoped.

Niall was supposed to maybe cut turf with Michael Donnellan today. We waited until eleven in the morning, wondering if he would come and what we would feed him if he came. No word, no alternative arrangement, no cutting today. Waiting, watching the weather. Useless time. After working in the garden for two hours, we decided to go to Ennis for our provisional driving licenses. In the back of my mind I was thinking they would naturally be closed. Everything here always is, the first time. We got there at five past three and sure enough, they had closed at three.

I am so discouraged with this country. We rang the man about our phone and he wasn't there. I feel defeated and think I've made an awful mistake. This romance with Ireland is a folly. In the evening, in the stillness, I have to fight to bring a smile to my face.

Finally the day arrived. Word came to our house in the now-expected contrary way. It was late in the evening. We were about to leave Mary's house after our cuaird.

"Oh, I nearly forgot to tell ye, Michael Donnellan is to give ye a day in the bog, please God, tomorrow."

Sleep that night was tense and fitful, for my mind was full of anticipation. We had heard so much of the mythos of the turfcutter; I feared I would not be up to a full day's work on the bog. It was rumored to be exceedingly hard work and that no degree of fitness could prepare you. There was something special, some undefinable quality about the nature of the work that made it like no other—or so we had been led to believe. Already in the village shops and pubs, men had started asking, "have ye started cutting yet?" I anxiously breakfasted and left the cottage that morning, carrying slan and fork up the three hill fields to the bog.

Back at the cottage Chris, too, was busy. It is customary for the turfcutter's wife to bring up the lunch, so that the work might not be delayed for long. Lunch consisted of glass bottles of tea, sandwiches, biscuits and perhaps a cut of cake. Most important, however, it was to consist of Chris's own turf-cooked brown bread.

She below and I above, we gave our morning to the ancient ways of Kiltumper. On the bog Michael Donnellan was already awaiting me. The day was fine, thank God, and clear across the open horizon we could feel the wind from the sea at Doonbeg. There was no sound but the stray half-blown songs of larks and thrushes. As I walked up, Michael was pacing the bank, examining how I had stripped it. It was a long platform of labor, and every one of the forty feet of turf had to be cut and dried if we were to have enough fuel for the winter.

A turf bank is measured in "bars" of depth, one bar consisting of a slanful, or spade-measure of turf (about twelve inches in length). A good bank might be six bars deep, to a depth at which the cutter would be working with bogwater up to his ankles and throwing up each sod to the top of the bank with the slan angled in an arc above his head. The nearer you come to the last measure of the bank, called "bar peak," the wetter the turf becomes. Brown, buttery stuff, it slides off the slan drippy and sloppy, and yet, with a touch of Irish logic, it is just this turf that dries the quickest and is the best to burn. The top bar, which to the hand seems dry and even feathery, is called "white turf" because it dries to a white crust, and is the last to dry and the worst turf for burning as it holds little heat.

Having explained this to me, without further ado, Michael began to cut the top bar. My job, less noble and certainly less romantic, was to stand on the heathery bank with two-pronged fork in hand. As Michael threw each sod up onto the bank, I had to fork it up and load it onto the turf barrow—a small wooden-wheeled, wooden barrow without sides. Once the barrow was filled, I threw down the fork, took up the barrow and ran away across the heathery bog to topple out the load and hurry back. By the time I returned, Michael had already pitched up a load of turf on the bank for me. In this way, I was always breathlessly behind him, but I couldn't drop more than a dozen or so sods back because then either the sods would begin to slide back on top of him, or, even worse, he would be forced to stop, cool his sweat, and wait for me to catch up. If I couldn't "keep it out from under him," my uselessness in the bog would become widely known, in Kiltumper anyway.

Barrow-work was not easy. The ground was soft and bumpy with little *pisogs,* or hillocks, everywhere. My Wellingtons slipped and the heavily loaded barrow sometimes toppled before I had intended. But there was no use trying to fix it; back I ran, pulling the barrow, doing what used to be literally "the asses' work" when a donkey and dray carried the turf from the bank to a place where it was laid to dry.

We cut the top bar all along the outer bank first, then the one beneath it, and so on. In this way we cut steps descending down into the bog hole. The necessity of the steps was immediately apparent, and so derives the timeless and impeccable logic of the turfcutter's little stair up from the cool, wet core of the bottomless bog, for the turf is cut to a depth greater than a man's height. Another explanation for the steps belongs to folklore: Once St. Colmcille went walking in Donegal and stumbled into a deep, stepless cutting. Saint and all, he was unable to get out for a considerable length of time, and it is said that he put a curse on any slansman since who has failed to leave behind him "the saint's stair" at the end of the bank.

It seems almost beyond words to describe that first day up on the bog of Kiltumper. After all, that was my work; there I was, nine to six, making, in the real sense, my living. And yet, it was work freed from the pettiness and tedium of schedules, memos, meetings office gossip and crises. There was pressure, I suppose. Each time I ran across the turf with the barrow, I could hear the slan turning out another sod on the bank behind me. I hurried about, perhaps even in the way I might have hurried through a corridor in Manhattan to meet some copy deadline. And yet. Here wind was blowing at me while I worked, my shirt sleeves were pulled up for a different reason, I could feel the weather on my skin and knew every moment that the work was not only good, but good for me. It gave me something. The day was all around us and we were a part of it. We knew every second of it even as we began to know and handle each sod of turf as it was cut from the earth. It was a moment when man and landscape seemed one. I cannot express how deeply satisfied I felt. But, of course, satisfaction came afterward. For the time being, there was only the unbelievable hush of the windy bogland and the steady rhythmic work. There was little talk—there was little breath for it. And by half-past twelve I found myself looking again and again across the bog meadow to where Chris was due to come with the lunch. When, at last, her colorful figure moved tentatively across the bracken and the bog (having dodged several bullocks and heifers), I was ready to drop. The five hours yet to work seemed beyond me, and I confess I might even have been glad of rain. No hope. The sun shone broadly back at me.

Down at the cottage, Chris had been busy all morning, falling, as she noted, into the grand scheme of things, baking brown bread and trying to figure how to keep tea warm until the last minute, without either stewing it, or denying it the proper three minutes to brew. It was a risky business. And so, too, with brown bread. As she later explained to me, there is no exact recipe for it. Rather, the measurements are rough Irish: Begin with a pile of plain white flour, add two or three fistfuls of bran, a slice or two of butter that is crumbled into the flour, a tiny palmful of sugar, a teaspoon of bread soda, a pinch of salt and enough buttermilk to make a sticky dough.

Up on the bog, Michael and I ate it like Christmas cake, it was so delicious. After several mutely taken mouthfuls, comment came in the usual way: Could we ever have another piece, Crissie? The quiet success of her baking would spread to the neighbors. Having bought flour from one of the shops in the village, she would return in three days to be greeted by the shopkeeper with a cheerful smile, "I hear your bread was lovely, Crissie."

For me, success was not so quickly won. Briefly revived, the half-hour break seemed to pass in a flash, and as Chris disappeared once more back over the crisscross hare tracks, over the banks of the bog, I was back at work on the barrow. The afternoon was hushed and warm and pleasant. As beads of sweat fell upon the sods, I began to think I had passed some obstacle; I had truly entered the West. Working away at an easy, natural pace, the turf itself seemed to be working me. Things began to fall into place; my terrific awkwardness passed. Michael smiled at me between strokes, for he, too, was undoubtedly relieved. And then, upon the infinite stillness of a dying wind, I heard the Song of the Cuckoo. Michael stopped sharply; he drew off his cap, and all the world seemed to pause in one marvelous moment of listening as the cuckoo sang on. His song was delightful and almost comic in the way it so closely imitated the exact sound of its name. "Coo-koo . . . coo-koo, coo-koo . . . coo-koo."

The double notes floated over the bog as the gray bird flew away, and glancing at Michael I understood we were to wait and listen longer. The sweetness of the birdsong uplifted me beyond description, for it was like a final welcoming, a solo performance of clearest pitch in the middle of the blue afternoon.

"He's singing for you," said Michael, nodding in the direction of the pine trees. "He's singing for you, all right."

As I took up the barrow again with renewed heart and energy, who was I to say that he wasn't?

CHAPTER
SIX

Our telephone finally arrived. An awkward black
contraption without any numbers to dial or push, it
hung lazily upside down upon the kitchen wall. It had
a little winder like a stunted arm that enabled us to
get the operator in the village. From the village, the
operator, in turn, had to crank Kilrush, and then they
would connect us with Dublin and the world. But the
telephone emitted no sound, for we were still not
connected. Rumor had it that, as Kilmihil 201, we
could not be added to the Kilmihil exchange. Switch-
boards come in 100s, they told us, and Kilmihil only
had the capacity to take 200 lines. Meanwhile, we sat
beneath the mute black thing on the wall and looked
out the window at the green patchwork fields and the
distant hills, beyond which, somewhere in telephone-
land, lay Manhattan.

Tiny droplets of red have formed on the fuchsia bushes looming so prominently around our garden. A signal for the summer to begin? It has been said to us many times since our arrival that last summer was fantastic. Sun from May to October. I am hoping that this summer will be the same. But the days of May have been very disappointing with unruly winds and daily showers. The May blossom—the whitethorn—with its tiny white flowers, so beautiful when it blooms over the countryside, has been set back this spring. There is hardly a hint of blossom anywhere. On the radio we heard of an old Mayo farmer predicting a long, wet summer. Secretly, I am preparing for the worst.

I collected a spring bouquet of meadow wildflowers: red clover, elderberry flower (Bishop's Wit), ajuga, buttercups, bluebells, early daisies, cuckoo flower, creeping speedwell, cranesbill, violets and cowslips. These flowers momentarily hold at bay the tremendous sense of isolation that envelops me when the skies are gray and wet.

Against the gloominess and a sense of being shut into a rainy corner, I set myself the task of clearing some of the tall pine trees that stand along the roadside in front of the house and block most of the view. Without the luxury of a chain saw, it was an all-day job, and since the wood would scarcely dry in time for this winter's fires, it was purely for the health of our hearts that I hacked away. From the kitchen window Chris checked on my progress and shouted out as the light opened in a corner of the sheltered garden and she at last could see out over the fields of sheep and cattle to the tree-lined horizon. And what a difference it made! Each day's weather would now appear to us over a broad vista of sky and meadow.

Huge patterns of clouds blew over the fields. We saw a clearing in the south; the more land we saw from the window the less isolated we felt. This, in itself, might seem sentimental reasoning, but to Chris and me the overwhelming gloom of sheer aloneness that hangs in the air in rural Ireland is a potent force. It is at once the greatest positive and negative thing about the countryside. For with it comes not only the tremendous peacefulness of life here, the undeniable sense of the spiritual, but also the consequent darker aspects of hopelessness and madness.

That evening we took a walk along the westward road to Cree. It had become usual now for a dull day to clear in the early evening, and as we walked the red and golden lights of an inspiring sunset were gathering in the remaining clouds. It was a magical eventide. And so when we came to the ruined old house nearest our farm, we climbed over the rusted gate to take a look. Before us was a long, graceful, curving avenue lined with hawthorn. After several years of abandonment the way had become overgrown with blackberry bramble and nettles. Weedy grass covered the avenue where once a grand carriage and horse had passed on its way up to the big house. Well in, off the road, the fields before it were nicely divided with stone walls; half a dozen roofless cabins bespoke a time when horses had been kept there. The battered stone house itself had a front veranda of sorts with steps rising to the front door. Once, we had been told, this was the grandest house in Kiltumper. People had come on holidays to hear music there, for it was the first and perhaps only house around to have a piano. As we walked up to it that evening, it was impossible not to be touched by the strains of sadness that hung about us. Kathleen, the woman of the house, had been an only child, and even in that grand elegant house she, too, must have sensed the queer edge of loneliness on rainy days in the West that was beginning to plague us. Where once she had played Mozart on the piano and gone cycling to the village, there, too, she had felt the sadness of living alone. It was said of her that she was "educated" and bicycled every day into Kilrush to the convent school. Kathleen knew things and read books and was left alone in her private world, her neighbors shy of her learned countenance.

On that sunset eve we made a hushed, cautious entrance upon the land around the house. In the dying light it was easy to imagine bygone glories. The faintest breeze was blowing, and in the fields bordering the house two wild horses, one black and one white, were galloping freely among the furze. From the house came an eerie chorus of minute sounds, too faint to be named, perhaps the scurrying of a great population of mice, or bats, or both. We didn't investigate further. One look through the gaping window showed us the nearly collapsed, woodwormed piano, and there beside it, the wheelless frame of an old bicycle. We were chilled to the bone, as if we had come upon the site of an isolated madness. The sound from within billowed with a gust of wind, the rafters creaked and we both at once had the sensation that somebody was there. The shadow of a ghost swayed the cobwebs and we were gone, hurrying away down the wild darkened avenue and hearing behind us that faint sound—leaves rustling, or bats flying, or the stirrings of lost melodies upon the worm-eaten chords of the grand piano.

It is a short step from ghosts to fairies. Belief in fairies is still so strong in some parts of the West that one of the fields on the eastern side of our farm could never be built upon. The reason, we learned, was that it harbored a fairy fort. There was no telling what ill luck might befall anyone who disturbed it. Our fairy fort rises on a mound of earth in a circle with a small hollow in its center from which a strange (shall I say fairy-like?) whitethorn tree grows at a twisted angle. It has a mystical beauty about it, and, true to the belief that one can always see another fairy fort from one fairy fort, it looks out upon a spreading valley where another mound rises from the green.

Besides this, there are many stories told in a half-disbelieving tone about various characters who were supposed to be "away with the fairies!"

Michael Donnellan told me how one of his relatives had, in truth, been the first man to fly more than a hundred yards, thanks to the fairies. This person was up on the thatch, mending it and looking over the meadows where the hay had been cut, when suddenly the fairies, who are known to enjoy pranks and games of all kinds, joined in a wind and made the thatch and the man with it lift completely away from the cottage and go flying across the field like an airplane.

"The funny thing was," said Michael, "not a hair on his head was harmed."

My own close encounter was less dramatic. It was a rare, beautiful calm day. We were up on the bog, Michael on the slan, me on the barrow, and we were working quietly.

"Whist, Niall, do ye hear the fairies?" asked Michael suddenly. His face was serious, his slan poised still, and his ear tilted to the West. "The fairies are passing. Look, over there, they're coming."

And over there, fifty yards away in an isolated spot of the field the blue windless day had been transformed by a wild whirlwind shaking the grass and heather and insects. And yet where we stood there was not the faintest breeze, only a strange murmurous sound as though a thousand tiny feet were dancing in circles through the grass. As we watched, the wind moved toward us, leaving a tranquil place behind. And suddenly it was upon us, we were in the middle of a most incredible, swirling, gusting wind. Hands holding to slan and fork, we did nothing. The fairies were passing. Our hair was blown about, and we looked at each other overcome with giddy laughter.

"That'd take the hair from yer head," shouted Michael.

I hardly knew what to say. I have known nothing like it before or since and stood amazed and dumbfounded until it—until *they*—passed, tossing the heather where they went and leaving us once more in an absolutely still, windless place.

"That's a sure sign of fine weather," he said.

Six little, yellow chicks are chirping. One week old and made of the softest yellow feathers. I made a little box-home for them from an orange crate, complete with a door and feeding trough. We've decided to keep them indoors for a few days during which time they will be hardened to the cold May weather and ready to move into their own whitewashed cabin beside the hens. These, I have to remind myself, are not pets and, unlike the hens, Audrey, Henrietta, Morgan and Thornton, cannot be given names. In ten weeks the chickens will be big enough to be killed for the table. But will I ever be able to kill them? They are adorable when they squeeze tightly together for warmth, each one no bigger than a newborn baby's fist. They chirp all afternoon and inspire care and kindness. We are like new parents fawning on them, our chicks. They are, like all additions to the farm, further evidence of our being here, of our actually, finally being here. Hard to believe that we left Manhattan only two months ago.

While I was contemplating the great switch in our life-style today, the room jangled with a sudden loud, startling cling-clang: the telephone actually rang! We are connected!

Niall gingerly lifted the receiver and there on the other end was the voice of Gregory, our operator in the village.

"Welcome aboard," was all he said.

Kilfenora and Corofin, Lisdoonvarna and Miltown Malbay. Music sounds in those names. It jigs and reels all across the county from Killaloe to Kilkee, from Carrigaholt to Ballyvaughan. It's the music of pipes and flutes and fiddles playing in even the smallest pubs all along the Atlantic coastline of Clare. Say Doolin, and everyone knows that you are talking about music.

Clare is famous for it: Irish traditional music. We had been told so many times, but after three hectic months we had still not yet found the time for a *seisiun*, an informal pub-gathering of traditional musicians. In the midst of work that centered around house and garden, music seemed too much an indulgence to justify our locking up and setting off early in the Peugeot while our neighbors were still busy making the most of the lengthening, though wet, summer evenings. But after all, it was partly in search of uniquely Irish things, like seisiuns, that we had come to Ireland in the first place.

One Thursday in the *Clare Champion* a large ad appeared announcing the *Scoil Samhraidh Willie Clancy*, a series of public lectures, classes and recitals in the community hall in Miltown Malbay. That was it, we *must* go.

Although he was no relation to the internationally famous Clancy Brothers, Willie Clancy was the most celebrated of the Clare tin whistle and pipe players. Born on Christmas Eve in 1918, he began learning music from his mother and soon mastered the difficult art of playing the tin, or penny, whistle. Later, finding work hard to come by, he moved from Clare to Dublin and from there to London, where, amidst many other Irish musicians, he became renowned as a piper. He was a founder-member of *Na Piobairi Uilleann,* or the Irish Pipers, and by the time his father died and he returned to County Clare, Willie Clancy was one of the most respected musicians in Clare—indeed in all the country. Since his death in 1973 his name and music have been kept alive in fond memory. The *scoil samhraidh,* or summer school, that is held in Miltown every year brings together for one mad musical week some of the very best traditional musicians not only from Ireland but from Europe and America as well. Its aim is to commemorate Willie Clancy while passing on traditional music to a younger generation. For one week in July Miltown Malbay is alive day and night with Irish music.

The evening was overcast—a prevailing weather condition which was disconcerting us increasingly. Chris herded our latest acquisition, three quacking ducks, christened Larry, Darrell and Darrell, in single file back to their cabin. We shut in the hens and chickens and loaded the Stanley with turf to keep the kitchen warm in our absence. As we set off we had music in our heads. The shortcut road to Miltown was a ribbon of gray unwinding below a glowering sky. It's a road with its own personalized signposts: Daly's immense and handsome Charolais bull on the right, the wrong turn that takes you to Mullagh, and the dip that suddenly rises to reveal the glimmering white breakers of the sea. As you drive that road you sense the mood of the ocean as you near it. By the time we reached the village, the roads were lined with cars.

People everywhere had the same look in their eyes as they left their cars behind in fields and on roadsides. Down the main street toward the church there were fiddlers and pipers playing, and from almost every doorway or open window came the swirl of hornpipes and reels. We felt we had come upon some marvelous celebration. It was truly a festival. Unable and unwilling to cram inside a pub, four young women began an impromptu Clare set-dance on the path outside. Many people, young and old, carried fiddle and flute cases and that evening they seemed to be always on the verge of breaking into music in spontaneous delight.

At the community hall we paid two pounds *Cead Isteach*—admission price—and entered for the main recital—a whistle and flute concert that was to feature the cream of Clare's traditional musicians. There was palpable excitement in the hall as students waited for their masters with tape recorders ready, and men and women sat with their children in expectation.

After a brief announcement, Michael Tubridy of Kilrush stepped onto the stage with his flute. Fingers flickering over the notes, eyes intensely shut, there was not a murmur anywhere as the lovely sad airs and sweet lively jigs made the hall seem like some mid-summer night's wood where fairy music was played effortlessly beneath the stars. Here were no special effects, no lights or costumes, only a parade of excellent musicians—Brid O'Donoghue, Bill MacNamara, Seamus MacMathuna of Cooraclare, and Mick Gavin of Doonbeg—each one playing with all he had for the pleasure of his neighbors. As we sat rapt, we understood the "traditional" element of traditional music more acutely. For as each flutist or whistle player came to play, the tunes were announced in a manner that gave them their place in time and county.

"I learned this reel from a man in Donegal called

Micko Dea who used to play it on the concertina. It's called 'The Road to Sligo.' " Almost every reel and jig had a similar history, the composer's name remembered and even, in some cases, given to the tune itself, so that in time, music and musician became one. Tradition was kept alive. In a mood of reverence the audience was hushed while the masters played. Except, of course, during some too-tempting hornpipe or very lively reel, when a faint but persistent rhythmic tapping of feet marked the beat.

The most beautiful music of the night came as Donnacha O'Brien was brought onto the stage in a wheelchair. After a long pause he positioned the whistle in his mouth and with butterfly-like flickering of his fingers began to play an air that hushed the hall with sadness. We could feel it weep over us. The audience tightened with sorrow and we could hear the wind blowing and the rain on the roof, but all that seemed to matter anywhere was the man on the stage with his tin whistle playing "The Lament of Gavin Wallace." The music was slow and melancholy. And it was easy to imagine the rugged landscape of Clare in every note, with the sea churning, the rain falling, and every road empty for miles.

We couldn't be left on a sad note: Micko Russell was to finish the evening. He came jauntily out on the stage and our mood shifted completely. Now in his seventies, his fame had preceded him. A great round-bellied man with a cheery impish face, Micko has a reputation for genius on the tin whistle, which he has been playing since he was a child. As he set corpulently down, his large frame resting upon a small stool, the whistle in his hand seemed tiny and lifeless. His eyes were watery, he breathed with difficulty. We waited. And then, quite suddenly, he placed the whistle to his lips, like a key to a door, and Micko Russell came alive. A wonderful fast jig came dancing from him and as he played his entire body swayed and bobbed in rhythm. He seemed, in the words of a different musical age, "turned on," for while the music played he was a dance in himself, all jiggles of fat and muscle, his eyes like birds in flight darting around the auditorium. The moment he finished, the instant he took the whistle from his mouth, Micko Russell was transformed back into an ordinary aging man sitting in front of four hundred people. It was as if a spell came and went from him. He was like a jolly puppet sprung into action by some magical puppeteer. Once he placed the whistle to his mouth again, the giddy happy-go-lucky hornpipes, jigs and reels of weddings and midnight dances, or *ceilis* took over. From here there was no turning back; on and on Micko played until toes tapped exuberantly, faces filled with with glee, and troubles were forgotten.

It was in this carefree mood that the evening ended. The crowd spilled out onto the streets of Miltown where more music was playing. It all seemed part of some continuous air or melody arising from the countryside itself. People were hurrying past with pints in hand. One reel mingled with another as a pub door opened and a seisiun emerged. On the street corner an impromptu American-style barbeque had been set up. Chris exclaimed and we hurried over as the moon nudged out from behind a blanket of clouds.

CHAPTER SEVEN _____

Against the romance of music and dancing, however, there was a more sobering reality: the weather. Irish weather is infamous. Mists, rain, fog, gale-force winds are the components of its reputation. But I was born in Ireland and lived twenty-three summers here when the sun shone brightly until eleven at night and days at the seaside were too many to count. Indeed the summer of '84 brought record heatwaves to the country. Was there any reason to suspect that this year was going to be *so* different? After a few bright days on the bog in May the skies turned gray and rain was part of every day. Except for three sunny days, the month of June was a washout. Each morning Chris went to the window in the kitchen and looked out only to find that Hayes' Hill was shrouded in a drizzling rain. Day after day, from morning until just before sunset, the rain fell and kept us from the garden. With no job to go to, with our main activity awaiting us outside the door, we were more a part of the weather than we had ever been in Manhattan. We couldn't simply take the train into the city, hurry along with rubbers and umbrella into a warm lobby, go up in the elevator, change in the office and sit down and wait for coffee and doughnuts. We were *dependent* on dry days, or at least semi-dry ones. Our cut turf on the bog would not be able to dry unless the rain stopped. A cold June meant that a fire must be lit first thing in the morning, and so our fuel began to dwindle quickly. So, like each of our neighbors, we began to watch the evening weather forecast most keenly and to sit each morning by the window looking for a sign of clearing.

Along with the inclement weather came the usual local opinions and predictions. Portents were announced. The cuckoo hadn't been heard since mid-May; one man remembered the beginning of a summer like this—the Black Summer of '47—the worst in living memory.

As the early days of July continued in the same wet gloom, we began to hear of St. Swithin. July fifteenth is Saint Swithin's Day (or Switen's, as he is known in Kiltumper), and the belief that accompanies it is known all over Ireland. It is said that if it rains on St. Swithin's Day it will rain for the next forty days. The origin of the legend is explained in the *Journal of the Cork Historical and Archaeological Society*.

> When St. Swithin, after being waked, was buried, his monks who dearly loved him, thought the simple "house of clay" was not befitting their Lord Abbot, so they determined to build a costly mausoleum which to their minds would more suitably mark his last resting-place on earth, and also show to the world how they

loved him even in death. But St. Swithin, who during his life detested ostentation of display of any kind, besought his divine Master (as it was afterwards revealed to one of his monks) to prevent such a useless expenditure of time and money which might easily be spent with more advantage in relieving the poor and needy.

Accordingly, when his monks had completed this beautiful and costly mausoleum they named a day (July fifteenth) on which the mortal remains of the Saint were to be exhumed and publicly transmitted to their new, and as they considered, more fitting abode. But the prayer of the humble servant of God prevailed, for early on that morning the floodgates of heaven were again, as of old, opened, and one continuous downpour of rain prevailed and thus continued without intermission for the succeeding days. The country for miles around was flooded, which gave all parties, St. Swithin's included, much concern. Thereupon they all prayed to God to less His anger against them and earnestly besought their good and holy abbot, Swithin, to intercede for them. It was at this period that he appeared to one of his monks, revealing to him how displeasing it was to God thus to spend their time in useless display, and forbade them ever interfering with his remains thereafter. The command was obeyed, and ever since, as a remembrance to St. Swithin, when it rains on St. Swithin's Day the succeeding forty days will be times of anxiety for the agriculturist.

And so we waited upon St. Swithin's Day. By July fourteenth we'd had six weeks of rainy weather, and, having heard the legend from many people, were, like everyone else, in a state of nervous expectation. The weather had begun to enter all conversations. Newspapers carried small columns with rainfall figures, and almanacs were consulted. Still, nothing was as crucial as St. Swithin's Day along our little road. After all, there was hay to be cut, turf to be saved. The night before, the weatherman on the television made no mention of the legend but neither did he announce any sign of a break in the weather. We were engulfed by low-pressure zones. We went to bed gloomy.

In the morning rain was falling. It fell all day without a break and for forty days thereafter there wasn't a single dry day. *Really*.

My garden, so fondly dreamed of from my desk in Manhattan, has begun to get away from me. Only weeds thrive here. Tomato, pepper, and zucchini plants sit forlornly through these sunless, cool days, although potatoes, carrots, and cabbage grow on regardlessly. My sugarsnap peas, the weak orphaned child of the garden, are blown about in the gale-force wind. We built the pea fence in anticipation of mild weather. Now, instead, the great black gusty days make the whole thing tilt and sway back and forth like a sail. Time and again, in Wellies and slickers, in the middle of July, I have been out trying to tie the vines back onto the fence, trying to re-anchor the fence, trying to win over the squall. Meanwhile, week after week, letters come from New York telling of heat-waves and droughts, of air-conditioning and water rationing, of dusty gardens going unwatered and red tomatoes coming into early ripeness. . . .

Rain, miserable, depressed, heartache. . . .

One blustery, gray morning we sat in the kitchen nervously waiting, a great pot of water simmering over the turf range. Down the road Mary was getting ready; before long she was heading up the road with a long carving knife in one hand and a white porcelain dish in the other: two of our chickens were ready to be killed.

As neither of us had ever killed anything bigger than a fly, and as the "book" on self-sufficiency had warned of the dangers of the job, we asked Mary to help us. That is, we asked if we might help her. Overnight the two unlucky fat chickens had been separated from the rest and starved. In the morning as we fed the others we could hear the muffled clucking from within the imprisoning cabin. We went back to the house in a knot of guilt. We were both regretful about the entire business, but tried not to betray it to our neighbors less they think us "chicken-hearted." But we were both very doubtful. Would Chris even be able to eat the thing, having known it for weeks on the farm? It was easy enough to eat supermarket chicken, but our own?

There was no more time for philosophy. Up the garden path in the rain came Mary with the long carving knife held out before her. "The Slaughterer of Kiltumper is here!" she announced gaily. Had we everything ready? Newspapers spread? A bucket? Scalding hot water? We had. Chris hung behind to keep the water boiling, and I went out with Mary to the cabin.

How many chickens, stripped featherless and frozen, had I seen? And yet, the living thing there before me seemed so immeasurably different. As we stepped inside the cabin and closed the door behind us, the two birds squawked in the semi-darkness. I imagined that their still, blinkless eyes *knew* as we closed in around them. Mary had the knife, I had the porcelain dish and felt tense enough for a fight. I hardly knew what to expect, and vaguely remembered once being told terrible tales of headless chickens running in a spattering bloody death dance. I could barely breathe. Then, in a moment, Mary had one of them. She picked it up by the legs and turned it upside down as its wings beat in the air and feathers flew. I put the dish on the floor.

"See, feel that now, Niall. Do you feel a little hollow?"

She was pulling feathers from the neck, clearing a place of red skin. I pressed a finger to it and felt a warm, little hollow.

"There," she said, "see." And suddenly the knife was sawing through it. Four clean, strong strokes and the head swung loose like a sack. I was holding the legs and wings, Mary was holding the head, aiming the blood as it began to spill into the porcelain white dish. The wings fluttered in spasms; the chicken swayed in my grasp and some of the blood missed, darkening the straw. The head socket filled with blood and was tilted over like an eerie cup, a spilling pool. The air in the cabin stunk, it was difficult to breathe, I was ready to be sick.

Beside me Mary was expertly bagging the still-dangling head.

"That's one done," she said, placing it in the bucket, picking up the knife, and going after the second. Then the whole process was repeated. From the blood collected in the little dish Mary would make blood pudding. Another head turned pale as it hung loose on a hinge of skin; another small, plastic bag over the head, and then we were ready. I opened the cabin door to daylight. It was raining still and off we ran with two dead chickens to the mortuary of the house.

"Is it done?" Chris wanted to know, peeping around the kitchen door.

"It is," I replied weakly. "Bring the water."

Suddenly it happened. Suddenly out of the blue (or in our case the gray) the fields came alive with activity. Unused to rhythms of the farming year, we knew nothing of the crucial timing of farm work. We barely grasped the urgency with which farmers complained of the weather. Their fields were dead under days of rain. Nothing happened. And then, very suddenly, on a milder half-dry day, the countryside was filled with the drone of tractors, balers and mowers. A gamble was being taken. Hay was being cut.

In West Clare hay has always been the way. Traditionally, the hay is cut on a dry mid-summer's day, turned several times, depending on "the weather" that's in it, and then trammed in cocks or haystacks for further drying before being saved and brought home on a happy note to the hay barn. Three consecutive dry days are needed. When the weather is fine, it's a satisfying time of year. The meadows are left clean and golden and the sight of meadow after meadow of haystacks is a refreshing one: a cycle completed. This year, however, the wet weather had long postponed the hay season and our neighbors drummed their fingers in a waiting game. Until one day—at the first sign of even slightly dry weather—the countryside was pitched into action. Tractors puttered back and forth along the road from early morning to late evening. Men, women and the older children were out with forks turning the rays with one eye on the pasty sky. Would they make it? Or would good hay turn into bad?

On the other hand, there are the silage-makers. Today, farm advisors counsel farmers to make silage instead of saving hay. With silage there is much less dependence on the weather, and a really good farmer can get up to three cuts of silage, as opposed to one cut of hay, off a meadow. The site of the silage pit must be concrete and situated in a place where the drainage from it will not reach any water drains or rivers—for it is a pollutant. The problem lies in the expense of the machinery. To make silage, which in fact is much easier to make than hay, requires one machine to mow and collect the freshly cut grass and deposit it, and another two tractors to compress the cuttings, which are deposited in a rectangular shape, by driving up and down over them so that a "wedge" is formed that is as airtight as possible. These wedges are usually fifty feet plus in length, twelve feet at the highest point and fifteen feet wide. The wedge of silage must be covered in black plastic and secured so no air can circulate.

To most of our neighbors hay is traditional and, although the saving of it is dependent on the weather and more time consuming, we are in a traditional place. Yet even here the new ways are setting in; while the hay-makers worked in the golden meadows, those who planned to make silage could afford to wait for better weather. They felt no urgency. They could drive out in the tractors, see where a day's hay had been cut and left abandoned in despair, as sheets of rain had come streaming down, and later thank God that they were making silage.

Tell me how it's going to be there, Niall.

Who could have foretold this? Who could have predicted the iron-colored days, the weeping skies, the mesmeric falling of desolate rain? How were we to imagine setting off up the hill of Tumper in the drizzle to "foot" the turf, stacking it with bent backs in places where puddles were forming? The battle to "win" home the turf began during the early days of July. For it was not enough to simply cut it and scatter it over the bog. The second stage of work was footing it. *Grogans*, or small stacks of turf, were made of four sods stood upright like a little teepee frame with a sod balanced on top. In this way the wind and sun would gradually dry them. We labored for our fuel up there in the windy wasteland in a different mood. These were not the bright cheery shirt-sleeved days of the cutting. Not the cuckoo days, nor the days of brown bread and tea picnics. No, these were grim, embattled days, both of us groaning with hurting hands over the rough, hardening sods, backs aching and wondering if we would ever get it down and stacked dry in the barn for the winter. We worked three hours and headed home across the squelching wet fields. The bog in this weather was becoming inaccessible.

"Have ye your turf home?"

"No."

"Is it dry?"

"No."

"Sure, it's a terrible old year."

Any dry day, any sign of any clearing, and every able man and woman in the village—those who cut turf—went to the bog. If we appeared in the shops we would be asked: had we been to the bog or were we going? Winning the turf, as it is so aptly called, is also women's work, and the boglands become places of silent, stooping couples working against the weather in hushed hoops of labor. In this way, between hay and turf, in the procession of the farming life, there always seems to be a nudging sense of preparation against the onset of winter.

Tell me how it's going to be there, Niall.

The wet summer had so far yielded little light for painting. The imagined summer of landscapes had not come about, and instead, with the easel mounted in the kitchen, Chris worked on pictures that looked always outward, as if waiting for a change. Awaited too, were the days at the sea, the swimming, the jogging, the T-shirts and swimsuits. All the light buoyant things of summertime. Under the pressure of gray skies we thought oftener of previous summers, of plunging into swimming pools after a day at the office, of corn-on-the-cob, of cookouts, of suntans. I thought of summer dresses and the sweet, sticky luxuriance of things in August. Chris talked of home, of salad days, of sleeping out, of crickets on a clear night, of reading Sunday's *New York Times* on the porch with a giant glass of fresh orange juice at her side and a doughnut, if she wanted one.

We were in the hardest days of our year. A trip to Dublin. That was to be the antidote, or at least the relief. And so, feeling somewhat guilty that we hadn't enough to do on the farm, we left Mary in charge of the animals and headed for the capital. Driving through Limerick, Tipperary, Laois and Kildare, Dublin was a holiday on the horizon. It was things to do on rainy days. It was movies and restaurants, it was shops and galleries, theatres and museums. It was six-channel color television and direct-dial telephones. It was everything we had left behind in New York.

In Dublin the weather was a subject of annoyance, but not of concern. Holidays, not livelihoods, were being ruined. At once, we saw the two-sidedness of Ireland quite clearly: the new and the old, the East and the West, the city and the country. Somewhere between these—the more modern, European-styled state and the ancient, traditional Ireland—lies the country at present.

As we walked around St. Stephen's Green, down Grafton Street and along by the high iron, green railings of Trinity College, we were more than ever aware of having come from the country, from the West. We had grown unused to even small crowds, to even just a little noise. And suddenly the hustle of *non*-rush-hour traffic was startlingly hectic.

Still, for two days we delighted in it. We hurried happily around with everyone else from shop to shop, looking, wishing to buy, but just looking in the end. That day Dublin might have been London or Paris for us as we gazed upon its offerings. Chris stocked up on art supplies, not being able to get them anywhere else; we browsed through every bookshop, and then, the sun shining down the streets of Georgian door-ways, we thought fretfully of Kiltumper. Were our animals all right? I suppose in a way we felt most uneasy about leaving the house and land. Not that anyone could steal it, but we had a sense of not quite trusting. Trusting what? It's hard to say except that we felt we were abandoning our adopted life-style, and, in a small way, betraying our own cause.

We had infused ourselves with energy and by the evening of the third day we loaded the car with bor-rowings—a small dresser (up to that point we still hadn't a place to put our clothes except for two open wooden shelves), a couple of throw-rugs, and a copper pot—and headed back to the West.

We left late and by the time we turned off the Ennis-to-Kilrush road and onto the familiar winding Fruar road, it was eleven in the evening and the last light of day was dying. We were back in the peaceable world. Chris turned to me and said, "The quiet is deceptive here. It's like driving through the village at mid-day when the place seems frozen, devoid of all activity. Yet behind every door something *is* happening."

She was right. For in the most unexpected places, behind the most ordinary doors, you could find the most curious things. It was months before we learned that there was a television and radio repair man who serviced the village's broken sets in his spare time in the evenings. Everyone seemed to know about it except us. Or that the creamery in the village, the place where all the parish dairy farmers brought their milk, also sold fertilizer, cattle feed, and silage covers.

We were driving along the one-car-wide by-road

that cuts through the countryside and is only traveled by those who know of its existence—the locals. Suddenly, in the middle of the road ahead of us were a cluster of men and a machine. I braked and pulled the car up sharply. Our headlamps caught faces peering at us wondering who the midnight travelers were. Some of them undoubtedly recognized us as the "Yanks" and directions were shouted and a flurry of activity ensued. The object of all the excitement was an over-turned tractor in the center of the road. In the midnight darkness inspired farmers were trying to right it while a gallery of neighbors in Sunday dress, cigarettes lit, eyes full of knowing unconcern, leaned on the stone wall and looked on mutely.

It was a busy little scene in the middle of the dark night; there are no streetlights here. Inch by inch we were waved around the fallen machine. I had the feeling we were part of some craftily prearranged night entertainment.

"This is just the kind of thing I was talking about," whispered Chris as men nodded to us. Others were already heading off along the road with the news of the accident. As our car drove on the lights picked them out: the newsbearers, men in brown suits and caps come out in the night to see the commotion and now heading back to the fire with conversation ready. We knew instinctively the rhythms of the whole scene, and knew enough to guess that we, too, would be part of the tale: "He blocked the Yanks!"

What we did not know was that already Kil-tumper featured us in other news, in a scene that had taken place in our brief absence.

We stopped at Mary's for the back door key that we had left with her. She answered the door in her dressing gown and spoke breathlessly.

"Niall, I left the key over . . . but ye can't go back."

"Why not, Mary?"

"Ye have trouble. Ye have bees!" What did she mean?

"They're in the bedroom," Mary said, "Joe and I were over to feed the animals and didn't we hear this queer humming and Joe went over and said 'Come here Mary, quick, look at all the bees inside in the room!' . . . And Niall, I never saw so many. Oh, there's hundreds of them now. Ye couldn't go back tonight." She paused to allow me to gather myself.

"They must have come down the chimney or something, Niall. There was some flowers and fruit in the back room, too."

I remembered that on the Friday evening before leaving Chris had set up a still-life in the window with lemons, oranges and a vase of nasturtiums.

Mary had guests in the spare room. "Will ye sleep in the sitting room on the floor? Ye could sleep on the mattress."

It was the only port in a storm; we were saved once again by our most amicable neighbor. I walked to the car with the delicate task of telling Chris without panic that she couldn't return to her bed tonight because it was the temporary haven of invading bees. I wish I could have had the composure to whisper, "Is this what you meant?"

Upon dreams of bees and a sleep full of insects we awoke with the problem of getting rid of them. By then, it seemed, nearly all of Kilmihil knew.

"Ye have bees, Niall," said the shopkeeper.

"We do, and plenty of them," I quipped back to her satisfaction, lest the world think we were terrified.

There were various counsels, as always. "Wear a sheet over yer head, walk into the room and wait until all the bees cluster about you and then throw the sheet over them," was what one man advised. And another said knowingly, "Run into the room and put down a big dish of molasses and they'll get stuck in it!"

Leaving my audience to mull further over our predicament, I went directly to the chemist and asked his opinion.

"Spray 'em," he said without hesitation, and ten minutes later, I was walking around the back door of the cottage with four cans of wasp killer. There, at the door, Mary had left a message scraped on a piece of slate, just barely legible: "CRISSIE, BEWARE OF BEES!"

I opened the door expecting to be attacked. Nothing. I stepped down into the kitchen. Nothing. No bees. Was it a prank? Perhaps they'd kindly departed I hoped as I opened the door into the parlor. A tremendous hum rose in the air and I froze. I had never heard anything like it. Opening the door I sprayed like a madman and saw perhaps a hundred bees clustered at the window, as if in a hive. I was reassured. There weren't so many.

Then the real humming arose. They were in the bedroom! The few I had done away with were merely an offshoot of the main body. I went outside and looked in the bedroom window. There, in a great hot swarming mass of black and yellow, were more bees than I had ever seen. The room was alive with them, crawling, buzzing, covering—a little hill of leggy activity upon photographs and papers, making the place their own. For two hours, jacket over head, and can in hand, running breathlessly in and out of that room until dead bees covered the carpet, the bed, the windowsill and the fireplace, I did away with them. They buzzed harmlessly and dropped in faint fury as I hurried time and again outside into the air for breath. They would not leave by the open window I offered them, but a cloying guilt gathered over me. What sort of farmer was I going to make? Once the terror had eased I realized that I had, perhaps, too hastily poisoned them and the chemical killer spray hung dankly upon the air.

What should I have done? Should I have known that right there in the village was a beekeeper? Like every other unexpected crisis there seemed to be an equally unexpected remedy, only this time we learned of it too late. In a wave of sudden exhaustion I went back down the morning road to Mary's, to Chris and a cup of tea. My heroics were praised, and a letter had come from Chris's sister Deirdre announcing that she was coming to visit! And soon!

"Tell me," began the cheery letter, "*exactly* what you did today."

Deirdre's coming! Thank God! I can't wait. What will she think of us now? Will she think that we've changed in the five months since we took that last train from Manhattan and flew to Ireland? I'm starting to get worried. Have I stressed enough the somewhat severe quietness of life here? Perhaps I've overdrawn things. Perhaps she'll think we're paupers without a kingdom and she'll feel sorry for us. And the garden, oh the garden! She mentioned in her letter wanting to see 'what must be by now a wonderful garden.' But as I look through the window, the rainy mass of sorry plants and happy weeds is anything but the splendor of which I dreamed.

We were anxious about our first visitor from America. How had our letters painted our life here? There was no great excitement to offer a visitor to Kilmihil; we drove into the village looking at it from the viewpoint of a new arrival. Now, of course, we had grown used to it; it was almost like home to us. But with Deirdre's imminent visit we were given over to inferiority complexes of the worst kind. The house, the garden, the unpainted canvases—the rawness of a new beginning. We, of course, knew the truth; we knew that the so-far wet summer had given us little chance to overcome the wilderness that still converged from the edges of turned soil; we knew that four or five months is no time to bring back a garden that had been a jungle for five years . . . but would a visitor appreciate this?

Our embarrassment drew us out in rainy weather, weeding among the cabbages and the sun-starved flowers. Our neighbors, sensing our concern, complimented us on how much we *had* done.

But had we? It would take a visitor to tell, someone who had known us in our madcap days rushing between office and the apartment, between the supermarket and the bank, with all the little chores that piled up for doing on weekends. Through Deirdre we would see ourselves as we were, here in Kiltumper Cottage. We counted the days, and in a last-minute panic that Kiltumper would prove uninspiring and downright depressing, we booked two nights at a bed-and-breakfast in Kerry.

When she arrived our worries dispersed like seeds blown away on the wind. We had underestimated just how different our life had become; to someone as curious and cheerful as Deirdre, everything was enthralling. All along the road our neighbors shook her hand and welcomed her "home." She was to be invited for tea at all the houses and asked right away how she liked Ireland? Had Niall and Crissie changed? For the better? She nodded that we had. Everyone nodded that we had. The best buns and scones and cake were brought out for the visitor.

Meanwhile, secretly, back at the cottage, Deirdre unloaded bags of gifts for us, some of the sorely missed things of New York—the Magazine and Book Review sections from *The New York Times*, two pairs of Levis, two giant jars of Skippy crunchy peanut butter, and packages of pesto sauce. For a week, we had the best of both worlds.

We looked at Ireland anew in Deirdre's company. With sunny spells making rainbows between the showers we drove out the western road where meadowsweet and pink valerian grew wildly, where Chris gathered knapweeds and mayweeds and harebells from fields by the sea, and where all three of us were full of wonder as the colors of Irish summer were awakened in a day of sunshine. Cerulean sky appeared after a morning's rain, green hills and golden meadows with hay trams stippling them in shadows, new grass, old grass, sheep, cattle, and everywhere black plastic-covered silage pits and the tractors buzzing until nightfall. The Peugeot purred happily around the bends of Clare, from Kilkee to Lahinch, Lisdoonvarna to Ballyvaughan. And every sight seemed newly discovered in the freshness of another person's presence.

The Cliffs of Moher in the afternoon light, crystalline and sparkling. There, from O'Brien's Tower, is one of the best views from any point in the West of Ireland. We had seen it before, and had seen, too, in an accepting, glimpsing way innumerable postcards of it. And yet. You stand there, all seaspray and wind, on the very edge of the country and you see the entire coastline of Clare running craggily away on either side of you. It is stunning. The drop to the light green ocean is sheer and awesome. Seabirds are loftily mid-distant. Out to sea shimmer the spread forms of the Aran Islands—Inisheer, Inishmaan, Inishmore—names austere and poetic as any this side of the Atlantic. The whole scene is entrancing, and it doesn't take a visitor to conjure you into the spell.

Inland from the Cliffs of Moher to the Burren and

again a sweep of changing scenery. Instead of sea and spray all is limestone rock and shale as Ireland's most unusual geography takes you down steep, stomach-turning Corkscrew Hill. The Burren. Here, thriving in crags and crevices of a natural limestone rockery are hordes of wildflowers and plants found nowhere else in the country. Chris named them for us: blue gentians, mountain avens, bloody cranesbill, and wild orchids. I reminded Deirdre of the chillier side of the place; the Burren was thought so barren that Cromwellian troops had claimed there was neither wood to hang a man, water to drown him nor earth to bury him.

Deirdre stared out the window. We drove on in a hush.

We crossed on the ferry from Killimer to Tarbert and entered the County Kerry. The coast road takes you by the fabulous sandy beach and reknowned golf course at Ballybunion. Then on into Tralee City and over the Slieve Mish mountains—Kerry green and Kerry gold. Soft weather is falling all around us as we circle closer to the larger mountains of Kerry—the MacGillacuddy Reeks, majestic in broken sunlight, their peaks in cloud. We each mention Nonnie O'Connell and think of her, stopped on a high road over a breathtaking view of the MacGillacuddies. It feels like a place of ancient haunts, of nobility and chieftains. Bracken-covered hills and field scabious, heather and green knolls. The Ring of Kerry. It's a place to be silent.

All around the Lakes we drove through the

serene, dark beauty of wild rhododendrons and native holly trees. We settled in Glenbeigh where high green hills rise to the south; the great flat six-mile sandy beach of Rossbeigh runs away to the west. Not a person anywhere.

"I *told* them there were beautiful beaches in Ireland!" Deirdre cried gleefully, her camera ready. In the morning, she took the Beach Gallop, while on the six miles of deserted seaside Niall and I went swimming in our underpants . . . and lost them in the freezing waves!

On to Derrynane, where Daniel O'Connell, the Liberator and the founder of Catholic Emancipation, lived. Derrynane, where the sun came out on a lovely quiet cove overlooking Skellig Island. It was the best day of the year so far. Kerry worked its magic on us.

Word came on the telephone when we returned; there was blight in Kiltumper. Mary herself was afraid she'd seen signs of it on her stalks. We had heard the warnings of the radio and sprayed twice already. Just after the half-past-one news, the newscaster had announced: "The weather over the next few days will bring the likelihood of blight." And so it had. Damp, rainy days and misty evenings brought it and suddenly the weather forecasts had a new urgency.

Blight, a fungal spore, travels on the wind and flourishes in dampness. It starts with a characteristic black spot on the leaves and eventually enters the potato tuber through the infected stalk. Within a few days, the leafy potato plant starts to blacken, wither and rot. If the tubers are severely infected, the potatoes are lost. Already this summer whole crops of the vegetable had been ruined, and here and there along the road you could see the withered potato gardens, spectral and black, or dug up early with the rotten stalks burning in a corner.

Spraying is only a defense. But for spray to work, the stalks must be dry. From the moment we heard the news of blight down the road, we were back once again as farmers, and all our touring and the scenery faded from mind. We inspected the stalks and leaves, we dug up a few potatoes and found them all right, and then we sat in the kitchen with Deirdre, watching the clouds and waiting for our moment.

A dry morning. There was no time for scruples, there was no time to weigh and balance the various arguments for or against the use of Dithane 405 to combat the blight. We wanted to save the potatoes more than anything else at that moment. They were our first symbol of settlement, our first planting on our first morning in Kiltumper. The image of their blackening into nothingness and the entire garden outside the front window disappearing before our eyes was too strong a terror. No, we couldn't lose them now. On top of all the rainy weather, that would have crushed us.

With the same implicit trust that was at work when we first set them in the beds of manure, we sprayed them. I was thinking this is how famine begins, quick, blackly and overnight, coming invisibly through the darkness in a year of bad weather. The spray mizzled in our noses and dampened our thighs as we waded among the furrows. Were there potatoes all underground here? We trod carefully, as if over jewels. I remembered a poem from schoolday lessons. Patrick Kavanagh's *Spraying the Potatoes* and the lines:

> He turned my way. "God further the work."
> He echoed an ancient farming prayer.
> I thanked him. He eyed the potato-drills.
> He said: "You are bound to have good ones there."

Good ones there? We wondered silently and sprayed madly while Deirdre watched us from the window. We were to have a feast from the garden that day: peas, onions, carrots, raspberries, one of the slaughtered chickens, and, yes, our first potatoes. The spraying finished, Chris brought in a handful to show and we all stood round as she washed them. This, I thought, more than anything measures the distance we've come from Manhattan. As we sat down at the table later, rain began to fall again. Had we had enough time? Had the spray dried on the stalks or was the whole spraying for nought? For that moment it didn't matter. Our favorite visitor was here to share in our first harvest dinner, and we put the thought of blight into a far corner of our minds. Instead we oohed and aahed over the flouriness of our new potatoes, the sweetness of the sugarsnap peas, and the distinctive flavor of our home-reared, organically grown chicken. It was a feast full of delight. It was a bright moment on which to look back . . . and from which to look forward. Chris gazed across the table at me, smiling.

Tell me how it's going to be there, Niall?

CHAPTER EIGHT

Sometime in July, when the rainy summer began to break down the holiday mood of the country and when talk of a farming crisis began to air on the radio, an unusual thing happened. Initially, only a small paragraph describing the bizarre incident appeared on the inside pages of the *Irish Times*: the sort of item you usually don't notice on the first reading of a newspaper, but later, coming upon it in the bathroom or when it is old and folded by the fire box, you spot it. It was a small article describing a curious episode in West Cork. The place was Ballinspittle, a village largely unknown until the summer of 1985 but ever afterward to stand for a phenomenon that gathered momentum and became major news in Ireland.

The first article we saw caused us no more than a moment's smile. It was the kind of thing you somehow expected in Ireland: at the small Marian grotto outside the village of Ballinspittle a statue of Our Lady had been seen to move by ten people.

Ireland is no stranger to miraculous happenings. At the now famous shrine in Knock, County Mayo, an apparition of Our Lady was seen by fifteen people in 1879, and after much debate the shrine was later made official by the Vatican. But a moving statue! It was too fantastic, and that morning (except for the few people in Ballinspittle) it was the subject of summer jokes. For example, in nearby Cooraclare a large statue of Our Lady carried the sign: OUT OF ORDER!

Down in Kilmihil schoolboys whistled at the statue of Michael the Archangel beckoning it to move. But in general the issue was treated with caution and wonder. Some said that it happened because at this year's Cork Film Festival there was to be a screening of Godard's controversial film on the life of Our Lady. It was a sign. To some it was clearly linked to the so-called Kerry Babies Tribunal, an investigation currently underway at the High Court in Dublin. Two murdered newborn infants had been found off the coast of Kerry, and the nation was alarmed. More light-heartedly, it was thought a trick by Bord Failte, the tourist board, at a time when, in the height of the summer season, rain was falling by the bucketful. For a week nothing happened, then it appeared again in the *Irish Times*: the statue at Ballinspittle had been seen moving. Longer reports followed. Apparently, crowds of a hundred were gathering nightly around the grotto saying the Rosary and singing hymns. When asked, eighty percent of them said they had seen the statue move. It moved its head from side to side, it opened and closed its hands, or, most mysterious of all, visions of Jesus Christ and Padre Pio appeared in front of it. The story progressed from the inside to the second-page headlines. Ballinspittle and the people who *believed* quickly became the targets of a whole series of jokes: about the Cork people, about the wet summer and about the Church.

"Oh, most Blessed Virgin, *sway* for us!"

However, there were believers—the Ballinspit-tleans. They had seen, and their lives were not to be the same again. The radio programs had daily interviews with them. What exactly was it they had seen? Again and again the same story emerged: The statue moved its head from side to side; it opened and closed its hands a few inches; it seemed to say things, although what it said was not quite clear.

Within a week the bishops were urging caution. Religious hysteria was growing in rural Ireland. Two weeks after the news of Ballinspittle reached the media, there were further sightings. More statues were moving. And in a clear arc around coastal Ireland—from Waterford to Cork and through Kerry and Clare all the way to Sligo—people began to mass around the many Marian grottos and shrines, saying rosaries and singing hymns. And the statues moved as if in miraculous response.

This was beyond anything Chris and I had imagined possible in Ireland. Television crews were sent out to Cork, Mayo and Sligo, but the statues didn't move for the cameras. Then again, for the camera *operators* and *reporters* they did. Self-proclaimed doubters and agnostics came forth and joined the believers. The country was turned on its head. There were new sightings almost daily. On a small country road in Coolens in County Mayo four schoolgirls coming home at night saw an apparition of Our Lady in the skies above them. The following day there were thousands gathered in the fields about the spot. RTE, the national television and radio station, had received more than a dozen calls after close-down one evening from callers claiming to have seen the face of Jesus vaguely outlined on the blank television screen. The country was in the grip of religious fervor unlike anything it had known in decades. There wasn't a person anywhere who didn't know what Ballinspittle meant.

Down in Kilmihil a small handwritten sign appeared in one shop window: now there was to be a bus to Ballinspittle every Sunday. For the rest of the summer it would be packed.

One Sunday morning in mid-July the round genial figure of a fifty-year-old man marched up our front path. He was Paddy Cotter, he said, and he came into the kitchen without further ado. We were by now used to the country way of gradually edging closer to the main subject of conversation, and for a time the three of us sat in the kitchen, having tea and talking about everything but the reason for Paddy's visit. We knew he would come to it in time, and as we waited and watched his eyes flickering across Chris's paintings on the wall, we began to remember something we had already been told: "Paddy Cotter, he's a man who is very interested in anything to do with the arts."

And so he was. "Do ye know they have this festival, a *Fleadh*, in Kilmihil every year?" he asked us at last. Yes, we were eagerly awaiting it, the musical event of the year in town, and a topic of conversation for weeks to follow. Yes, we knew. A full year ago, coming upon a copy of the *Clare Champion* at a newsdealer's on Forty-second Street, we had read the program for *Ceol Kilmihil*, literally "Music Kilmihil."

"Well," said Paddy, "this year I'm thinking of having a bit of an art show in the Fleadh and would Crissie be a part of it?"

Chris had never imagined the rush of activity which would mark the first showing of her paintings in Ireland. The gallery, as it *had* to be called, was Matty Melican's unlived-in house down on the main street in Kilmihil. In this exhibition, however, the "artists" were not to be simply artists; they had to be workmen too. Floors and walls needed scrubbing. "Crissie, have ye any old pail?"

My first exhibition. And what a gallery! The floor-boards are dangerously loose, more than one stone wall has bits of plaster falling away and the wainscotted walls of green and pink and Naples yellow are stained with grease and soot. In the kitchen, where an old stove still stands, the light is poor and the walls need washing. But Paddy is not a man to be discouraged. He shrugged at the amount of work that lay ahead. "Well, it won't be New York," he said to me, "but it'll be something all the same."

Within a couple of days of Paddy's visit, Chris was down at the gallery with brush, hammer and nails. The whole place needed going over. While Paddy talked excitedly about the other local artists who would be part of the first-ever Kilmihil Fleadh Art Exhibition, Chris groaned and wondered: what would a New Yorker think of this? The light was terrible, the place was musty. Then again, who would come into Matty Melican's to see the paintings when there would be music playing in every pub in town? The whole project seemed doubtful. But like everything in Kilmihil, within moments of its inception word had leaked out, "Ye're to have paintings in the Fleadh, Crissie?" Now there was no turning back.

With the continual rain, there was no possibility of carrying the easel out into the fields; landscapes remained half-started, half-imagined, orphans of the season's ruin. Instead, while the work went ahead on the gallery, Chris hurried to finish the first large canvas of our days here, a great colorful picture looking outward from our crooked kitchen where the door is always open, where the sugan chair is always waiting to welcome a visitor. This picture, still wet, was to be Chris's main contribution to the exhibition, and she hoped there was a cheerful simplicity in it that might let people know how she felt in Kiltumper.

Small plastic flags of green, white, and orange fluttered in the rain. They had been hung the length of the village, passing the community hall where the ceilis were to be held and where the two large fish-and-chip vans had already settled for the weekend. Two old-fashioned loud speakers hung at the cross-roads and staticky Irish music filtered from them. It was Friday afternoon, and three hours later the Fleadh was to get into full swing.

We had already seen the programs which were being handed out at the shops and stuck in windows about the town. The Fleadh was to begin on Friday evening; there would be pub and street seisiuns; there would be dancing at the crossroads at eleven o'clock; and there would be ceilis every midnight in the community hall. Already musicians had arrived. Fiddle and flute cases hurried through the street. The members of the famous Liverpool Ceili Band had been dispatched to the various houses where people had agreed to give them lodging. That Friday afternoon in Kilmihil there was no one about but Chris, Paddy Cotter and a couple of young artists who were hanging paintings in Matty Melican's. The gallery was finished just as it was due to open, and all in all the sixty-eight paintings that covered the walls made a good display. Hastily, Chris had typed up a brochure with titles and prices, and in the same haste Larry Blake, the headmaster of the Kilmihil Vocational

School, had made copies. Everything was set. Then the rain bucketed down.

Friday night was a washout. With the usual timid curiosity of the Irish—I won't go in if there's nobody in there—a gradual stream of people moved silently through Matty Melican's and viewed the paintings. It was a success, Paddy whispered and smiled, for although little was said, there was interest. A new dimension—bringing art into the Fleadh— had been achieved. Chris stood shyly in the corner and smilingly received our neighbors' warmest congratulations and praise. "They're lovely pictures, Crissie." And in its own innocent way, too, the exhibition of paintings was a lovely thing. This was different from a gallery showing in New York. There was a vast gap between the murmurs of the initiates, flicking through glossy gallery catalogs, and the instant and gratifying exclamation: "That's Kathleen's place in that one. That's over by Downes's, look!"

Meanwhile the skies continued to pour, cars were double-parked the length of the town and the speakers at the crossroads played music to nobody at all. With wary looks and hurried nods the short journey from car to pub was quickly made. Inside the pubs the Fleadh was taking off on schedule. There were packs of musicians, and every opened door revealed the same thronging crowd, with fiddle, concertina and whistle players sitting around a table full of pint glasses, with tapping feet and red faces all around. By eleven the rain was heaviest and the programmed street seisiuns were canceled for that night; there was to be no dancing at the crossroads. By the time Chris and I locked up the gallery and headed back to Kiltumper the streets were deserted and only the haphazardly parked cars gave any indication of the secret festival of music that ran on into the small hours of the morning.

It rained again the next day, and the next day

after that as well. Ceol Kilmihil was the wettest ever and the tramp of wet boots through Matty Melican's front door grew fainter as the weather worsened. There had never been a year like it, we were told. However, as Paddy had remarked before the Fleadh, "If there's rain, sure nobody will come, and if there's sun, sure, nobody will come." (Presumably, in fine weather the farmers would be out until sundown since heretofore they had been unable to make hay.) All of the street sessions had to be abandoned, and only in the warm, smoky pubs did the Fleadh live on, sometimes marred with too many hours at the bar and too much drinking without a break for air. We moved through the weekend with a sense of not quite definable disappointment.

Still, there were two events to come, the set-dance competition at midnight and the first-ever Kilmihil parade which was scheduled for Sunday morning after last mass. For a week before the Fleadh Mary the hairdresser had been solidly booked. It seemed almost every woman in town had a new "do," and by the evening of the Senior Set Competition they had all gathered inside the community hall. It was wonderful. Bashful, suited and shaved, men changed out of their farming clothes for the occasion and came as gallants—Claremen as good as any for a jig and a reel. Up on the stage the Liverpool and Tulla Ceili Bands belted out the music and you could touch the excitement with your hand. Here at last was that happiness we had always associated with the word *Fleadh*, for it meant something more than a festival of music, it meant a holiday for farmers. As we watched the nimble dancing and the practiced clockwork-like steps that men and women had known since childhood, we momentarily forgot the pouring rain, the ruined garden, and the lost summer.

By Sunday it was obvious that the weather would not change for the remainder of the holiday weekend, and any event would have to skirt around it. We heard in the gallery after last mass that the parade was threatened: it was lashing rain. Within minutes, Paddy Cotter, busy, bustling organizer, was down the street with a blue pen marker and a handful of sheets of paper. Signs had to be put up: the parade was to be postponed until Monday. Johnston's, Daly's, Cotter's and Saunders' shops, and a string of telegraph poles displayed the message, and in the usual word-of-mouth way it was passed along. Ten minutes later the street was emptied of people waiting for the parade. The Fleadh organizer resolutely promised that it would take place the following day.

Monday afternoon there we all were at the crossroads, standing opposite the graveyard and waiting for the parade. The rain for once had held off. A little crowd, we stood and waited in a huddle on the steps outside the church without any idea of what to expect. Chris was thinking of New York parades, of fanfares and St. Patrick's Day. But that wasn't what we were to see. Half an hour after the scheduled start the parade appeared—from behind our backs! It was heading down past us to the starting point. "Don't look," I whispered to an astonished Chris, "we have to pretend we haven't seen it." She bubbled with laughter and watched as the entire parade did an about-face and came at us up the street. The parade consisted of six long trailers disguised as floats; representatives of the athletic club, elegant costumed women from the Irish Countrywomen's Association; a young Barry McGuigan; an invisible man; a gun club float with painted brook and waterfall and stuffed pheasants; and Paddy Cotter, smiling gleefully from a float, momentarily turned into a well-known character from Ireland's own soap opera, *Glenroe*. The parade passed to applause and laughter, and everyone admired it, waving at the final float even as the held-off rain at last began to fall.

You can forget it for a while. For a while it's only out there, streaming down the windowpane and spilling from the clogged gutter. You can concentrate indoors and try to dismiss the weather. But it happens. A storm blows up. It's August and you're helpless to ignore it. What sort of weather is this, for God's sake?

Last night's wind kept Chris from sleep and this morning we opened the kitchen shutters with dread. There it was: The pea fence was blown down and the thin tendrils of the sugarsnaps had been ripped away. The months of struggle, the battle against the jackdaws to get the seeds to germinate, the securing of the fence, the tying and retying of its pins in the squally July, and now this, the rude end of this season's crop.

By late morning, with the wind-driven rain still churning the treetops madly, we had mustered the courage to go out and inspect the damage first-hand. Sure enough, the crop had been brought to an early end. But as we raised up each bruised or broken stem and plucked the pods, we saw that there would be a healthy harvest all the same. This was the end of something, the end of one of those early days in Kiltumper Cottage when innocent faith had seen us out planting for the summer of growth. This, our first real harvest from seed to crop, contained within it the lessons of the West: the raw seasons, the unexpected storm and the unexpected harvest all the same.

No car came or went on our road as the scarcely noticed rain softly fell, and Chris and I filled plastic bags with peas, bringing them inside to the kitchen and the weighing scales.

By noon we were cheered as twelve pounds of peas lay heaped across the table.

The phone jangled into life and startled us one day, and Mary's cheerful voice came loudly on the other end.

"There's a fellow gone down to ye. He came here and I sent him back the road. He's looking to see Tumper's Grave."

At Chris' insistence I pulled on the Wellies and headed up the back meadow to meet the stranger. He was from Dublin, Mary had added, almost unnecessarily. For in these parts only Dubliners or Americans come looking for giants' graves. After all, we ought to know; looking for Tumper's Grave was one of the first things we had done when we arrived here.

As far as we knew, the name of our townland, Kiltumper, had no proven derivation. There were two main versions of its history—the pagan version and the Christian version. The Christian explanation cited the fact that *Cill* in Irish meant church and *Tuimpe* was literally a hump, giving the meaning "church on the hill." And as the land does rise dramatically to a hilltop with a spectacular view across the southwest tip of Clare, this origin has held some sway in the textbooks. There are, however, no signs of any church foundation, or building of any kind, up on that windswept hill.

The pagan explanation is much more agreeable and imaginative. Tumper, you see, was a giant. A fierce and infamous warrior, he was able to hold an average man in the palm of one hand, and could squeeze water from a stone with the other. There is some, slight, evidence for this explanation. For up there on the hill of Kiltumper is a mound of grass, about twelve feet long and five feet wide, with a broken circle of stones about it. This was supposedly Tumper's Grave.

Heading up the back meadow I expected to meet someone on holidays with a woolly notion of finding giants. After all, there was little enough for tourists to do in Kilmihil, and besides fishing in the serene beauty of Knocklough Lake, it was hard to imagine what anyone would do here on vacation. Halfway up the hill meadows I saw him, a young Dublin man moving with slippery caution across the flooded ruts of the tractor path. He had no boots and already his city shoes were the worse for it. With a shy uncertain glance down the hill, he stopped when I called out to him and looked at me as if I was about to clear him off the lands.

"I was told I could come up," he said, "I'm just looking for Tumper's Stone."

"You mean Tumper's Grave," I said to him. "It's up on the top of this hill."

"No, Tumper's Stone. I've seen the grave before but I never saw the stone and I'm doing an article on Irish *cromlechs*, or stone circles, and one of them, mentioned by Borlase in his book, *The Dolmens of Ireland*, centers around something called Tumper's Stone." He paused and looked at me. "He describes it quite clearly, so it should be here somewhere."

I was a bit taken aback, but surprised and delighted, too.

"Well, let's go up and look for it."

"I'm sorry," he said suddenly, as we set off, "my name is Conor Newman."

And in a typical, coincidental Irish way, I realized that I knew him. He was the brother of someone I had gone to college with. We had been neighbors in Dublin.

We went up the windy hill looking for giants. The wet land sucked at our steps and the cattle moved slowly away beneath a glowering sky. With the sweeping landscape stretching for miles all around us, it was easy to imagine a configuration of giants, great footsteps tramping over the bogs and a bellow and a song from Tumper's hill.

We arrived at the mound, and Conor paced it, kicking at the stones that circled the spot, gazing down the hill, and across to the west where the cliffs of Kilkee can be seen jutting into the spray of the wild Atlantic. It had the right orientation, he said. They buried their chieftains in an east-to-west grave like this and often just below the crest of the hill. However, Tumper's stone and its cromlech could merely have been the demarcation of a place of religious or judicial importance. Perhaps Tumper was buried elsewhere. But it looked like something all right, he added, and moved off into nearby clusters of furze and bracken. For a moment the word *chieftain* had worked magic on me and I stood there, my mind full of ancient warriors, mud huts and turf fires. A giant's head lay beneath my foot. *He* had walked these hills centuries before.

Leaving Conor to wander alone before he would come down to lunch with us, I hurried home to Chris like a schoolboy-knight who had slain dragons. We were on Tumper's trail, we were going to find a cromlech, a burial chamber; there was a giant up there! Within minutes Chris was in on it, fixing sandwiches and soup, and by the time Conor arrived in sopping wet shoes and socks, we were all set to gulp down the food and hurry back up the hill. Mind you, you'd really want to know what you were looking for, because quite honestly, it looks like nothing up there but grass and stones and cattle.

But there was more news.

"I didn't find Tumper's stone", said Conor, "but I did find what I'm pretty sure is a megalithic tomb on your land. And as well as that I found a quern stone. It was too heavy for me to bring down, but between the two of us maybe we could go up and get it after lunch."

Our excitement was matched only by our ignorance. We had no real idea of what a megalithic tomb or a quern stone was, so lunch became a lesson in ancient history.

At its simplest, a megalithic tomb is a burial chamber dating from roughly 2500 years before Christ; it consists of a large capstone and a heelstone, with several small subterranean stones filling the crevices. It would contain the body of somebody of significance and would most often include some kind of earthen pot or chalice as an offering to the gods at the gateway into the afterlife. The quern stone, dating from about 500 years later, was essentially a rubbing stone used to mill grain. And the smooth indentation and finish resembling the back-and-forward motion of stone against stone could be seen on its surface.

We added to Conor's information our very own "fairy fort," which is actually a ring-fort. The ancient Irish lived in nomadic conditions and in times of danger fled to the enclosure of their forts. The remains of these circular forts, which were sometimes made of stones but usually built of earth or clay, look like raised mounds.

Everything we were to do that day was abandoned to the tracing of giants. We lent Conor the spare Wellingtons and set off with our meal barely eaten.

In ancient times, Kiltumper was a thickly populated region, but whether the demarcations of the townland have since changed or the area has simply shrunk through emigration and hardship, there are now no more than six houses here, compared to the now-thriving town of Kilmihil. And yet, walking up the sloping meadows and thinking of old history and the possibility that once there was a settlement of sorts around that windy hilltop, we got an eerie feeling of shadows and ghosts. The quern was not a stone dropped there by some passing cart; there, in what had been a bog for two thousand years, a human hand had put it down to stay . . . until Conor's had picked it up. As Conor explained it, finding the quern stone was not insignificant; it gave evidence, half-buried up there in the encroaching bogland, of a time when tradesmen, villagers and peasants lived close by. The ring-fort was further evidence that Kiltumper, from as early as ancient times up until the famine years, had been a populated place.

Quern stone and megalith. Chris fingered their cold damp textures like puzzles, *feeling* the passing of time. The three of us shifted the weight of the quern among ourselves as we carried it down the hillside, and rested it by the site of the newly discovered tomb. Conor showed us the capstone, the heelstone, and there, with a few divots of grass pulled away, was a deeper-than-arm's-length crevice down into the secret chamber itself.

Our megalithic tomb, however, went undisturbed. Rain was coming on across the skies to the west, and with the quern as a trophy we were ready to clamber homewards. We knew *he* was up there, our Tumper, and we were not about to interfere. Walking into the fresh face of misting rain, it was enough that we had come upon a giant; we had touched history.

And still it rained and rained. The wettest June became the wettest July, which became the wettest August, and the summer was lost. Further reports of a now-desperate farming crisis took over the headlines. An appeal had been made to the disaster relief fund of the EEC, and Austin Deasy, the Minister for Farming and Agriculture, became a national figure as he helicoptered across the swamped farmlands of western Ireland and diagnosed the worst year in Irish farming since the 1800s.

Hay was lost, potatoes blighted, and the weather seemed to hit directly at those few vital things upon which the smaller farms depend. An article in the *Irish Times* described how a sixty-year-old bachelor farmer in Mayo with thirty acres had gone out on his tractor and looked at the soggy mess of cut hay that lay ruined in his main meadow. Leaving it in hopeless abandon, he had gone home, closed himself into the cottage and hung himself in despair. In rainy Kiltumper we read that with hushed sympathy, a small tragedy from the summer of '85. Many less dramatic stories went unreported. The whole countryside watched the skies for sun.

Although not quite farmers, in our own way we too were caught up in the gloom. To the drumming of each morning's rain on the bedroom window we turned back toward a half-sleep of disbelief. Under the drowning weather the garden was cut off from us; Chris watched weeds thrive where flowers should have been and threw up her hands until anger sent her out, rooting about in every kind of dismal weather. From the typewriter at the window I watched as she heaved up the stunted fruitless mangle of our tomato plants, leaving a bare wound of uncovered ground. Meanwhile, on television's *Gardener's World*, perfect crops and mowed lawns teased us like a sunny day.

But more urgent than the loss of the garden was the increasing threat to the cut turf, lying in puddles up on the bog. We had stacked it in grogans months before, handling for a third time each and every one of the hundreds of sods that we depended on for our winter's heat. In ordinary summertime, the turf would have solidly dried and a tractor with a creel could have carried home the entire cutting in half a day. This year there was no such possibility. The turf, under the constant deluge, had never had a proper chance to dry; only the top sod, balancing on the tip of the grogan, was fully ready to be brought home. The rest of the turf, often lying on wet ground where it soaked up the water like a sponge, was almost as wet as on the day it was cut. So, too, with the bogs themselves. The narrow passageways over ditches and through fields had all been flooded and no tractor could come close enough to our bank to be easily loaded. Instead, we were to go "bagging it." With half a dozen great heavy plastic fertilizer bags found around the cabins, I left Chris one morning and went up the hill meadows to the bog. Picking off only the dry top sods from each grogan, I filled the bags and felt a burst of hope, as if after all it wasn't going to be so hard to get the fuel home. I shifted one bag at a time, from the bog to the big ditch, from the big ditch across the Bog Meadow and from there across Upper Tumper and past Tumper's Grave and down through the grazing cattle to Lower Tumper, and from there over the wall into the Big Meadow, and there, at last, I emptied one bag on the floor of the hay barn. I made the journey six times, for we had no tractor and I didn't feel free to ask our neighbors at a time when I knew they were most busy on their own. After six journeys and half a day's work in light rain, a very small heap of turf lay piled in the hay barn, less than enough for three wintry days.

Of course we had underestimated the community of our neighbors. Within a day of that first effort, Michael Downes down the road from us told us to get sixty bags from Sean, fill them and carry them out just over the bog ditch, and he would get his tractor up there to bring them home. Michael Donnellan would do the same. And suddenly, thinking sixty bags a time, Chris and I saw a glimmer of hope.

Together then, up on that bog that had so quickly become familiar land to us (we knew the hare paths, we knew the sally bushes and the bracken, the short-cuts between banks and the heather-covered bog-holes), we spent days bagging it. It was rough work. The bags were unwieldy and, without any way to grasp a firm hold of them, they slid from wet fingers even as we humped them onto our backs and out across the bogholes. Silently working beneath a gray drizzling sky we gathered the winter's turf. Across the bank from us, Mary and Joe were doing the same, heaving it out in a stack of bright green and yellow bags. Years ago, in childhood summers at the Clare seaside, I remembered seeing these lone stacks of unnatural-colored plastic bags in a mound in the mid-dle of brownest bogland. Then I had no idea of what they were and imagined them to be the leavings of some untidy farmer. That day, and others, up on the bog with Chris, I came to know more intimately than I had ever dreamed the stuff of the West. It was cursed unglorious work and brought little satisfac-tion. For even when as many as sixty bags had been shifted out to drier land, there remained almost ten times as many on the puddled bog. And it seemed as if they would never dry. In the squelch-ing, sinking bog the task of almost manually drying each sod of turf as we turned them again and again, rebuilding the grogans and turning sods face-out to the west wind, seemed more than impossible. In Irish the word *bog* literally means softness, and to conjure from that softest of sounds the tough, hard substance of dry peat was a feat of no little imagining.

Marshaling our efforts, Chris loaded the bags and I shifted them. It was husband-and-wife work, a task nicely divided by our separate abilities, and in that quiet and primitive labor was as rich a bond as any we could imagine. Mucked and tired, rained on and worried, we trudged home, past the cattle, dreaming of a bath.

Where are all our promised visitors? Where are all the helping hands that were offered at our going-away party last March? Now, when more than ever we could use the help to win home the turf, there is no one. Plans have been canceled; Ireland is not on the cards for this year after all.

Chris groaned when she opened yet another letter from America. We'll never manage to bag all the turf by ourselves, she said, for even two dry days would see only half of it down from the bog and into the hay barn. And suddenly, looking out from the rainy kitchen window across the tangle of the garden and the distant swamped and muddy fields, we were struck by the full realization that this was not a holiday or a game for us, this was a life, and that a couple of extra hands would have been a vital help.

September fifteenth. The statues were still moving. The *Sunday Tribune* carried a list of thirty sighting places all across the country. There were reports almost daily of new extraordinary incidents and visions. There was news of statues in Clare. At Glenbrien, two countrywomen said they saw a statue of Our Lady moving. At Cratloe, another two women saw another statue move, and nightly gatherings of over three hundred pilgrims claimed to have seen the same thing, as well as visions of the face of Padre Pio superimposed in front of the face of the statue. Besides these reports there were literally dozens of unofficial sightings. A statue in Ennis was added to the list. And with these in mind, we wondered, what was the chance that our own statue was moving, too? After all, only a hundred yards from the house, back along-side the boundary wall of the farm was a Blessed Well with a blue and white statue of Our Lady. Earlier, in Our Lady's Month of May, Chris had helped Mary in the annual task of whitewashing the shrine and pre-paring it for the advent of pilgrims on the last Sunday in the month. Perhaps, there, right beside us was another of the extraordinary summer phenomena.

Perhaps. But if there was it did not move for us.

Sunshine! A morning shower misted across the land and was gone; a great beam of light quickened us to get outside. A hasty plan was drawn up: Niall was to go to the bog to fill bags, Chris was to paint up in the back meadow. We attended hurriedly to the hens and ducks. The flickering of light about the hay barn was the first real glimpse of summer. Elsewhere tractors were sputtering in echo to each other. Men were out in the fields, the roads were full of machines, even the cattle seemed happier. It was one moment in a lost summer and to everyone it came like a reward. Hoist-ing the great wooden easel like a mast, and bringing the paints, the jamjars of turps and spirits, the rags and the canvas, we were the image of hope moving up the fields beneath a rare blue sky.

Chris set up her day's work in the middle of a meadow overlooking Kathleen's bounds and the ruin of her ghostly house. Chris wore a sunscarf for the first time in six months. The painting she created contained an image of joy in wild landscape, the hostliness of Kathleen's, and the anxiety caused by the oncoming afternoon clouds. By evening when we carried canvas and easel back home, we felt the glow of satisfaction: Chris had begun a painting, Niall had shifted forty bags of turf. We had seized the day.

CHAPTER
NINE

We had heard he was coming a day before he arrived. Father Linnane, the curate, was in Kiltumper. He had already been to Conway's and O'Shea's and was likely to be at our house by midmorning on Friday. As new parishioners from abroad where we had not been the most diligent Catholics, we were wary. The priest in Ireland is a figure of such standing that there was just a hint of fear in our kitchen as we awaited his arrival. Could we tell him that Chris found some accents almost impossible to decipher, and that we hadn't yet quite grown used to the sometime agricultural scent that wafted through the church on a packed Saturday night or that, well, we didn't go to mass *all* the time? There was no need to fear. Father Linnane was kind and gentle, quite unlike his counterparts in Irish literature.

In the West of Ireland over ninety percent of the

123

people are Catholics. Yet it is not uncommon for the local curate to know almost all of his parishioners first-hand. At Saturday-evening or Sunday-morning mass, he is there inside the gate to meet young and old as they come to the church. He knows them well, knows the limits of their lives and knows how deep their devotion runs. Twice yearly one of the two priests in the parish tries to visit every home in the village and townlands. The priest's car putters away from Kilmihil in mid-morning, heads off down narrow *botharins*, to every modern bungalow, as well as to the run-down cottages of bachelor farmers or widows where the light is dim and the comforts are few. And it is a measure of the importance of his position in the community that every house, no matter how poor, will try to welcome the priest with a generous cup of tea.

By two o'clock in the afternoon Father Linnane had not arrived and we began to think that perhaps he had passed back along the road, missing our house behind the high screening fuchsia hedges. But it was not so. The hospitality of Kiltumper had simply delayed him in a welter of teacups and biscuits. By half-past two he was walking up the garden path to meet us at the front door with clasped hands and a blessing.

"You have a lovely spot here. God bless all," he said, and stepped inside the kitchen.

Down from the pulpit and sitting in front of the fire, he seemed full of good will and friendship. Once he had inquired about our health, he moved the talk to that most important of subjects: "Who is it now are your wife's cousins?"

Cousins, uncles, aunts, nieces, nephews, grand-fathers, granduncles and even simply neighbors are the keys to knowing someone in the West. Everyone is closely related from the days when a farmer went no further than the neighboring townland to bring home a wife in his donkey cart. The villages are full of cousins and in-laws. Literally everyone is related to someone not far off. On the several occasions when we have picked up some local farmer in the car on the road to Kilrush or Ennis, the very first question has always been, "Ye're from Kiltumper, well, do ye know so-and-so, he's a cousin of mine up there near ye." The entire community is knit close like this. Cousins are the coordinates by which each person is defined; their *relation* to the world at large. Even when someone leaves to live in America or England, it is cousins and old neighbors they meet with first.

Father Linnane could know us better by first knowing who Chris's cousins were and how she fit into the local landscape; with each answer he became more at home, and there in the kitchen of her grandfather's birthplace he puzzled out her connections. A sense of personal history was spun before the fire. And we heard again the fragments of stories about "The Big Breens," about Big John, and Jack O'the Grove, the fruitful apple trees that used to grow in the front garden, and the nights of music and dancing that went back more than a hundred years. As he spoke Chris's place in the parish became more rightful, and mine, too, through marriage to her. For despite Father Linnane's brave efforts ("Williams? Are ye anything to the Williamses in Kilrush?"), as a Dubliner I had no claim to Kiltumper, except for the friendship I had won by giving up the world to come here. Chris was our ticket to belonging.

The visit lasted for an hour and might have continued longer had there not been three more houses down the narrow western road waiting with kettle on the boil for the priest. By the time Father Linnane blessed us again in going, we felt we had come more intimately into his parish. He knew us now. We were another link in the chain of related people. We belonged.

To know the real story of the West of Ireland spend a day in Shannon Airport at the foot of the stairs to the departure lounge. They come in little clusters, farming families dressed in their best clothes, with a son or daughter moving slightly ahead in anticipation of the dreaded moment of goodbye. Mothers' faces are damp with tears, fathers are stiff with emotion, and they all grasp the rails of the moving stairs. It is joyous and sad at once. An old Irish image, the farewell, has lived on through centuries of immigration and is as real today as it ever was. There will be half-hearted quiet talk that he or she has gone to "a better place," and later in the car back to the farm words about the people who have already "gone over," and sure, won't they have a great time. There will sometimes be bravado and talk of big money and opportunities. But there will always be tears when the boy calls from the Bronx and asks to know if the calf is well, or when the widowed aunt misses her cheerful niece who has flown away to a job as a waitress in a restaurant on Thirty-fifth Street in Manhattan.

Shannon Airport is an emotional place for people in the West. More than an airport, it is the escape hatch to America for the young and the symbol of Ireland's massive unemployment problem. Often brand new suitcases fly one way to New York in the hands of passengers who have never even been as far away as Dublin before.

We were there for our own leave-taking that afternoon. Chris was returning to New York for two weeks to see her family. It had been decided; she was to go alone, I was to stay behind and take care of the farm, readying the place for the oncoming winter.

And suddenly there I was. Nighttime in Kiltumper with winds lashing about the darkness. It seemed as if the cottage was larger than before as the brisk stormy weather rattled the windows. Drafts of all sorts crisscrossed the kitchen and for the first time I began to feel the cold inside the house. I sat close to the fire to write, imagining how in one brief afternoon Chris had vaulted into the heart of autumnal Westchester county where that day's *Irish Times* gave the temperature as seventy degrees. I wrote a few notes and again had the sensation of the utter stillness of the house. I scurried out around the cabins. Tumper's Hill was very dark. In the black windy distance few houses showed a yard light. Only two nights before we had come upon a fox on the western road, and so I resecured the hens' door and hurried inside as the storm spat rain. It was the worst kind of Irish night, and alone in the quiet of the house I felt a sharper loneliness than ever before. Although I had open invitations to all of our neighbors' houses, and already Pauline and Michael and Mary had fed me a feast, I stayed in, reading quietly, and catching a glimpse in my mind's eye of the reasons why the West of Ireland was the birthplace of so much music.

A hint of suddenly dry weather became three dry days in a row in the middle of October, and as before the hills were alive with tractors. No word from Chris. Michael Donnellan would bring down some more of our turf if I could bag it and have it ready. And so I was alone in the bog for two days, bagging turf. It was noticeably colder. The winds that blew from Glenmore were sharp across the open horizon of bogland. The bloom had gone off the heather, and still in places the ravages of the summer showed in puddles and drains oozing over dry fields. Still, the turf was drying in the windy, pale sunshine and after two days' work there was "a handy piece" of it stacked in the hay barn. What is Chris doing today? I wondered as I clambered up Tumper with an armful of plastic bags. Madison Avenue seemed like a vague dream.

One day I was sitting in the kitchen with two

young neighbor boys, Peter and Francie. It was a quiet Sunday morning; later on I was invited down to Downes's for my dinner. We were playing a game of cards when suddenly Francie let out a cry, "Niall, there's a taxi here!" And before I even had time to say anything, the boys were out of the house and running back by the cabins to see. It was the first time they had ever seen a taxi on the Kiltumper road. None of us had any idea who it was and for a minute we hung around the gate waiting to see who would get out. A distinctly American voice was laughing with the cabbie and when the door opened it was someone I had never expected, but a wonderful surprise all the same: Jane, the indefatigable office manager at the company I used to work for in Manhattan. She and her husband were on a week's whirlwind tour of Ireland, Scotland and England. They had arrived at Shannon at eight o'clock that morning and had set out to find Kiltumper in a taxi. Four hours and two punctures later they had finally almost given up the quest that should have taken less than an hour. But Jane had promised at the office that she would find me and take back a photo. And there she was.

Jane and her husband said the cottage and the countryside were everything they had imagined. I was thrown back into the world we had left behind and found myself excited to hear of the comings and goings, the sackings and the deals of publishing. What was happening? Who was doing what? I remembered what it was like to be part of a company of people, a team of disparate personalities, with all that praise and all that backbiting, all that teamwork, and all that selfishness, too. I didn't read *Publishers Weekly* anymore. I had no idea what the best sellers were and as we were sitting in the kitchen drinking tea, I missed some of the excitement of the advance *New York Times Book Review* best sellers list and the cheeriness along a corridor when *ours* was Number 1. Seeing

Jane was a test of the dream. For me it held up that Sunday morning. I was grateful to Jane for coming, but secretly wondered if the dream was still holding true for Chris in New York. Or was she dreading coming back?

I feared that when Chris returned from New York she would have gotten too used to luxuries again. If the winter settled in early she would come back from the golden foliage and sunshine to gray glowering skies and damp weather. I looked out on another dry day, knowing full well that it would rain or sleet the moment she returned. I realized that off the kitchen there are five doors: bathroom, hot-press room (the closet where the hot water tank is), back door, front door, and garret. Unless we could get the big fire lighting properly it would be impossible to keep the room warm for the winter. I ran around the cottage for days trying to make it seem more homey and wondered each moment how Chris was feeling in New York. I tried to look at Kiltumper through the eyes of Manhattan. I worried.

I am really surprised. I hadn't anticipated that I would be subject to culture shock. After all, I have only been gone for seven months.

The things that surprise me the most are the ordinary things of everyday existence and *not* the expected contrasts—the racetrack atmosphere of New York, or driving on the right-hand side of the road again, or just the sheer, vast difference between our remote farm in Kiltumper and the affluent suburbs of

New York City. No, instead I find myself shocked by simple housekeeping things as I catch myself thinking: where shall I put the garbage? In Kiltumper I throw it into the Stanley Range as general fuel, or, if it won't or can't burn, I throw it into the bin that we take to the dump once a week. Then again, the hens and chickens are eager for the waste. Everything has a place, and I know where it is. Home again here in New York I cringe a little as I watch the scraps go into the bin and witness with awakened conscience the unnecessary waste.

I find myself wondering in the middle of the day: will there be enough hot water for a bath, or for the dishes, or for the clothes? But of course, in New York, there is always plenty of hot water at any hour of the day. There is instant heat, too. Once again, I was walking freely about my mother's plushly carpeted floors in bare feet. I wore a loose, cotton T-shirt and felt the warm air outside on my skin. But until now I have never really felt the full measure of all this luxury.

I can wash the clothes in a machine. All those months of washing clothes in the bathtub and hanging them, without the luxury of a spin-dry cycle. Not to mention a dryer. It's not that people in Ireland don't have washing machines. *They* do. Only *we* can't afford one, and the local laundromat is thirty-five minutes away.

And food! Glorious food! All the foods that I can't get in Kiltumper: asparagus and fresh broccoli, pizza and pesto, fresh corn-on-the-cob, frozen yogurt pops, and real fruit juices. In Kiltumper the choice of juices is very slim: orange, pineapple, apple and sometimes grapefruit. Grape juice appears on the shelves of Quinnsworth (the equivalent of an A & P) in Ennis occasionally, but raspberry or cranapple or apricot or pear are unheard of. To be able to go into a supermarket again and find . . . everything.

I've had one of each: bacon cheeseburger, takeout Chinese, brownies, Dinardo's mushroom pizza, loads of vegetables for lunch and dinner, and doughnuts on Sunday morning with *The New York Times*. I will never get used to, or accept, the dull unimaginative diet of the Irish. But there may be hope: a pizza shop is to open in Ennis soon. Or is it just a rumor?

Living in Kiltumper is sometimes the epitome of tranquility (when I can put up with the rain and damp). Peacefulness has become a real part of me. When I took the commuter train into Manhattan this morning and edged into the rush of people I discovered two things. First, it was easy for me to resume my old habit of walking fast up Madison Avenue and passing others like a sports car, and second, that all the noise, the busy throngs of people, the steaming, exhaust-spewing trucks and the honking cars *didn't* assail me, as once they had. Kiltumper has given me an inner peace.

October-blue sky and magnificent foliage raise my water-logged spirits. The trees and the landscape are so inviting and colorful, like nothing else anywhere. Nothing in the world compares to an October in the Northeastern United States! I will miss the snowstorms. But I wonder, "Has winter begun in Kiltumper yet?" I put aside feelings of deprivation and a hesitancy to return to Ireland and spend as much time as possible walking outside.

Before I leave I must stock up on some art supplies that will fit easily into my suitcases. I buy a turtleneck and some American-style undershorts and socks for Niall; for myself long underwear and flannel pajamas. My mother has treated me to Clinique cosmetics that are difficult to locate near Kilmihil. I have seen four movies since I've been home and have been taken to dinner several times in these two holiday weeks.

Having had a good dose of the sorely-missed American life-style, I am prepared to return to Ireland. Here goes.

A foreign sound ripped through the quiet of Kiltumper: the buzz of a chain saw. After a disastrous summer few people in the West had enough turf for the winter. Besides which, the turf that had been won home would not be of good quality. The sods would contain little heat. And so, the sharp angry buzz of a chain saw, in our back field cutting down three ash trees, reverberated through the countryside.

Ash, we had been told, is the best wood to burn in these parts.

> Ash, fresh and green
> makes a fire
> fit for a queen.

It doesn't need to be seasoned like other wood but will burn fresh the day after it's been cut. The farm with a stock of its own ash trees survives even the worst summer in a hundred. But at what cost?

There is not a plentiful supply of wood in Ireland today. The countryside was once thickly wooded. But during centuries of British rule, the forests were constantly cut and cleared to supply the British Admiralty with timber to build the Royal Navy. British ships of Irish wood conquered the seas. Meanwhile, *coineadhs*, or laments, were written for the ravages suffered by the countryside. As every Irish schoolboy learned, a stricken voice cried out:

> *Cad a dheanamaid fasta gan adhmaid?*
> *ta deire na coilte ar lar . . .*
> What shall we do without wood?
> The last of the forests have been ravaged

In Ireland there is always a link back into history. And whether acknowledged or not, the buzzing of the chain saw that afternoon struck a deep discordant note of sadness evoking many stories.

"There's a man down in Kilmurry sure can't stand the sound of a saw working. He's driven pure mad with it. He'd be out screamin' at ye to stop before the tree'd fall. And there's another fellow down by Cahermurphy won't let ye within a mile of his place. Anytime ye'd be out cutting around him at all he's out watching everything ye're doing in case ye'd be cutting down one of his favorite trees or disturbing the fairies or something. Oh, people can be very choosy when it comes to timber. They don't like ye cuttin'. Sure, I suppose it's a bad sign if ye have to be cuttin at all."

A bad sign in a bad year. The whole feel and smell and sensation of timber seems foreign. Just as everything about the bog and turf seems indigenous. Is this just a fancy of ours? We don't think so. Turf, not timber, is the stuff of the West and the bog-and-heather landscape seems to reverberate everywhere, all the way from the speckled rough texture of tweed cloth to the weathered, aged faces of the farmers. It alone tells the story of the poor land and the years of hardship in living off it. As I split the ash blocks and Chris stacked them in the cabin, we had the feeling of being rich in having trees to cut. Our neighbors had no trees. And as the ax flew through the air into the ash with a loud clean crack, we were grateful to Chris's thoughtful ancestors and the planting long ago that was to give us fuel after the worst summer in our history.

The statues were still moving, although not as frequently as first reported during the start of the summer. One morning's radio news featured a violent incident that had shaken the country. The most famous of all the "moving" statues, the one in Ballinspittle, was attacked by three Dublin men. While a crowd of people stood praying, the three vandals vaulted the barrier in front of the grotto and slashed at the figure of Our Lady with a metal bar, shearing off one of her hands and one entire side of her face.

By the time we heard the news, they had been caught.

Samhain. Oiche Shamhna, Hollantide, or Halloween. An ancient feast time in Ireland, it is still celebrated here with many of the old customs. For days we had been hearing the children talk of it. For them the main excitement was the thought of dressing up in costumes and going about the roads asking for apples and nuts, and then coming back to the house for Halloween games such as snap-apple and ducking. These Samhain games date as far back as two hundred years ago, and they remain today the main fare of the holiday as children try to bite at apples floating in water or hanging from cords.

But Halloween is more than games. Traditionally it is the last day before winter begins on November 1st. It is also a day of special foods and many forecasts for the year ahead. For the main mid-day meal many homes would serve *colcannon,* or *pandy* or *champ.* This consists of mashed potatoes mixed with cooked green cabbage and chopped raw onions, flavored with pepper and salt. Served in a big round dish with a pat of butter melting in its center, the colcannon is often loaded with penny or twopenny pieces wrapped in tin foil, adding a touch of excitement as the children scoop away at the food to find the money. Another common Halloween food is *boxty,* or mashed potato cakes and milk. But of all the traditional foods, by far the most enduring is the *bairin breac,* or large fruit cake. The breac contains a ring, a coin, a button, a thimble, a piece of wood, and a tiny rag or a pea, each of which foretells its finder's future. To find the ring means an early marriage, the coin predicts wealth, the button, bachelorhood, and the thimble, spinsterhood. Ominously, the piece of wood means that the finder will be beaten in some way by his or her marriage partner, and the found rag or pea means a life of absolute poverty. Once upon a time in houses too poor to afford a cake, these things were put into the colcannon. Nowadays, most houses have a breac, either homemade or bought, and on the day following Halloween the children run around the road with the news of who got what.

Mary remembers other Halloween games from her childhood, games which seem to be gradually dying out with the increase of television and more sophisticated pastimes.

"Once," she said, "we used to pick out two old nuts and name them after some boy and girl who were said to be courtin'. Then the two nuts would be put together, side by side, down onto the grate in the turf ashes, ye see. Well, we'd all watch them then, and we'd know which nut was the boy and which was the girl. And after a time, ye see, one of the nuts might jump out of the fire, and ye'd say, well that means she's going to leave him, or he's going to be fighting with her, or whichever it was of them. And sometimes of course the two nuts wouldn't jump at all but just burn away quietly together, and that meant the two would be married and live happily after."

Another game involved placing four plates on a table. Water was poured in one, a ring put in another, earth in the next, and straw in the last. A person was blindfolded and led to the table and asked to reach into one of the plates. The water signified a journey across the sea; the ring, marriage; the earth, death; and the straw, prosperity. But, as Mary quickly added, "In our day we never used the plate with the earth. We were afraid to know we were going to be dying," she said, capturing the strange mixture of belief and ridicule in which the Halloween customs are held.

In addition to the games that remain today, other traditional Samhain customs involved a belief in the ever-present world of the fairies. On Hallows Eve, or All Souls Night, the fairies were said to be abroad in the darkness, sweeping about the countryside. The people were so afraid that they might inadvertently incur the anger of the fairies, that on Halloween Night anyone throwing water or waste out the front door would first let out a cry of warning, *Seachain!* (Beware!), giving the fairies ample time to stand out of the way.

Stories of this tradition are still common in the townlands about us. "Oh," said Pat, one of the best storytellers, pulling his cap down a little over his eye, "in those days people believed a load of quare things, d'ye see. There was the *puca* then, of course, and he was a dark black beast'd be out traveling around the roads in the night of Halloween. And there was many people said they saw him, too. It was on that night, d'ye see, the *puca* could take ye away with him, to the fairies, and ye might never be seen again in the land of the living after that. Then, of course, when we were going to school in our day we were told that on Halloween, when the puca would be out, he'd be spitting on all the berries that'd be left on the bushes, and after that ye couldn't go eating any of 'em at all." He paused and looked over at us with his hands on his knees and his eyes wide with wonder. "Of course, then, there's many people wouldn't believe that either. But at that time, now, d'ye see, there was a number of stories around from people who said they'd been away with the fairies, and others who said they'd seen a house packed with the souls of the dead, or that on this night they'd make out the fields and the hills and everything were covered with returned spirits, d'ye see?

"And then there'd be some stories of strange things happening and noises and that. There's a house now, out the road there, ye've seen it maybe, 'tis strange-looking because, d'ye see, the gable end of the house comes right up at the very edge of a window, and there isn't an inch to spare between that

136

window and the end of the house. And do ye know why that is? When that house was built it was about three feet wider. But soon after the people moved in they had a spell of fierce bad luck, cattle were going wrong on them, and children were getting sick. And anyway in the end they had to do something, there was no living in the house at all. And it was then they were told, and I don't know how they knew, but anyway hadn't the house been built in the path of the fairies." Pat paused and let out a sigh. "D'ye see they had to cut three feet off the house so the fairies could pass. . . . And the day they done that they never had any more bad luck at all.

"Oh, there was a power of great stories then! There was this farmer having terrible luck with his animals. So he went to the priest and asked him what he could do about it. Because in those days long ago the people believed in spirits and the like. The priest, then, said he would say a mass in the farmer's house, and at the end of the mass the farmer was to drive all his cows through the house. Now, in those days, d'ye see, the houses had the front door and the back door across from each other, and anyway when this farmer drove his cattle through the kitchen where the priest was saying the mass he was told to tell the priest when the last one was passing. Now the farmer knew that the priest meant to cast all the bad luck of the house onto the last beast as it came through. D'ye see? The bad luck would be on the beast and that beast was meant to die in order for the spell of the bad spirits to be broken.

"Now, this farmer was a mean man and he didn't want to lose this animal. So, he didn't tell the priest when the last beast passed through the house and out the back door. And do ye know what happened?. . . . After the last beast had gone through the house . . . the priest dropped dead!"

137

Why are we here?

It was Chris's question asked quietly on a rainy evening when the day had brought little but frustrations. She was calling for a reassuring voice to say: We are here for the quality of life, we are here to write and paint. And with the question and answer came the inevitable inventory of our recent efforts. Are we being 'creative'? Does so much freedom actually inspire us more than the snapped-at moments we had in New York? What have we done?

The large, colorful painting of the kitchen door and window with the fields beyond hangs in the studio/parlor like a statement; so, too, did the one summery day landscape of the back meadow, the stone walls and Kathleen's ruined house. In a pile on the kitchen table are the half-filled sketch books of Chris's numerous drawings. They form a record of endeavor, a compendium of impressions that hold promise for the future. Yet, Chris's self-portrait, entered in a national competition, came back to us with regrets.

My first novel, written intermittently over five years in Manhattan, was at last finished during the wet summer days, and had gone from the cottage out into the world like a bundle of hope. A first radio play, scripted by both of us, was being readied for Radio Telifis Eirinn's Peadar J. O'Connor competition. The first two of a number of Kiltumper poems had been sent to the *Irish Press*, a first-ever screenplay had been started between us, and I was thirty pages into a second novel.

Still, we were full of doubts. Letters came politely inquiring how the "work" was going, and by evening time, sitting by the fire, we wondered. Was it enough? From the vantage point of New York the prospect of a year in the West of Ireland free to write seemed to promise countless projects and the chance to get things finished. After eight months we had the nagging thought that we hadn't made enough of it. How can we explain? Michael Viney, one of the first and certainly the most public of all movers-to-the-West, said that a man and woman digging in a garden are just that. They are not composing poetry or prose, or looking about for suitable subjects to paint. Simple as it sounds, it is nonetheless an important fact: digging is digging, and nothing else. Dreaming in New York, however, having never spent an entire day just turning earth, I confess to imagining that words and images would fill my head while I was out digging the spuds or turning the turf, that the work itself would be so poetic that the writing would flow from it, naturally, as it were. In our experience, this is a fallacy. I know no one who is handy enough with a shovel that it doesn't take most of their concentration to dig straight ridges or even a proper planting-hole.

What, then, *is* the relation between this kind of life and art? For Chris and me it is something almost undefinable, an invisible thread that runs through the heart, and ties together the *feeling* of the day spent outside, and the peacefulness that follows, maybe days later, when you finally get to sit down and write. I think of Patrick Kavanagh, one of the most celebrated of modern Irish poets, who lived most of his early life as a poor farmer in Monaghan. His poetry was made of country life, lines written out of unglorified experience, catching something of this ambivalence between the richness and the demands of living a life in the country. In "Inniskeen Road: July Evening," Kavanagh perhaps captures it best.

I have what every poet hates in spite
of all the solemn talk of contemplation.
Oh, Alexander Selkirk knew the plight

of being King and government and nation.
A road, a mile of kingdom, I am king
of banks and stones and every blooming thing.

We *are* kings of every blooming thing here. A poo1
apologia perhaps, written as we found three days passing without any progress on books, paintings, or anything else. But our wood was neatly split, our hen
house was cleaned out, dead trees cleared off the garden wall, and a splendid broad view of the hills opened
up for the winter ahead.

CHAPTER TEN

We had bad news. After a protracted series of checks and rechecks, beginning in New York and ending here on a rainy day in November, we discovered that we could not have children of our own.

That is said so easily in a sentence, but Kiltumper became a different place for us. As the days blew and hailed on the edge of winter we were beaten into a difficult silence. The cottage seemed the most remote place in the world and the haggard, barren landscape an apt setting for the sheer aloneness we both felt. It seemed fitting that we should face this pain here, by ourselves, in the terrible quiet of West Clare.

Without the escape of a daily job, we were in the gloom all the time. Beyond the kitchen window the unattended garden grew ragged in the rain.

One Sunday it was announced from the pulpit: the first meeting of the drama group would take place at eight o'clock sharp in the vocational school the following Wednesday night.

We were ready for it. We had already heard much about the past successes of the group. During the 1960s, in the able hands of such natural thespians as Paddy Cotter and Noel Conway, Kilmihil frequently won awards leading toward the ultimate competition —The All-Ireland Amateur Drama Festival. In recent years, however, the group had been disbanded as interest lagged.

Wednesday night, eight o'clock sharp, we were there at the school. Nobody else was. Windows were dark, there wasn't a soul about. Half an hour later, and two trips back and forth through the village, there was still no sign of anybody. Had we confused the day, the place?

We hadn't. Within minutes Martin Keane, a friend, arrived.

"Aro ye the only ones here?" he asked with no surprise, letting us into the school. "This is very bad, so it is."

As Martin had secretly suspected, no one else arrived to attend the first meeting of the Kilmihil Amateur Drama Group, although he promised that there *were* half a dozen people who *wanted* to be in a play. They couldn't come that night, so we drifted back home having gotten no further than agreeing to meet again later in the week. One further thing was quietly agreed: if at all possible, this year's play would *not* be by John B. Keane.

Well-written, traditional, parochial dramas of provincial Ireland, the plays of John B. have for years been the staple of regional drama groups. They are entertaining, enjoyable, accessible plays; the audiences are certain to love them and for this reason,

142

as well as for the fact that they are plays which tell a story, they are huge favorites when it comes time for a group to choose a play.

Secretly then, Martin, Chris and I conspired on that first dark evening outside the vocational school to look all week for a play to propose against the works of John B. Keane. Brendan Behan, Sean O'Casey, Oscar Wilde, J. M. Synge, Tom Murphy, Brian Friel, Tom Kilroy, Frank McGuinness and Hugh Leonard were all possibilities to us in our innocence. We searched the libraries, thumbed playscripts in the Ennis bookshop, and came to the second meeting with a handful of possibilities. It was going to be a good year for Kilmihil drama.

At the second meeting a half-dozen people appeared—Noel Conway, Kathleen Devine, Lucy Blake, David O'Connell, Martin Keane, Michael Mescall and ourselves, the newcomers. It was a rambling, uncertain kind of meeting. Plays were mentioned and actors for them, but at the end of two hours nothing had been decided. And then in the usual Irish way, just before the meeting broke up, we got down to business and two plays were proposed: John B. Keane's *The Year of the Hiker*, produced from somebody's pocket, and Hugh Leonard's *Da*, which Martin energetically laid down on a desk. "I love this play," he said, "I think it would be great to do it." There was a strained silence, nobody touched *Da*. "Oh, *Da* is a very funny play," Chris added, throwing in her bit and picking up the script, "I saw it on Broadway with Brian Keith in the part of Da." Faces were impassive, unimpressed.

"What's this *The Year of the Hiker* about again?" somebody asked, picking it up to read.

After three more meetings, *Da* won the day in a half-hearted and uncertain way, because Chris and I had the outnumbering votes. There was not a mood of great excitement among the cast, but two things were

143

decided at once: I was to direct the play, and Chris was to design the set. God help us.

Within a week the play had been cast. We were one player short, but never mind, we'd find one, we assured one another. We gathered in the vocational school and huddled in our coats to read the script. It was heavy going. On Tuesday and Wednesday nights lines were read slowly, lifelessly, in the empty room, and I felt secretly that we had undertaken too much. Much of the comedy of the play seemed unsuitable, too sophisticated in a way for the real talents of the actors. Besides which, the play takes place on the day of Da's funeral but involves a very clever kind of continuous flashback allowing the character of Da to appear onstage throughout. "Oh yes, very clever, altogether," as someone in the village said to me with a disconcerting, totally unimpressed expression.

At the end of the first reading some quiet reservations were expressed that the play might be unsuitable for the audience, but we pressed ahead nonetheless. After all, isn't it the job of community theatre to raise the appreciation of its audience? We were full of good intentions. And by the finish of the first night's rehearsal when the players dispersed into the evening with scripts in hand there was a mood of good humor and many jokes about the comic scenes in the play.

Three weeks into rehearsals, the first act well underway and everyone warming to his part, no Young Charlie had yet been found. Word had been put out around the village and there seemed to be genuine interest in how the play was going. There was a real sense of community which was new to us, and at the cottage Chris made the first sketches for the set. We wanted it to be the best-looking, best-directed play Kilmihil had seen in years.

At last we found our Young Charlie. He read with enthusiasm and seemed pleased to be in the troupe.

144

But throughout the reading the colorful and bawdy language of some of the passages caused concern. "This is a bit rough, lads, isn't it?" asked Young Charlie. From this clue we should have surmised the rest.

It didn't take long before we had lost our Young Charlie. A wave of disappointment weakened the optimism of the cast. A rumor was gathering momentum in Kilmihil, though neither Chris nor I had gotten wind of it. Finally, after one evening's reading in the cold schoolroom it was brought out into the open: was the play too risqúe? Nobody wanted to admit it. Neither Martin nor I thought it was even slightly unsuitable. But the others? A long silence and a shiver of apprehension answered us. We decided to go over the script noting objections. It went like this:

"Page 16, OLIVER: There was a girl who took pride in her appearance. With the big—well, it was you know—chest.

CHARLIE: Tits."

A plaintive voice surfaced through the laughter "Could we maybe say "boobs" instead?"

But rumor had taken off. We came upon it repeatedly as we tried to find a replacement for our disenchanted Young Charlie. "The play the drama group are doing this year is very rough, there's some ferocious language in it."

From as far away as Lissycasey, Cahermurphy and Knockmore, many had heard. No young man would come forward to take the part. No one would even take a copy of the script to read as we drove around Kilmihil trying to get somebody to give it a chance. The more we tried the more it seemed the news had preceded us; the rumor was more powerful than the play, and swelling with it was the general impression that this strange new play was brought in by yer man from Dublin and his wife from the States. There were knowing looks in the town, and no possible Young Charlies anywhere. "I think we're going to be run out of town," Chris whispered as we left the butcher's, having had another Young Charlie's quiet, but nonetheless firm, refusal.

After seven weeks of rehearsal and a hopeless search for the one missing member of the cast, it was finally decided. On a damp Wednesday night in the brightly lit classroom, a vote was taken in a gloomy mood. The nays had it. *Da* was abandoned.

Our garden is a rack-rent, ruined place. It needs desperately to be tackled. And tackling it is just what I'm doing. No words can explain the bond that exists between me and this place. I can't even explain to myself the determination and passion with which I throw myself into rescuing the Kiltumper garden during these last lingering days before the frosts of winter. I guess I need the garden as much as it needs me. It's a constant symbol of my state of mind, a witness right there in front of the kitchen window. I *am* making an impact on something. Couch grass, nettles, and Japanese knotweed—once planted here years ago for its tiny mass of white flowers that appear in late summer and now truly an escaped weed with foot-long roots that reach far underground—these are my enemies.

On the creative side, I am resurrecting the small wild strawberry patch that I began in early spring. Secateurs in hand I stoop in the soft rain to rescue a dozen wayward plants. An abundance of cowslips, and polyanthus and primulas are gladly separated from the choking grasp of the couch grass roots that network the place where—I hardly dare say it—I have envisioned a perennial border. There is a lovely old Rose of Sharon, with round yellow star-like flowers, which needs to be moved away from the path that leads to the house. And lupines and montbretia and a sweet-scented wild rose bush of rose madder petals. But they're all overgrown, all a nuisance in their present positions, tumbling and knotting across the path and brushing you with their leaves and petals full of raindrops as you come up the garden.

Two giant old hydrangeas, of sickly pink color in late summer, stand out like sore thumbs and are oddly planted off-center at the front of the two sides of the garden. I move around them with the secateurs. Perhaps this is the last Kiltumper Cottage is to see of them.

This work is good therapy, and there is so much of it to do. Waiting for the weather to bring out the sun is pointless. We are out in the rainy garden digging over the western side of the path (where the potatoes and peas grew). The tangled roots of the nettles come away easily enough. Finally, the beginning of a perennial border, with saved plants, new plants and plants from Mary, is appearing. Of course, *now* it looks nice: black earth and healthy plants: who knows what it will look like by spring?

Comhair is an Irish word for which there is really no English equivalent. Literally, it means *help*, but in the context of the West it has come to mean something much more than that. The *comhair*, as it was called long ago, was the word for the powerful sense of community in a place, whereby men and women "gave" each other days, sharing labors on the farm and on the bog. In a time of great poverty it was this kind of teamwork that enabled each farm in a townland to get turf cut, to get the potatoes in, and to tram or bring in the hay. The men might be at O'Shea's today, they would be at Breen's tomorrow. *Comhair*. It is the mechanism of community.

Since we arrived in Kiltumper we had already witnessed many examples of it in the kindness and help of our neighbors. From television aerials to chimneys, to turf, to spuds; we had help with them all. And if the modern days of tractors and machinery have made each farmer a little more self-reliant, there is still a strong sense of the *comhair* between them.

The day we were finally to dig the front garden into ridges for the winter, Mary and Joe came down the road with shovel and fork in hand. We were delighted to have them. Mary is a fury in the garden, pulling weeds wherever she sees them, and demonstrating in a moment just why she has the prettiest flower garden in Tumper. And Joe, beside her, is a skilled man with the fork. So easy and peaceful, he makes a mockery of our sweating and bustling efforts, as he seems to make the ridges mound up before him in an ancient, timeless rhythm. We have never seen the like of him before. He spits into his bare hands every few minutes to keep the wooden handle from slipping from his grasp and smokes his cigarettes every half hour, resting huge cracked and thick hands on top of the spade. He bends one knee, resting his foot on the top of the blade, and looks across Hayes' Hill. He rarely says a word.

We were delighted when he reappeared two days later to give us another helping hand. Joe explained that if the garden was laid to rest in these ridges over the winter, where more of the surface was actually exposed, two things would happen. First, the frost would kill any roots exposed to the air, which in our case was a lot. And second, the process of freezing and thawing repeatedly over the winter would help to break down the heavy soil into fine tilth, facilitating spring sowing.

As Joe and Chris and I began that afternoon on the eastern half of the garden, my mind was full of gratitude and thoughts of the *comhair*. Here was a man, I thought, giving his time without personal motive and sharing his knowledge and skills with us.

148

What a staggering contrast this was to the days of Manhattan. I sunk my fork into the earth while Joe lit a cigarette and watched on. And then the afternoon was pierced with the jangling of the telephone. It was Michael Donnellan. He had promised to bring a neighbor, Sadie, into Kilrush for her eye-test that afternoon, but his car had just broken down. Could I take her instead? By rights I couldn't. Joe was here to work with us, and in any other world I shouldn't have left. But this was not anywhere else, and even as I said yes, giving over the afternoon to taking an elderly countrywoman the twelve miles to Kilrush, I realized that this was yet another measure of our coming into the community. We were part of the *comhair*.

Omens of winter: the sounds of hammering as our rotted and airy back door was torn out and replaced by a new teak one. In the evening we moved around the cottage with two candles—not for the romantic light, but to track down the innumerable gusting drafts that traveled about each room. Keen gales blew down from the ceiling-boards, and as Chris's candle was snuffed out altogether, we hurried back to our seats by the fire and turned to each other with the same expression: what is an Irish winter in this cottage *really* going to be like?

We had hardly imagined it, or if we had, it was only to compare it favorably with the blizzards during which we would walk up Park Avenue into a tunnel of cold too severe for words. No, Ireland never got *that* cold, never got any real snow. And so when clocks were turned back in November, and the days were shortened dramatically to end at four in the afternoon, winter struck us with the force of a new idea. All about us the towns were moving in a different rhythm, and for the first time the idea of entertainment began to surface. What did people do here on all these dark nights? They went on the *cuaird*, they went to the pubs, and they played the local card game, 45, which we were slow to learn.

The first short days caught us by surprise. We found ourselves closing the wooden window shutters early and spending the night between the fire and the television. The winds made noise in the Grove and billowed the curtain over the front door. Made timid by the sheer darkness and the roughness of these nights, anyplace seemed too far to go. In a voice of gloom Chris asked me, "Is it going to be like this, then?" Were we to be winter-dormant until spring, harboring ourselves in the kitchen with the quiet, lonely pain of childlessness? Was this it?

Of course not. Among the things we missed from our previous life, foremost were the varied entertainments of New York: the movies, the theatre, and the all-night, multi-channel TV programs. We especially missed the movies. Irish television, although not as broken with commercials as its American counterparts, leaves much to be desired in terms of programming and professionalism. Besides which, it shuts down every night before midnight as the announcer bids everyone a good night's sleep, never imagining that there are creatures like Chris who are just then readying to watch something. Irish TV was not the answer to diverting us. But an ad Chris spotted as she pored over the *Champion*, our local newspaper, proved just the thing: an announcement for the Ennis Film Society.

One night we gathered in one of the grand upstairs rooms of the Old Ground Hotel. The place was freezing. Rows of straight-backed chairs with red velvet seats had been arranged facing an impromptu screen. We moved into our seats with some nervousness, holding the society's season program and our new membership cards. Chris draped my coat around her legs and her breath steamed the air as she pointed out the fine high ceiling. This was actually an old chamber for assemblies, converted for the night into a theatre. Looking around at the score of other patrons, most of them sitting in the awkward seats by themselves, I saw the same movie-starved, vaguely apologetic faces everywhere. We had all come out in the wind and rain to be here. "No popcorn and cheese doodles," whispered Chris in my frozen ear as the projector was cranked up and the film rolled.

It was a 1979 movie, and not the kind of film we would have gone downtown to see a year ago. The contrast between this and the Ziegfield in New York was staggering. The screen was mounted slightly at an angle, which left one side of the picture out of focus, the sound was very poor and occasionally rose to a screeching of tape when nothing the characters said was audible. And still we watched it. No one clamored for their money back when the film got caught and the frame jumped madly on the screen, leaving the soundtrack to continue on its own; no one left when there was a five-minute break between reels and the picture came back having altogether missed a scene; no one shouted when the shadow of someone's head blacked a corner of the screen.

"It won't always be this bad," I said to Chris, who was silent for a minute. I was afraid she was too disappointed to speak. We got into the car quietly, and then suddenly in the half-moonlight, she burst out into uncontrollable laughter! "What a great night out. I really feel like we've been on another planet."

"Are there ever any exercise classes around here in the wintertime?" Chris had asked down in the village one day in September.

"Well, now there were, once, Crissy. Why, are ye interested in having some?"

"Well, I'd like to go to one if there was one

around. I used to take classes before I came."

And so it came about. The first week of November as I stood at the counter of a shop in the village I was asked when would Crissy be starting her get-fit classes, because Lissycasey would be starting theirs in two weeks and Kilmihil would want to start theirs before then.

"I see," I said, seeing nothing at all, and wondering if Chris had gone ahead and organized the classes but had forgotten to tell me. Needless to say, she hadn't. No one was more surprised or dismayed to discover that she was going to be teaching get-fit classes on Thursday nights in the community hall to the ladies of Kilmihil. Once again we had been given a lesson in how our community worked. Women had already been told, the word had long gone out, and perhaps everyone in the town knew that Chris was going to give the classes—except Chris herself.

So the intricate machinery of starting up the classes was put into action. An afternoon visit to the big house of Father Murphy, the parish priest, procured the necessary approval for the classes to go ahead. The hall was rented for two pounds a night. And as for advertising, well, it was barely needed. Kilmihil is a place of powerful word-of-mouth, as we had already discovered with the drama group. But, for any unfortunate in the outlying rural townlands too far away to catch the news, one final touch was needed— an announcement must be made from the pulpit at Sunday mass. That alone guaranteed that everyone would know.

We sat in St. Michael's on Sunday and heard Father Linnane announce the beginning of get-fit classes; Chris caught the curious glances of the women as she walked through the village, and everyone wondered: what would these classes be like?

That first Thursday night Chris got ready early. All our neighbors in Kiltumper were going to give their support, and like everything else that is new here, no matter how simple a thing, there was a tangible air of excitement which was infectious.

"If the women in my exercise class back home could see me now, planning to lead Irish country-women in a forty-five-minute exercise routine, you know they could quite possibly die laughing," said Chris, going out the door without the slightest idea of what to expect.

Down in the community hall, almost forty women were waiting, in murmuring unease, for her to come. Dressed in everything from dresses and skirts with heeled shoes to tracksuits, coats, and boots, they were a formidable group unlike anything she had ever taught before. This was a night out more than a class for many of them, and facing Chris in the big cold hall, they were prone to the giggles. But, like a true American, "what the heck," said Chris; some exercise was better than none and the women of Kilmihil were eager to learn. To them, she was Crissy, an American get-fit teacher, and in *their* eyes she was in terrific form.

The classes ran for twelve weeks; twelve weeks which would see more than half of the women drop out at various stages and for various reasons, but more than fifteen stalwarts continued. Together with Chris they huffed and puffed in the icy air of the Kilmihil Community Hall to the music of Michael Jackson. That made a strange contrast. How different this was from all those classes Chris had been to in the States. Only one thing was the same, the motive. At the end of each session the women lined up to weigh themselves on our bathroom scales. There were groans and smiles, and a round of good cheer when it was announced: "Annie has lost five pounds!"

It would be fair to say that the women of Kilmihil were unused to the kinds of exercises that Chris gave them. For instance, the giggling and abashed noises which resounded throughout the room when she demonstrated The Hydrant—so called because the motion resembles the action of a dog peeing—could be heard in Carey's or McNamara's Pub across the road. A sit-up, as we know it, was unheard of, and judging from the groans and laughs, the abdomens of Kilmihil women were weak, although their arms may be as strong as men's.

The women were shy and quiet for the first few weeks and embarrassed by the open manner in which Chris tried to encourage them to do the exercises. As she explained her difficulties to me I began to get the comic picture.

"I mean," she said, "when one sits on the floor with legs apart in order to stretch from side to side, it definitely requires that the legs be at least more than two inches apart. Irish women just won't open their legs!"

Six weeks later, Chris was shyly approached by one woman in the class: would she agree to speak before the Kilmihil branch of the Irish Country-women's Association? Indeed she would. To be asked was an honor, and to refuse would have been ungracious.

The Irish Countrywomen's Association is a nationwide organization that was formed in 1910. Its aim is the promotion of "better living in rural Ireland." It has succeeded by organizing in small western villages up and down the Atlantic coastline whole series of demonstrations, lectures, debates and plays. It's a lively organization and over the years has covered everything from cookery and crafts to civil defense and set-dancing.

We had already heard about the Kilmihil ICA women long before we rightly knew who or what they were. Maura Cotter was one of them; so were Lucy Blake and Kathleen Devine. But just what they did on those monthly Tuesday nights when they gathered in the upstairs classroom of the vocational school we had no idea, and in the weeks following Chris's first invitation to address the ICA on the benefits of exercise Chris was especially nervous; what had she let herself in for? From the night she was invited until the night arranged for the talk, she heard nothing of what was expected of her. She was an American and would be unlike anyone else who had addressed the group in the past year. In a way, she felt, she would be on display up there, talking in front of them. Certainly there wouldn't be a single woman in the audience who wouldn't know just who this speaker was. Her relatives would be known, and she would have been fit into the "picture of Kilmihil," all before she walked into the classroom. For heaven's sake, what were they expecting? A lecture? A demonstration? With a handful of notes on exercise, and a bundle of nerves, she arrived at the school at eight and was told that she wasn't needed until half-past nine.

Chris still didn't know what was expected of her by the time she was called into the room at nine-thirty. With her notes on cardiovascular fitness and flexibility in her hand, she stepped up to the blackboard, looked down across the desks and saw in an instant that the women were not dressed for exercise. Rather they were ready for a real evening out with heels and earrings and lipstick. Chris was to do the exercises *for* them. As they sat in expectation of the demonstration about to begin, Chris noticed from the corner of her eye that the back tables were adorned with colored and patterned linen and whipped cream cakes, apple tarts and sandwiches.

Looking down over the kindly, interested faces of the ICA ladies, she introduced herself and felt at once that same Irish country feeling of hospitality we had already met so often in the houses of Kiltumper. Here were women out on an evening trying to find more for their lives, to enrich themselves in a place where the most common and easiest thing to do was stay at home, watch the television, or sometimes go to the pub. They were genuinely pleased to have Chris as their guest speaker, and their pleasure communicated something special and touching. They did want to look better and feel better, and they looked on Chris with earnest, open minds.

She talked about the necessity of exercise and the importance of starting out simply and slowly. She answered questions and demonstrated a variety of routines. From their chairs, with their coats still on, the women accompanied her in a number of exercises that can be done from a sitting position. They smiled and applauded when she finished. One woman asked when would she be starting the classes up again after Christmas.

And then they all adjourned to the spread table beyond for tea and an array of delicious homemade cakes.

CHAPTER ELEVEN _____

Drive through almost any town or village in Ireland and you will come across a monument of some kind or another. It will be somewhere around the main square or by the bridge over the river. Years will have darkened it, men and women will pass it everyday without a glance, and children will run their fingers over it without any idea of just what it is. And yet, it is always there: the plaque on the wall or the stone Celtic cross monument carved with narrow, barely legible words in Old Irish. Such monuments are everywhere around Ireland. They are the cold souvenirs of seventy years and commemorate the heroes who died in the struggle for Irish Independence between 1916 and 1922.

Today in Ireland there is an ambivalence about the revolutionary past. Republicanism in Ireland today too often means talk of the Provisional IRA and

157

the troubles in the North. After seventeen years of ceaseless bloodshed in Northern Ireland the ordinary man in the South no longer praises the heroes of the past without a shudder at the present. In the months that we have been here we have begun to notice what might be known as a revisionist phase in Irish history. That most tender and emotional subject for all Irishmen, Easter 1916, seems to be transforming ever so slightly in the public mind. Things are not quite what they once were.

Still the monuments are there. Having been in Kilmihil six months we had often noticed the stone cross monument that stands eight feet tall in front of the community hall. But until one day in November we had never managed to make out the script upon it. Then, happening by it on our way from Ryan's, the butcher's, one morning, the light caught the words and Chris and I stopped in the street to read them. It was like fingering a Braille tombstone, reading those chipped Gaelic words by touch and deciphering, with a shiver, the name of Sean Breen, who died for his country, April 1920.

There was more to this story we found by inquiring.

A native of Kiltumper, John Breen was born in 1899 and educated at Clonigulane National School. When he left school he stayed on in the parish to work on his father's farm, and when the Kilmihil Company of the Irish Volunteers was founded in 1917, John Breen joined up. By 1919, at the age of twenty, he was Quartermaster of the Second Battalion, organizing and training the company, taking them for long rugged marches across the hills and bogs of the West. On a Sunday morning in April 1920, John Breen was commanded to lead an attack on the Royal Irish Constabulary patrol in the village of Kilmihil. It was a drastic move. As the policemen were at morning mass in St. Michael's, the ambush was planned. Peader

McMahon of Boulnameal, Martin Melican of Glenmore and Jack O'Dea of Lacken, took up positions under cover about the community hall. On the other side of the street Michael Killoury of Clonakilla and John Breen prepared for the first shots.

The mass ended, and the crowd began to emerge. There was a moment's pause when it seemed the policemen were not to come out at all. And then, there they were. Shots rang out at once. Three policemen fell and the crowd scattered in terror, crying out and racing down the street from the church. More policemen appeared in seconds and a gun battle raged. Then, while the crowd was still caught, trying to shelter from the crossfire, the police prepared to throw grenades. The Volunteers were forced to make a hurried retreat. McMahon, Melican, O'Dea and Killoury made it safely away. But as John Breen came forward to divert the police from throwing the grenades where the innocent would have been killed, a bullet hit him. Bleeding heavily he escaped behind Ryan's. Within hours he was dead.

It is not an unusual story, and yet even in excerpts from a letter written in Kiltumper by John Breen's mother to her sister in Australia, there is an extraordinary evocation of the feeling that lies within it. She wrote:

Kiltumper, April 28th, 1920

Dear Sister,

Sorry that my letter is not one of joy. Perhaps the saddest in the history of our family. But we have one thing to look to with pride and joy that my darling child has been ever devoted to his religion and his country. It had been my wish to

be with him in his last agony, and to offer his
poor soul to God. He could not speak, but he
moaned heavily. His powerful countenance was no
longer discernible—his heart's blood flowing.
He was a true soldier of Ireland. He gave all to
Ireland. How many a lonely glen and valley did he
call on his duty, he never missed and how he'd
try not to let us know when he'd return. "Mother,
I can use my silken paws sometimes like the
cats." He was the most affectionate child that
ever lived. If he wished he could have saved
himself, but I hope his innocent death has saved
the multitude. What a hard life his poor
comrades have . . . there is a big price on their
heads. They have to seek the lonely mountains
and bogs for shelter. The country is full of
military.

Catherine

It was only days after we had heard this story and
come upon the letter that we were up at *Tobar Ri
Domhnaigh*, the blessed well, which is at the boundary wall between our land and Sean Melican's. There,
on the wall of the small shrine to Our Lady, is a
roughly weathered brass plaque. Again fingering the
words in that little secretive grove of trees, we made
out the name and epitaph in Old Irish: "Sean O
Bhrian, who Died For His Country."

Within days of that discovery, the Irish Taoi-
seach, Garret Fitzgerald, signed the Anglo-Irish
Agreement. It was a historic and bold move to bring
about the final and lasting peace of Northern Ireland.
On the cuaird at Dooley's, the news of the agreement
was met by one old republican with a mock sneer.
Turning to me through the smoke of his cigarette with
eyes that had seen action and the old heroic IRA men

of the past, he gave a small laugh: "Them old lads," he
said, "is just all talk."

Tonight is Thanksgiving. Thousands of miles away
America has stopped for the holiday. Families are
together and turkeys are roasting. All day today my
thoughts have measured the differences in our life
now. Throughout the day I have had a nagging sense of
being out of step, isolated; the ordinary business
around the farm only serves to heighten this. There is
no Thanksgiving in Ireland. No, no celebrations, and
in their absence a strange atmosphere of vacancy pervades the house. Around the henhouse, out by the
turfstack, the day seems extraordinarily lonely. Nothing is happening, and happening all day at that. I am
quiet and homesick. Our hand-cranked telephone system takes forever to get through to New York, and the
frustration of then hearing a faint, tremoring busy
signal on the other end is enough to knock the wind
out of you.

But this lonely, self-made isolation and vacancy
also has a beneficial side-effect. Knowing full well that
our absence is felt around at least two Thanksgiving
tables, we imagine, too, those who think of us here,
and try to see our lives from their perspective.

There is one common question, whether asked by
Niall's friends in the civil service in Dublin, or on the
staticky telephone line from a Manhattan office: *What
do you do all day?* In leaving New York for Kiltumper,
we have left behind the simple answer to that question; we have no jobs, as such, nothing that in one
word could encapsulate or explain our everyday lives.
Nothing that circumscribes our time. No listing of

small, petty duties, or description of the more pleasant tasks of the farm, is enough to answer that long-distance question. In the end we have often found ourselves picking up the listener's doubts, and feeling that, in some way, we are cheating, dropping out from real life. We are as unreal as leprachauns.

Today, Thanksgiving, we know that whenever our absence will be spoken of by friends who are beginning their long holiday weekend away from the office, there will be that question: "What do they do all day there?" With this in mind, we putter through today in Kiltumper in the mood of people who know they have learned some unproveable truth. What is our business here? we ask ourselves, and answer in the words of Thomas Merton, "our business is life itself." Someone, as Thoreau said, must be Inspector of Snowstorms, Inspector of Sunsets, and to those professions Niall and I have added a passionate host of others. Walking with quiet loneliness back along the western road in the hush of early evening, together we are Inspectors of Wildflowers, Secretaries of Sunshine, Surveyors of Meadows, Auditors of Birdsong, Clerks of Clouds, Vice-Presidents of Hilltops and Valleys, Bogs, Trees and Everything.

Seven o'clock the shutters are closed over and the candles lit. I bring the last of our summer's chickens from the oven. Tonight is Thanksgiving, and with wind blowing and the fire flickering in the hearth, we give thanks. We go back to work tomorrow.

A year ago we had imagined Christmas in Kilmihil. Then, just beginning the secret countdown of our hundred days, we pictured it as something entirely different without knowing what it would be, only we knew it would be nothing like New York. For one thing, in Kilmihil we would be alone. There would be no close family down the road. There would be no office Christmas party, no Christmas bonus; we would no longer be able to afford lavish gifts or even plain ones. No Fifth Avenue lights, no Tiffany's windows, no Christmas catalogs in the mail. Without an idea of what to expect we pictured Christmas in Kilmihil and felt a little sad.

By the end of November, as one way of life had begun to replace another, so, too, the image of a Manhattan Christmas had faded. Chris and I sat in the kitchen and made a little list of gifts for neighbors and family. In the nine months that had passed our expectations had changed greatly. It was only through a visiting New Yorker's startled remark that we could appreciate just how sparse our existence here was. By now we felt *almost* at home here. But Christmas was to be the true test. As the days drew closer to the twenty-fifth, we feared we would be overcome with yearning across the ocean.

By the first week of December Mary and Pauline down the road had already cooked two Christmas puddings, boiling them on top of the turf range for eight hours each. Christmas cakes would be baked within the week. Christmas—the biggest feast of the year—would be prepared for all month. Word filtered down to us: over the holidays in Ireland no one works between Christmas Eve and New Year's; people go frequently on the cuaird. It was important to have a good stash of cakes, puddings, biscuits, and mince pies handy.

A year ago, we would have cringed at the thought of the calories and cholesterol. But now our first reaction was to ask for recipes. In this part of the world the quality of the welcome you offer visitors is the measure of your worth. Money is not the deciding factor. Far more weighty is the taste of your tea and the sweetness of your cake. As several trips down to the village confirmed that first week of December, the whole place was alive with baking. Bags of sugar, flour and fruit left Kilmihil in their dozens. On a cold clear day from Tumper's Hill you could smell the countryside cooking.

Along with cakes, pies and puddings, a second important element of the preparations was the order for a turkey. Already Anne O'Gorman, one of our most industrious and cheerful neighbors, had a booking for each of her twenty turkeys. Walking free-range about the farm, they were guaranteed delicious, "Kiltumper turkeys just ready for the Christmas, Niall," as Mary put it. But for us no such order was necessary. We had saved our final chicken, we had sacks of our own potatoes in the cabin (so much the better for having beaten the blight), stored onions from the summer, and five pounds of sugarsnap peas in the freezer.

It was not, of course, only for visitors that the homes of Kilmihil were busying themselves. The same sense of expectation and preparation that filled the houses was mirrored in the church. The sermons of Advent were really and tangibly felt. From the altar Father Linnane spoke of the infant Christ coming into each dwelling in the parish. Sitting in the pews you could feel reverence and agreement. On Monday the women of the house started at one end and began their Christmas cleaning, moving from room to room in preparation. We were drawn into it. Pauline and Michael, two of our best and closest neighbors, had bought paint for their parlor, and new linoleum and armchairs had been ordered also. They hoped the job would be done before Christmas. We didn't need asking. In the spirit of the *comhair*, and in the gathering and infectious spirit of *the Christmas,* as everyone called it, Chris and I walked down the road daily to paint their parlor. We had hearty meals and a feeling of satisfaction in our work. This, too, was part of Christmas. What we were experiencing in Kiltumper was a real survival of traditional Ireland. Reading about country life and traditions during the nineteenth century, we came upon the same descriptions of Christmas preparations. Here on textbook pages were described exactly the details of scrubbing, tidying and whitewashing that were happening all around us. That would never change. For both of us it was the first telling image of what Christmas was to be like in Kiltumper.

No sooner were rooms cleaned and tidied than the question of the tree arose. Mary answered us by saying: "We'll cut one, Crissie." It seemed such an obvious thing to do; but was it really done? On a cold bright day in the second week of December Mary arrived up the garden path to prove it was: we were going hunting for Christmas trees. We set off down the road with the small bushman saw in hand. Up across the fields, over stone walls and wire fences, the three of us trooped like a little pilgrimage. The sun was shining. When we moved among the thick evergreens on the top of the hill there was such a lush peacefulness that it seemed there was nothing else in the world happening at that moment. Into the midst of the trees we went, thinking Christmas.

To pick from a line of ready-cut Christmas trees outside a supermarket is one thing. To pick one from a forest is quite another. Up there in the vast green stillness it was impossible to remember the small cleared space in the parlor where the tree was to stand. We changed our minds a dozen times, moving ever deeper into the trees.

It took some time to decide. Finally, we took two of the smallest evergreens from beneath the shade of older more established trees, just as the forestry men would do in the months to come. And yet, the smallest trees were still very sizeable. Having cut our chosen ones, we moved them out into a clearing and studied them. They were perfect. With Chris's help I hoisted ours onto my back. Mary did the same with hers. Chris gathered the saw and the shovel. The sun was still shining. I shouldered the tree and passed it to Chris while we clambered awkwardly over the stone walls. There was a calm green joy in the afternoon air. Down the hill we marched, two trees over our shoulders and our hearts full of the still, quiet expectation that was Christmas.

There are no bags of cranberries here. After a furious search in Kilrush and Ennis, I wrote in desperation to Deirdre in New York. SEND BAG OF CRANBERRIES IMMEDIATELY. VERY IMPORTANT. And in the meantime I decked the tree with the small wooden figures we had collected over previous Christmases. Niall can't believe that I managed to remember to pack these decorations, each one marked and dated on the day it was given to us, as well as a string of lights. I guess that I imagined this Christmas tree and our sitting tonight on the bare floor beneath it when I had packed our things that exhausted last night in March before we left America. Our tree will look different from others. In Ireland, it is not uncommon to deck the tree with cards and balloons, festooning it with the postman's daily deliveries. And of course no one uses strings of cranberries, not to mention popcorn.

Sitting beneath the tree in the bay window, I think tonight what many Irish people think of at Christmastime, of those far away, of those in America. Alone in the hush of night we light candles and drink hot chocolate sitting in the soft glow of the tree lights, saying not a word and writing Christmas cards until we are tired.

We had slowly come to realize that there were things that we were doing that we could never have achieved in our previous life-style. "Achieved" is of course a little grand. But since coming to Kiltumper I felt we had gradually acted on our countless artistic or creative impulses that had been for so long held at bay. In New York Chris had spoken often of her deep desire to write a novel; many times she had made brief beginnings on a page torn from a yellow pad, using a sick-day in bed. I suppose that is not uncommon. I feel it was having dared to take up the challenge of moving to Ireland that freed our energies. Forty pages of a manuscript had gathered in Chris's folder as we headed into the winter. Ahead of both of us were the long dark days which we hoped to fill with words and paint.

I had begun again to write poetry, something I hadn't done in ten years. It has always seemed to me that to write lyric poetry well required a state of near innocence in the relationship between the poet and the world around him. Allowing myself that most romantic of views I had held off writing any poems at all, waiting, knowing that everything should feel right, in balance. In Kiltumper life seemed to encompass poetry, even demand it. There are so many things in the wild natural world of the West that seek celebration. Following that impulse I began a sequence of Kiltumper poems using the place-names, legends and lore around us. Out around the hay barn or going up across the Big Meadow I found myself for no reason remembering the Gaelic I had learned as a child. One such word, *duachais*, means everything to do with a place, its rootedness, tradition, its lore. I remembered it, said it over and over. It seemed an entirely apt expression for the same rainy fields I walked. Quietly I went up Tumper's Hill letting the rough and tender sounds of Irish infiltrate my English.

LOGAINMNEACHA
(The Meaning of Place-Names)

Upper and Lower Tumper,
the Big Meadow and the Bog
Meadow, and *Gadie na scoile*

Overside the haggard
where once the Hedgemaster
taught rhythm and rhymes.

Tobar Ri Domhnaigh,
Our blessed well by Melican's
Bounds where Bridgy Griffen

Got back her sight.
I wandered up there once
dallying in the names of fields

until it came to me:
duachais, duachais
a feeling-sound of name

meaning and place, by which
every noun bled to verb, and
every field raised its voice.

Out of the same impulse of freedom to write all kinds of things, together we had written a short radio play. "At the Heart of this Place" was a brief drama about an American who arrived in Clare to live in his grandfather's cottage, and the son of a farmer who was about to leave for the States. We wanted to enter it in the National Radio competition for amateur drama groups. I was nervous about showing it to the Kilmihil group. We were relative outsiders still, offering a play about one of the most tender subjects in the country.

I need not have worried. The play was accepted

by Martin Keane and entered at once. In the days following its entry word went around parts of the town. "I hear ye've written a play," said the woman in the post office. "We have," said I, "and wait till you hear what we've said about you!" She laughed, wondered about it, and let me go with a smile.

A month later the word came back from Dublin. The play had been chosen as one of the semi-finalists in the competition; now the Kilmihil Players had to send in a recording of it. This was a more serious matter. It would mean that on successive Sunday afternoons for the next month four members of the drama group would come to our house to work on the play. Chris would produce it and, as I had already agreed to be director of Synge's *Well of the Saints* (Kilmihil's newly and hastily chosen replacement play for the West Clare Drama Festival in March), I would play director.

We had a feeling of satisfaction in having written the play which was far different from any literary feeling I had ever had before. I realized that literature need not be a rarefied animal of publishing and academia. In the West it was something "live," like a football match. Kilmihil was in the semi-finals, the only town in the county of Clare to have made it that far. Hurray for Kilmihil! Come on Kilmihil! There is no feeling like it, it was so closely a thing of the community. For the first time ever I had the sense of an artist's proper place in a community. Michael and Pauline, Mary and Joe, Michael and Breda, J. J. and Mary, all our neighbors had praise and congratulations for us, just as they always had an admiring word whenever they looked in at Chris's various canvases hung in the parlor. They were not afraid to talk of our enterprise. It was only overseas or Dublin visitors who gazed at those paintings, nodding, shrugging, cut off from their instincts and from saying anything, lest it be the wrong thing.

By mid-December, with the full-length and the radio plays well into rehearsal and our chronicle of life in Kiltumper more than halfway written, the people around us had completely accepted us. They made us feel we belonged. How different that feels is hard to describe. I stood in the front door one evening looking out across the fields and the mizzling rain, trying to think of a word for a poem. Karol Downes, a seven-year-old boy in Wellies and rain jacket came marching up the garden path carrying the stick which he used to drive cows along the road. He was covered in muck, spatters of it flecked his face as he looked up at me happily in the doorway. "How's it going, Karol?" I said to him. "All right sure, Niall." He smiled, "How are all the books going today?"

And then it was Christmas. High winds were blowing and I was outside climbing up the holly tree. For weeks the prized red berries had been covered over with the netting from the pea tent to save them from the birds. Daily we had thrown crusts and scraps onto the frosty garden in the hope of diverting their hunger. Sprigs of holly were in great demand. Not least by Chris, who sat in a pile of spruce twigs, acorns and holly in front of the big fire making Christmas wreaths. Many of the gifts this year were to be home-made; wreaths for Mary, Michael and Pauline, Breda and Michael, J. J. and Mary, a tied ribbon on a bucket of our best spuds for Ma Williams, one of Chris's lovely pastels for Da in Dublin, a sketch of the traditional sugan chair for Regis in Baltimore, a packed, Christmas-wrapped box of our own dry turf for Declan and Patricia. There was the labor of love in each of them.

In Kilmihil preparations for Christmas were reaching a climax. Santa had arrived in Johnston's, and children gazed in the window filled with toys: big plastic tractors, trucks, coloring books, and, of course, cowboy guns. They stood in the cold, looking at the wonderful toys while their parents went "to get the Christmas." At Johnston's, Saunder's, Daly's and Cotter's, there was brisk business as people from the outlying townlands came in to stock up for a fortnight. Boxes upon boxes of food supplies were carried out the door, the last one or two of these being the customer's Christmas box from the shopkeeper himself. This is an old custom in Ireland, still carried on in towns like Kilmihil all through the West. The shop where you have done your main business all year will make a present to you of a packed box of groceries, the size of the present being in proportion to the amount of business you've done in the year. So, as Chris bought the last of our needs to "bring home the Christmas," Mrs. Johnston bent down behind the counter and looked around among the boxes on the floor, each one with a name written carefully on it. "Crissie and Niall," she read. "There you go, Happy Christmas."

We took it home as if it were treasure. Unpacking on the kitchen floor we laid out three pounds of tea, four pounds of sugar, three packets of custard, a bag of flour, some marrowfat peas, two tins of beans, a bottle of red lemonade and three packets of biscuits. We were well stocked and prepared. Our Christmas cake and pudding were waiting in the cupboard, I had split a hundred ash logs over the previous days and stacked the corner of the hearth high with fuel, Chris had bedecked the kitchen with hanging cards. And then, with only two days to go, the postman arrived with a package from New York. Cranberries!

Perhaps it is something to do with being on high ground or the distance to the North Pole. Perhaps the West of Ireland is a first stop on an all-night journey,

171

but whatever the reason, here in Kiltumper Santa Claus arrives at around six o'clock on Christmas Eve. All the house curtains are shut tightly. The children are scrubbed for mass, their Christmas clothes laid out on the beds. Outside *he* very quietly arrives and unloads gifts, laying them by the front door. Once everything is unloaded Santa goes to the front door and gives three sharp knocks before hurrying away around the hay barn or the cabins. "Santa's here!" cries one of the children and they rush for the door, opening it to find the little pile of gifts on the ground in front of them. Faces are turned to look out into the the darkness, up and down the road and up into the sky. There is no sign of him. All the presents are carried inside. One child shows another how Santa had brought just that same tractor in the shop's window he had wished for so hard.

A moment later Grandfather, or a neighbor, will come in through the back door. "Has Santa been to you yet?" he'll ask with a broad smile.

Of all the traditions associated with Christmas Eve by far the most prevalent today is the lighting of the *coinneal mor na Nollag,* or the big Christmas candle. Blessed candles had been on sale in town for weeks. In each household the coinneal mor would be lit at darkness and placed in the front-room window to burn there until morning. The origin of the custom is that the candle is lit to show Mary and Joseph that, unlike the inn at Bethlehem, this house would always welcome them. In the same way it is customary in many houses to leave all doors unlocked that evening and when going to bed to leave some food in three dishes upon the kitchen table as a welcome for the "travelers to Bethlehem."

Following tradition, tonight on Christmas Eve at half-past six Chris lit our *coinneal mor* in the kitchen window. It was a signal of sorts, shining out across the dark fields before us just as it was shining out in homes all across the country. It was a warm silent message of hope and welcome. It was our house, our townland, village, and country sending out slivers of light into the world. Standing at the front door we gazed out beneath a clear sky impossibly packed with stars. The heavens seemed loaded with them. There, and there again, Chris pointed to the tiny flicker of candles in cottages all across the valley. Christmas in Kiltumper. Upon the floor in the great kitchen hearth a big fire had been stacked high, sending dramatic sparks from the ash logs high into the night. By half-past eight we were ready to leave for mass—midnight mass in St. Michael's at nine o'clock.

Driving down the road we stopped in to wish Michael and Pauline a happy Christmas. The seven Downes's were in a riot of excitement and cleanliness as Santa had come to them already. Mary and Joe were in their Christmas best, waiting for a lift down to the church. Down in Kilmihil St. Michael's was jammed. The whole town jigged toward the church in new clothes. Last-minute presents and food supplies moved out of the shops like crazy, tractors and cars sprawled all along the street. The town came to a halt just as the choir falteringly began to sing and Father Linnane and Father Murphy walked out to the altar.

On Christmas Day we woke up after our private midnight feast. Chris's first-ever "plum pud' and Christmas cake" had been delicious. We gave each other the small presents we could afford—socks for Niall, soap and perfume for Chris. Later, we drove across Ireland under the hoops of a half-dozen rainbows. The car was loaded with potatoes, turf, eggs and paintings to bring as gifts. We sang as we looked out at the peaceful meadows of Tipperary, Laois and

173

Kildare on Christmas morning. It was so quiet that the landscape of stilled animals and low, sweeping mountains evoked a pastoral mood we were both happy.

Peter and Francie were to go on it. For a week before Christmas they had been excited enough to rush out from the house and announce it to anyone who passed: they were going on the Wren.

Hunting the Wren, or Going on the Wrenboys is an old Irish custom which has now died out in all but the westernmost counties. It takes place on St. Stephen's Day, the twenty-sixth of December. Originally, some weeks before Christmas, a crowd of boys from a village would go off in a pack hunting with a great hullabulloo through fields and hedgerows for the little bird, the wren. Once found the wren was quickly killed, his body was bagged, and another little bird hunted in like manner. Then, on St. Stephen's Day, the Wrenboys, as they were known, would attach the bodies of the wrens to a large holly bush and carry it off in procession through the streets shouting and roaring like murderers and singing the Wren Song outside homes until a ransom was paid to make them leave.

Nowadays few wrens are killed, but the strange custom of the Wrenboys lives on. The day after Christmas the stillness of Kiltumper came alive with them. Peter and Francie joined up with a gang of their schoolfriends under the guidance of a teacher. They held their holly branch aloft and marched from farm to farm, startling the afternoon with the bustle of giddy happy voices. From across the fields you could hear them coming, the Wrenboys singing the same Wren Song that was older than the days of their great-grandfathers:

174

The wran, the wran, the king of all birds
St. Stephen's day was cot in the furze,
although he is little his family is grate
put yer hand in yer pocket and give us a trate.
Sing holly, sing ivy, sing ivy, sing holly,
a drop just to drink it would drown melancholy,
and if you draw it of the best
I hope in heaven yer soul will rest,
But if you draw it of the small
it won't agree with the wran boys at all.

Christmas is a time of children. That was inescapable. All around us we saw children and pregnant women as we struggled with sadness against our own bad news. Since that awful day we had suffered silently in Kiltumper, smarting at simple things—ads for nappies, toys for little boys, a pretty little girl's dress. Letters from America came, full of kindly advice: artificial insemination, technology today, scientific advances, and a plethora of other catch-all solutions all impossible in Ireland, all hopelessly hoping to save us from our pain.

It would be a lie not to chronicle this, the often unspoken undercurrent of sadness which was ever-present that winter in Kiltumper. "What are you painting these days?" asked various letters to Chris, while in the cold parlor we both knew that canvases were lying untouched, white.

It came and went, and came and went. We were alone with it, crying together when some well-meaning letter made it seem as if all we had to do was call a specialist or fly to some clinic. Who, after all, could understand how things looked to us from the rainy green expanse we were living on? We could not explain it to anyone—neither the fact that such things as artificial insemination were banned by the church in Ireland, nor that neither of us felt that was the

175

answer anyway. At the risk of receiving everyone's continued advice and judgment that we were simply feeling sorry for ourselves, we said nothing. I answered no letters. Together we took long quiet walks back the wet road to Kathleen's. The sky was a glowering gray. Cattle moaned with cold and huddled by stone walls, mucking the line of shelter from the east wind. In our hearts we clung to each other, our bodies not touching, we felt so senselessly bruised in those days. Rain was falling. Rain seemed to be always falling.

CHAPTER TWELVE _____

A letter came with good news. The first of the Kiltumper poems was accepted for publication in the *Irish Press,* a national newspaper. I was paid thirty pounds for two of them. It was valued cash which we counted far more gladly than any Friday's paycheck reduced by taxes. Our spirits were high; it was a sign, an omen of encouragement at last, indicating that we were on the right road. Mary, Pauline and Michael were genuinely delighted for us. Thirty pounds, let me see. I thought of things for Chris, she thought of spring seeds for the garden. Then, finally, she looked up from a catalog and across the table.

"I know," she said, "let's give a party for the people of Kiltumper."

Nine months ago, before leaving New York, we had imagined throwing a party at the cottage as soon as we had arrived. What had happened to that idea?

The time it took us to settle into the cottage, make it comfortable, buy more than two cups, two saucers, two plates, all the while joining in the rhythm of the community as potatoes were set, turf cut and won home—that time passing made parties seem out of place. Besides which, apart from weddings and wakes, the notion of a party was a foreign one in Kiltumper.

In the mood of Christmas though, the place was ready for it. On a cold Monday morning we went out in the car, driving the narrow lonely roads of Kiltumper. We stopped in the middle of the road and left the car, going to knock on doors with the invitation to come to our party on New Year's Eve. Everywhere the invitation was received happily; we felt like messengers of good will. Our guest list, being composed of our neighbors in Kiltumper, brought together twenty people of one, if not two generations older than both of us. Anywhere else that would have been unthinkable; our party would be in stark contrast to other New Year's Eve parties we had attended. We pulled up the car on the rainswept western road and I hurried in to knock at O'Sullivan's. A voice from within bid me enter. I unlatched the old door quickly—too quickly, and, as it swung in on the breeze, a great cloud of smoke rose into the kitchen from the fire. There, blinking at its side, sat Mikey and his wife. They hardly knew me through the smoke, but then each rose to vigorously shake my hand in welcome. Welcome to their house. I was seated in the best chair by the fire, turf was thrown on, and Mikey lifted a bottle of Powers whiskey from the floor at his feet. I felt like an honored guest, though I had only come to ask them to the party. Mikey's wife, Nora, was busying herself washing a glass—making me cringe a little with embarassment for they had no running water and every drop that was heaved up the road from the well was precious. Still, the pride of these people runs deep and the welcome must be given. It's the cardinal rule in the West.

"We're thinking of having a bit of a party down at the house. We'd like the two of you to come," I said at last. There was that same delighted expression on their faces which we would meet everywhere we went with the invitation. Then Mikey looked over to Nora. I understood. He was partially lame. They had no car.

"I'll come and collect the two of you on the night," I said, and went out that door realizing I was recrossing the threshold of one of the very few traditional cottages where a life of hardship and struggle had imbued the old people with something special and ardent. They were people of whom, they say in Irish, their like will never be seen again.

They were all invited and would all come. Mary and Joe; Breda and Michael Dooley and Michael Donnellan; Michael and Pauline; Paul and Kathleen; Tommy and Tom; J. J. and Mary and Martin; Sean, Tom and Mary; Mickey and Nora; JohnJoe and his tin whistle, and the guest of all guests, our guest of honor, Mary's eighty-four-year-old mother, Nora.

Largely confined to her bed and the chair by Dooley's fire, Nora was rarely out of the house anymore. She sat quietly in her corner whenever we made a cuaird up the hill to see Breda and Michael. She was alert and full of welcome; she remembered the old ancestors and stories out of the past and could still draw tunes from her concertina. When Nora said she would be happy to come we knew that the party was to be something special.

All the women would bring breads, scones and cakes, and in the three days before the end of the year, Kiltumper was busy in preparation. Guinness, Harp and whiskey were stacked in the back hall. Out in the hay barn I split enough ash logs to build the fire high for a long night. Chris was busy cleaning and cooking, wondering where everyone would sit, how the men would behave, would they all gather together in the other room and leave the women sitting by the fire alone? Would JohnJoe play music for people to dance sets to? Or would the night be shaped by the powerful shyness of Irish people which we knew only too well? It was a strange irony that the very same race who were near-legendary carousers, dancers, musicians and storytellers were also the most bashful people anywhere in the world. As the three days before the party hurried by we wondered nervously: how in the world would it all go?

Six o'clock. A clear cold night and the fire in the hearth was stacked high. Chairs we had borrowed from Mary and Pauline ringed the kitchen floor, leaving free a center rectangle for dancing before the fire. An old table, none too steady on the slanting floor, was packed with glasses of all descriptions hastily gathered from our neighbors earlier in the day. On the counter across the kitchen were the buns, scones, brown bread, cake and biscuits of a feast. On the range were three different kettles of hot water for the tea, and next to it, in the warmest seat in the house, was Nora's special straight-backed chair. I was to collect her within the hour. I passed the time in a fret of anxiety, fussing with the fire, moving chairs, and moving them back again while Chris seemed calm. Quietly she put a cassette in the tape recorder: the jigging music of the Kilfenora Ceili Band set the scene.

I couldn't wait until seven. Everything ready too early I set off for Dooley's in the car to pick up Mary and her mother, and Tom and Mary. The house, when I got there, was abuzz. Everyone wanted to look his or her best, not least, Nora herself. Her long white hair braided behind her, a stole over her shoulders and a brooch on her blouse, she was helped out the door on her walker, leaving the house that night for the first time in a year. She was delighted with herself; we were delighted to have her. When I carried her down the steps into our kitchen she sat in her chair shaking Crissie's hand over and over in thanks for the invitation. I headed back the road in the car to pick up Mikey and his wife feeling the warmth of satisfaction. It was going to be a good night.

The sky was full of stars. There *was* a moon. Inside the kitchen, ranged around on the furthest chairs with their drinks in hand sat Tom, Michael, Mikey, J. J., Martin, Paul, Tom and Tommy, Michael, Sean, and Niall. In an inner ring, closer to the blaze of the massive fire, sat the women, quietly tapping their feet to the jigs and reels that played from the tape recorder. Everyone was chatting. Nothing too exciting was happening.

"Crissie, I think it's time for the tea," whispered Mary, trying not to be noticed.

Tea? All the men had been there over an hour and had glasses of whiskey and stout. The women had sherry or orange lemonade. Tea?

"All right Mary, you help me," said Chris, getting up and going across the room.

Breda joined them and a major tea-making operation was set up, all the kettles were boiling, the teapots were scalded, the bread sliced and buttered, cold meats, salads, cakes and biscuits, put on individual plates, and all the while the men seemed not to notice until the moment one of the women came over to them with a plateful of food and a mug of tea. "Tea, Crissie? Oh, lovely, thanks." It was the way of the West. In a flurry of activity everyone was served, and served again if they had missed anything—Breda's ginger cake, Mary's scones, Pauline's bread, Kathleen's tart, Crissie's carrot cake. Compliments were passed to every house in Kiltumper.

After supper the mood began to change. The fire was so warm that the front door was opened on the starry night. Carrying the empty plates back to the sink, Mary hummed and danced three steps to the ceili music. Then, like an entrance in a play, the back door swung open and down the two steps into the kitchen came JohnJoe with his tin whistle in his hand. "God Bless ye all," he said, drew up a chair in front of the fire, looked around at all of us and started up a tune.

J. J. was the first to take to the floor. A big genial man with a happy face he looked anything but a dancer, and yet he moved to the music with light-footed ease and grace. He had been dancing these same steps to the very same music ever since he was a boy. Following his lead, others were called up, and called again and again if they didn't get right up to the women who stood waiting on the kitchen floor. Within a minute it seemed the room was swaying with a crowd, dancing one-two-three, one-two-three in a mixture of old-time waltzes and traditional Clare sets. Their shadows flickered on the ceiling as they swung right around in front of the blazing fire, laughing and nodding to the jigs. Men teased any man who left the dance too soon, and a great yelp of laughter burst out as time and again the couples collided in the small kitchen and re-formed to dance on. And on and on. JohnJoe played for all he was worth, a bottle of Guinness on the floor at his side. Chris was already familiar with Irish dancing and flew round and round in the company of every dancer, her dress flashing across the fire. From his seat beside mine, Tom, leaning on the bad leg that kept him from joining in, nodded at her. Leaning to me as the music jigged on, he said, "I'm seeing in her now the Old Breens come again." It was his highest compliment, having already unraveled for both of us his many great stories of the old days, and of the near-fabled generosity and *spiritedness* of the family. I looked at Chris. Her cheeks were alight, she was beautiful with dancing. Urged to the floor I bumped along with her, with

Mary, Breda, Pauline, dizzy, as our little cottage seemed to spin like a top with Irish music.

There were breaks for breathers, breaks for the women to stop laughing, breaks for the men to slip out the front door to pee in the moonlight. Then there was the call for songs. "Come on Sean, sing a song for us! Come on. Good man!" Shyly in the corner, Sean said he knew no song. "He has a grand voice if he'll use it, ye know," said Michael in my ear, and raised again with the others the call for a song. There was an expectant hush; there was no announcement. From his place in the corner Sean began to sing.

It was the kind of traditional Irish singing that is unlike anything else. It wavered on the air like a clear keening, shaking the singer a little as the sound of a sad ballad stilled the room. There were murmurs of appreciation and praise. "Good man, Sean," whispered Michael, gazing across at him, his marvelous rich voice as good as any, his clear blue eyes fixed on the ceiling. From her place by the range Nora followed each note with a nod of her head. At that moment while Sean sang I had no thoughts about anything. The world was a simple place with cattle outside in the fields and songs sung around the fire in our kitchen. Paul sang after Sean with a voice just as good. At a minute to midnight, Chris ran through the house closing the front door and opening the back one, to let out the old year. Glasses were filled with whiskey, there were words of hope for a better summer in 1986, and then it was announced: Midnight! Chris ran to the back door and shut it, and then through the kitchen to the front door, letting in the New Year. It came, fresh, clear, and full of stars, to the calling of toasts. Nora smiled on everyone and raised her glass. JohnJoe set himself down by the fire, took a sip of his Guinness and started up the music.

The night danced on without notion of time. At another breather, J. J. hushed the company with a sudden announcement: "Once upon a time ago,"he began, "and it was not in my time nor in yer time either but it was a time all the same for all that, there was a man walking along the road in Kerry when up before him rode a great host of fairies on horseback. 'Come along now with us,' they said to him, 'and we'll take you to a great feast we're off to this day.' And the man looked up at the leader of the fairies and said, 'How can I go with ye and I with no horse to ride?' And the leader of the fairies looked down at him and said 'Do ye see that *buachailan* [a thistle], there's yer horse for ye' ".

Peals of laughter broke out as J. J. continued the long fabulous story of the man and the fairies, taking us into the New Year to the sound of laughter. Nor was that all. When the music began again, he flew into the air with a solo shoe-snapping demonstration of Irish step-dancing, clicking his heels and jumping into the steps to the shouts of the men and women gathered around.

There was more dancing. More music. Into the morning the party reeled with good humor and laughter. Everyone was happy to be there. It was something new for Kiltumper. Or rather, it was something very old and simple which had all but disappeared in the West, the night of traditional music, tea and dancing in the kitchen. It felt right. As our neighbors left to go home, thanking us with the same fierce sincerity with which they had welcomed us to each of their homes, we felt we had given them back some of the warmth they had given to us.

As we dropped Tom off at his front door in the moonlight, he leaned over to the window to thank us one last time. "That night," he said, "was every bit as good as one of the old weddings or wakes."

One hundred days. Over the Christmas the count began again. In a hundred days we would have been in the house one year. Over the New Year that thought kept ringing in our minds. Could it really be a year? The New Year's wet weather kept us indoors. In the heart of an Irish winter we looked to the last hundred days of our private year and made a careful inventory of the things we had left undone. Those wintry days—not quite cold, not quite dry—were perfect for the making of resolutions. New schedules of paintings and sketches were drawn up, a daily three pages of writing demanded, seeds ordered from catalogs for early setting in windowboxes, routines established for the biweekly trip to the dump with our tin cans and bottles, a rationing scheme proposed for our remaining turf and timber, and a farm plan mapped out for the garden and for poultry—fifteen chickens, how many ducks? In our January enthusiasm we knocked our plans into shape like a new boss.

If you live on a farm, no matter how large or small, then it is a sin not to farm it. In West Clare if you're not lucky enough to be a dairy farmer, then your only other option is to be a cattle farmer. Since we had arrived in spring it had always been in the back of our minds that one day the moment would come when we would have to decide whether to lease the land again to a local farmer or try our hand as cattle farmers. In our seats by the fire counting our hundred days we decided that we'd go farming. Stocking the farm was our goal. It would be evidence that we had gone all the way.

On a quick visit to Ireland—four nights, and eighteen rainy holes on three of the country's most famous golfcourses, Lahinch, Ballybunion, Killarney—Chris's father, Joe, came to see us. On a dark evening walk back along the western road by Kathleen's avenue Joe stopped and looked at me with a steady eye. "Do you *know* anything about farming?" he said. "No," I said. We walked on a little bit. Rain was falling. Cattle in fields came blindly up the land toward the road in the hope of feed. As we went along, a trail of them followed us inside the stone wall, a sighing, snorting audience for our conversation. As I walked I remembered job interviews at Madison Avenue advertising agencies. "Do you think you could do it?" asked Joe. The cattle behind the wall paused, the clouds in the darkness were darker still, and there we were, two men stopped on a country road about to decide a future. I told him about the course. It was agreed with a gentleman's handshake on a lonely botharin that if I took the course Joe would pay for the first four cows and we would keep their calves as our living.

The Certified ACOT Farmer Training Course had been advertised in the *Clare Champion* months earlier. ACOT is the National Agricultural Advisory Board, and places in the course were supposed to be difficult to obtain. A hundred hours spread over two months, it fit so exactly into our hundred days that Chris had persuaded me to apply even before we knew for certain we would be buying animals in the spring. One day in January I got the notice of acceptance: I was to be present at the Kilrush Community Center at half-past ten the following Tuesday. I was to bring a pencil, and my Wellies.

The next three days were unnerving. Having spent five years in college, having thumbed countless books, here I was about to be part of a class in which I was certain to be the dunce. Already I dreaded the first day. It was going to be like going to school for the very first time and as the familiar feeling of anxiety welled up in me I questioned my wisdom in having mentioned the course to Joe. Chris tried to help: "You *do* know something about farming," she said, unconvincingly, as the two of us stood in the front doorway looking out at the young Downes children driving nineteen cows homeward to be milked.

In fact, the course was *not* for novices. It was for the elder sons of established farmers and offered a substantial exemption from inheritance taxes as an incentive for anyone who graduated with a farming certificate. The other men enrolled in the course had spent all their lives on farms and I'd be sitting among them like a Martian.

The day before the course was to begin I realized my Wellies were punctured and leaky, and so immediately I went down to Kilmihil and bought a new pair, black and glossy. That evening I quietly took them out in the back meadow and carefully muddied them from top to toe.

How do you approach your first day at farming school? Well, you try to look as casual as possible, as if you had just stepped in from the fields where you were scattering dung or spreading slurry. The pencil you were to bring could be already lost or chewed to a stub. A little muck about you is no harm. Standing around in the big room, ignoring the rows of chairs, there were forty-two of us waiting for something to happen. Neighbors who knew one another were laughing to find themselves there, others were edgy and felt confined. At last a man carrying a box of papers came through the door. "Well, ye're a quiet lot," he said. "Will ye sit down and don't be afraid of the chairs." In the rumble that followed seats were established; without anyone saying so they would become our permanent positions, each of us heading for the same seats week after week until the course was finished. When I looked up I found the only two women in the class were sitting beside me.

Farming in the West of Ireland is different from farming elsewhere. Here the wetness and poverty of much of the land and the relative smallness of the holdings have meant that the western farmer has had little expectation of progress. He is the traditional Irish farmer, his home a single-story cottage, his land, around forty acres, having often been divided and passed from generation to generation. Stone walls crisscross and meet everywhere in his fields, sometimes separating no more than half acres. On these hilly, boggy or rocky lands he scrapes a living. He is not entirely successful and the government, categorizing him as living in a "severely disadvantaged" area, pays him the farmer's dole. Even with this, the farmer in the West does not compare to the man who wakes in the splendid fertile farms of Tipperary and Ireland's Golden Vale. In the West the farmer will always be poor. It almost seems a condition of the landscape. He will run his place with the minimum of machinery, cutting hay to winter his cattle, and doing things much as his father and grandfather have done. His farm will provide a living for only one son or daughter.

It was against this background that ACOT offered the farmer training course. They knew the situation well and hoped that by attracting the sons of farmers who would eventually be responsible for the land that they could instill in them some of the modern practices of efficient farming. After all, elsewhere in the world farming had become a science, a huge business of fertilizer tonnage and measured weight gains, a studied mathematical practice of profit and loss, while in the West of Ireland it still retained all the hit-and-miss elements of years gone by.

When Tadhg Murphy stepped to the front of the class that morning in Kilrush and looked down on the forty-two of us he seemed aware of the burden of persuasion that lay upon him. He knew that in matters of farming, experience and knowledge of the land often counted for more than theories. He knew that the fathers of some of the pupils would be waiting at home to contradict everything he told them. But he did have one advantage. Almost everyone in the class that morning who was actively farming was running into the same problem. The same fear had begun to nag them as the month of January ran on and the real hardship of the worst summer in a hundred years began to make itself felt. In a place where the poorer farmers still rely exclusively on hay as winter feed for cattle, last summer little hay could be made, and the quality of any that was made was appalling, without feeding value. All over the West animals were beginning to weaken from malnutrition. Within months they would be dying in the fields. When Tadhg began the course with the words, "How do you know if you have enough winter fodder left at this stage?" everyone hushed and listened.

During the afternoon session we went out on a farm trip—testing and measuring silage. The task of converting rural Irish farmers to making silage was one of the main objectives of the ACOT advisors, for although the cost of harvesting was greater, the hardship and risk of a bad summer would be greatly decreased. From the moment silage was mentioned discussions began. Conversations were carried on out the door as, with a few general directions and a time-check, Tadhg Murphy dismissed us. Packed into cars and tractors of all descriptions, we set off in convoy from Kilrush.

Three men from the class joined me in the car and talked about farming as I drove. I muttered, nodded, and agreed when they spoke of ruined hay, sick cattle. But I knew nothing about the real hardships of farming. I felt like a fool. I was only playing at farming; these people had years on me, it was ridiculous my coming to the course. As we passed occasional farmers on our way, they stopped to look at the long line of us, the trainee farmers. I imagined a little laughter in their eyes: as if you could teach farming, learn what only the land itself knew, what only the land itself could teach you, and in long hard slow rainy windy lessons at that.

When we arrived at the farm I parked the car on

the side of the road. A cold rain was blowing and I took out my muddied new Wellies with a low heart. There were cattle in a field next to me: what breed were they, were they sick or healthy, well fed or starved, two-year-olds or three-year-olds? I hadn't a clue. As all the young farmers strode among the cattle with an easy, knowing familiarity, moving them with the whistle and yelp of drovers back across the land, I felt like turning round and driving home. For God's sake, what was I doing there? I didn't know a blooming thing about farming.

In the country, when you buy a newspaper the first thing you turn to are the deaths. Sometimes it seems no other news is even read. The deaths are what count. The reasons for this are quite simple. In the West relations are all-important, everyone is related to everyone, and this extends even beyond distant cousins to neighbors of cousins, cousins of neighbors. The bond of community is vital and funerals are one expression of that bond. As the cold short days of January and February gathered into a long hard knot of time there seemed to be a continual stream of funerals in Kilmihil. At first we hardly noticed them, and then, as conversation turned ever more frequently to "what time is the funeral?" another element of last summer's ruin became apparent. Little turf had been saved in the rain and, in the hard black weather of the beginning of the year, old people were quietly dying. Who could say for sure that it was coincidence?

There was no oil heating in these houses. When you woke, dressed and hurried about the hay barn in the east wind to gather a few sticks to try and begin the fire the air was freezing. If you had sods of turf any water or dampness in them would be frozen solid, making for heavy, heatless fuel. It was hopeless.

There were stories of men and women too cold to get out of beds that were stacked high with coats and blankets, and tales from the West of desperate measures—soaking wet turf in paraffin and blazing the whole house down, or of great boughs of bog deal smoldering in kitchen fires, and rubber tires being thrown onto the flames. It was the saddest winter, the winter that at every turn was a reminder of the summer just gone, and of the constant struggle for life which was and is the West of Ireland. You have to live through it to believe it.

Kilmihil was like every other parish, huddled in the cold, waiting the long wait for spring. Back in our cottage, looking out over the stilled whitish frost-burned fields we waited, too. Then one morning Michael called from down the road: there was bad news, Mary's mother had died in her sleep during the night.

The death was in the papers later that day. Nora had died quietly in her bed with Mary and Breda sitting by her. It had been the most peaceful passing and now she would be waked at the house while we waited for her other daughter, Eileen, to come from England.

That morning as Chris and I walked down the road to offer our sympathy to Mary, the fields of Kiltumper seemed hushed and still. Everything here is a mirror of everything else, and in a strange way the countryside was bleak and mournful with death. Nothing was moving in the chill wind, and without quite knowing what to do or say, we entered the house of tears.

It is at moments of crisis or pain that the force of love between neighbors is most powerfully expressed. Nothing matters but to comfort the sorrowful and help with the ordeal. In the dim light of the kitchen, with the blinds down, Mary was crying helplessly by the fire while trying to organize what was needed for the wake: chairs, tables, candles and five brass candle-holders. Our neighbors undertook these simple errands, and brought whatever was needed up to Dooley's. By mid-morning we were on our way up there, bringing Mary in the car with extra chairs and glasses. It seemed as if every road led there; there was a powerful sense of the name and spirit of Nora in every mind. Over the next three days of the wake and funeral it would be said time and time again: she had been at our party on New Year's Eve and never enjoyed herself in recent years as much. That happy memory was to stay with us, for in Nora Donnellan, Chris and I had been lucky enough to meet one of the truly generous old Irish people. She had seen a world change before her eyes, and seen, too, enduring qualities of friendship and community in Kiltumper. The stories of her playing jigs and reels on her concertina in the kitchen were like country legends. She was of a kind that was disappearing from the West, one of the old stock, welcoming, musical, kind, generous and good natured.

In the brownish-yellow light of a small bedroom, Nora was laid out in a long white dress with her white hair braided behind her. A small missal and rosary beads in her hands, she lay between the five candles in peace as Chris and I knelt beside her in the room to say a prayer. There was a serenity about it, made even more peaceful by the small sounds of clicking rosary beads, the flicker of tiny flames in the hearth and the steady murmur of prayers. We left as more and more friends and relatives began to arrive.

Nora was to be waked for two days like this up at the house. Father Linnane came; neighbors, friends and anyone who had seen the death in the papers called in. The parlor was continually set with plates and cups, and every mourner pressed with urgent hospitality to sit and eat. There was no getting around it. In thanks for the expression of sympathy came the insistent offering of a meal—tea or stout, cakes, scones, baked meats, salads and tarts. This was an inseparable part of being waked at home in the West, a traditional way of remembering the dead and sharing time, welcome, and hospitality with those who remembered with you.

The day of the funeral was a bitterly cold one. A freezing wind tore down the length of the street from the Village Cross to Johnston's shop. Kilmihil was crammed with parked cars, and outside St. Michael's men in heavy coats stood quietly, waiting for the mass to begin. The church was full that day; there had been a second death the previous morning and now there was to be a double funeral. A thick, pervasive atmosphere of grief settled into the rows of seats like a fog. You could touch the sorrow, feel it hush the little building of the church so that nothing sounded but the cruel wind outside blowing endlessly across the fields, across the bogs and mountains, the leafless, birdless winterland. The sound of prayer began, came bodyless from the sad air itself and filled the church with a steady hum. When Father Linnane and Father Murphy came out to the altar the murmuring tide of prayers rose, and fell, then eased to amen. Into that silence, that sudden vacancy in which the souls of the dead might have paused, looked back, hung in the balance, there came the quiet assured and reverent voice of Father Linnane. He named Nora Donnellan and she was alive for everyone there. During the mass, from above in the choir loft at the back of the church, a sad soft air was played on the concertina.

After the mass, the crowd poured out and waited on the street. Then, wheeled to the church gates came the coffin. From here it was carried to the grave. And so, quickly organizing themselves in the cold, six men lifted the coffin to their shoulders. There was a shuffling, a steadying, and then off they began, followed by immediate relatives and all the rest of us.

Down the center of the street we slowly moved into the face of the bitter wind. The whole town stopped. No cars came up the street as the dark procession of people shuddered forward and the coffin was taken over by another six men. On past the cross and into the old graveyard. The sky was heavy and gray. Between headstones the wind whistled and took the petals from fresh flowers. In an instant they scattered away across the land like fairies. White-faced in the weather, Father Linnane stood at the grave with a final prayer. And then Nora was buried.

That afternoon and evening crowds of people went back up the road to Dooley's, to drink tea and porter, to eat bread and scones and to share the time. But at that moment by the grave in the wind, tears were stung from sad eyes as it began to rain. A grand, lovely old woman had died. Father Linnane whispered in a final blessing: may perpetual light shine upon her.

CHAPTER THIRTEEN _____

Through the cold wet weeks of December and January Chris had been watching the "rick," or stack of our turf in the hay barn slowly diminish. By the first of February the ash logs had been burned and there was turf for a week, no more. We had a fuel crisis, and as the year turned its coldest yet we were trying to light smaller fires. Everything was fuel for us now, milk cartons, newspapers, the smallest branches of ash. If the fire could be lit later in the mornings it meant so much turf spared, if it could be allowed to die down before eleven at night it meant more heat for tomorrow. It also meant hasty night retreats to the bedroom and more hesitant waking in the chill mornings. Lying in the bed at night we watched our breath steam on the air and wore the sheet like a glove over our hands; it was literally too cold to hold a book. The temperature was not any different in our house than it was in other cottages just as old; the difference was that we had grown used to warm, insulated rooms in America, to comfort zones. Here you had to have thicker blood and wear as many layers of clothes as you could around the house. It was not inviting to take showers or baths. We found ourselves delaying before stepping from the very last dribble of the hot-water supply into the bracing room air.

Chris and I battled daily to readjust our minds and our bodies to the cold, one of the hardest things to get used to in our life here; not that it was *that* cold outside, but the thick stone walls of the house itself were cold, the floors were cold; the drafty air cut through each room and left you closing in around the fire, the only immediate point of warmth. Our neighbors looked at the last of our turf, nodded knowingly, and said, don't worry, God is good.

And He was. The days of February froze hard. Michael came down the road, with forty plastic fertilizer bags. If we filled them with turf and carried them out a little from the bank itself, he would go up and get them down for us. The frozen land would hold the tractor; he could travel the bog now as he had not been able to do all summer and autumn long.

Chris came with me. Up on the bog we went bagging in the wind, where the cutting days, the song of the cuckoo, the brown bread and tea, the heather in bloom and the sweat of work in shirtsleeves seemed a dream. The bog was now a desolate place. You could see for miles over the flat brown top of the windy world. Hare tracks, fox trails, the stamped prints of straying, hungry cattle, were all crisscrossed at junctions up there going nowhere. Down in the bogholes where we had kept water bottles to slake our thirst, there was now a floor of ice, reflecting white sky. Our stacked half-year's turf was a sad sight, white-capped in frost. Sods were hard as concrete, the water in them frozen solid. They would never make good fuel now, but after drying in the cross winds of the hay barn they would burn, and that was all that was important.

All the afternoon Michael went up and down the mountain in the tractor, each time with a little more difficulty as the ground thawed beneath him, each time with greater satisfaction as he took away more than three months' fuel.

At the end of the day we stood outside in the wind around the stack of turf. "You've a handy bit now, Crissy," he said. "We have," she said, and smiled thankfully.

All through the night the rain seemed endless. In the darkness the trees in front of the house thrashed loudly and threatened to fall. We were both sick. A sudden attack of food poisoning had lifted us out of sleep and now we were crouched together, unable to move from the bathroom. For five long hours the illness held us there while the storm knocked the night about. By half-past seven in the morning I managed to crank the arm of the telephone and have Gregory, the operator down in Kilmihil, call the doctor.

Medicine and medical practices here in West Clare are a world apart from their specialized, competitive, highly priced and by-appointment-only counterparts in New York. With nationalized medicine, the business of health in the West is not a wealthy one. Queues of farm men and women wait in the Kilmihil clinic every Tuesday and Thursday for their pains and problems to be diagnosed, pick up their prescriptions and head home in their tractors without ever having to spend very much, if anything at all. For specialized care or tests, you go "over" to the General Hospital in Ennis, thirty miles away; for specialized operations you are sent "up" to Dublin, your best suit on and your small suitcase in hand.

Although we both knew Dr. Carthy by sight

neither of us had ever needed him. He was a young man kept busy by his work, traveling all over the parish, caring for babies as well as people of ninety. He was a central figure in the community, heard everyone's grievances, was present at births and deaths, and in between times doctored the various physical and psychological wounds of a people who were largely hesitant and often skeptical of the powers of medicine. There were no names of drugs on everyone's tongue here. The vast array of brand names and colored boxes meant nothing, and the decision to take even an aspirin was rare. The body was not considered a thing on which to waste great vanity or care, to pamper or display, but almost a part of God's landscape, something like a tree, a shrub, suffering the pains of time as patiently as possible. It was against this background that Dr. Carthy practiced medicine.

He arrived at the cottage early that morning, letting himself in the back door and coming to look at both of us with quiet assurance. He had stopped at the chemist along the way and picked up a bottle of green medicine. He spooned it out to both of us. I motioned to where my wallet lay, but Dr. Carthy waved aside our offer of money for both the medicine and the care. "I'll let myself out," he said, "you'll both feel better later in the day."

And sure enough, we did.

I have been making a list of the phrases used by Irish weather forecasters. Every evening following the nine o'clock news the weatherman comes on. He stands in front of a very small chart with baton in hand. On the chart the island of Ireland seems at first glance a miniscule blur of land and the idea that it could possess a weather of its own, or indeed several, seems comical. The camera zooms in on the satellite picture, and there through the dense white cloud cover you can just make out the eastern coastline. The West is entirely lost under weather. The baton points to where it might be and the hesitant voice of the weatherman says "There were some heavy showers in the West today, some of them of hail, and I'm afraid . . ." the baton swings out into the white expanse of rude winter Atlantic, ". . . for tomorrow it looks like being just as bad."

The wind is howling outside and I am afraid the windows will fall in. We are sitting on either side of the Stanley range. As the weatherman says goodnight, a map of Ireland is shown on the screen with wind directions, cold fronts and the abbreviated forecast. This last I find the funniest. I have yet to see *all* the phrases of the same weather forecast tell of fine weather. Rather, all bases are covered. We read: "Sunny Spells, Rain Later, Clearing to Showers," or "Bright Spells, Heavy Winds, Rain."

Tomorrow we are to expect winds of gale-force eight and weather which is described as: "Cold, Occasional Showers, Some Very Heavy Winds." It's not much to go to sleep to.

One night, the weatherman appeared on screen wearing a raincoat

There were two weeks to go. After a checkered year in the revived Kilmihil Drama Group—a year in which one play had been chosen, rehearsed and abandoned; a first-ever radio play produced and entered in a national competition; and a second full-length stage play chosen and rehearsed somewhat shakily—the Kilmihil Players were about to present J. M. Synge's *The Well of the Saints* at the West Clare Drama Festival in Doonbeg.

The cast was nervous and uncertain; for weeks

beforehand there had been talk of Doonbeg and the festival, and always the talk had been of competition. It slowly became clear to us that the Kilmihil Players were going there to take over the community hall in Doonbeg for one of the ten nights of the festival and to give the performance of their lives. The actors would be playing to the house and also to the adjudicator. It was she, sitting alone at the back of the hall and making notes throughout the play, who graded each group and came to the stage every evening after the performance to read aloud her criticisms of the production. No waiting for the morning papers here. She would address her comments to the packed audience and on the final night of the festival announce the winners.

During the last jittery weeks before it all began, down in the classroom where we rehearsed there were horror tales of previous adjudicators down through the years, of actors and actresses in tears in the wings, of dreadful Kilrush or Kilkee productions winning out over Kilmihil, and of grossly unjust criticisms and favoritism. To Chris and me, hearing this for the first time, it made the week of performance loom like a little war. The prospect of such cutthroat and intense competition was nerve-wracking, especially as lines were still not learned by heart.

The group had to undergo another false start and stop. Kilmihil's entry form was returned in the post. We had been rejected for this year's festival. The reason? Our application was late, and the Doonbeg committee did not know that Kilmihil had intended performing a play. It was hard to believe: Doonbeg was ten miles from Kilmihil. The news was a major shock to the cast. Was it going to be another play fully rehearsed but never performed? It would be enough to collapse the drama group for another few years. But again, in Ireland no rules are hard and fast, and a simple refusal to accept the committee's decision impelled Paddy Cotter to his phone. We had not heard the last of this, he said. And so we hadn't. Midnight phone calls and the local politics of persuasion swung into action. Two days later a phone call from the secretary of the festival committee declared us in; Kilmihil was to perform the final night of the West Clare Drama Festival. The winners would be announced at the end of the evening.

Mad excitement. Everyone in Kilmihil knew. "Are ye all set for Doonbeg?" asked Mrs. O'Shea in one shop. "We'll be back to cheer ye on," smiled Tessie Garry outside the church. Meanwhile, on a trip to Doonbeg to check out the stage Chris had uncovered a major problem: the Doonbeg backdrop was of an eighteenth-century interior and totally unsuitable for Synge. Our play required an outdoor set, she said; we would have to paint our own. In a hectic week—finding a wig for Kathy, a blouse for Lucy, hammers, a cartwheel and an anvil for David, a saint's sack-cloth robe for Michael, and all the other minute details that were the final touches on the production—Chris had to paint an outdoor scene twenty-five feet wide and ten feet high. Behind the closed doors of the community hall, with Larry Blake hammering together his ingenious "forge-cum-church," she climbed up and down the step-ladder painting hills and mixing forty shades of green. It was terrific.

One of the actors failed to show at the final rehearsal. The cast was on edge; they forgot lines they knew. Looking up at them against the still-wet backdrop of fields and mountains from the back of the hall, Chris turned to me, said nothing, and ever so slowly shook her head.

Larry loaded the van during the afternoon. The forge, the anvil, various papier-maché rocks and all the props were stacked in a heap as the traveling theatre got underway. We hoped it wouldn't rain as we followed the van. It was three o'clock, five hours to showtime. At Doonbeg the deserted hall looked a mess; the previous night's production had left the aisles scattered with candy wrappers and bottles and the stage had been emptied of everything. Now it was a bare, uninspiring community hall in the middle of West Clare.

The mounting of the set that afternoon and the steady assemblage of a stage fit for Synge was extraordinary. As Larry hammered and sawed, and Chris sat for the first time ever at a lighting board she would have to work from the back of the hall, I found myself walking across a realized scene of the eighteenth-century crossroads which until now had been two stools set crosswise in a bare schoolroom. We all felt that tightening theatre feeling in our stomachs. Down there, with the little lamp beside it, was the adjudicator's desk, over there the curtains that Martin would pull, there, there, and there, too, the unseen hideaways for our three prompters.

By half-past six the lights had been set, the stage mounted and the hall swept clean in readiness for what Kilmihil had to offer. Quietly the actors arrived. In a small dressing room where the message "Good Luck Kilmihil" had been lipsticked on the mirror, they got into costume while Chris was adding last touches to the set—rushes, grass, moss and ivy, and a large standing branch of whitethorn. Seven o'clock, with an hour still to go, the doors were opened as Chris and I slipped out into the damp night, taking our nervousness down the road to the Igoe Inn.

Walking back we saw the crowds gathering in the darkness. People from Kilmihil had come early to get the best seats. Pauline was there with Peter and Francie; so was Tessie Garry. Faces we knew were scattered throughout the place, and the expectation in their eyes made us feel even more anxious. An unlabeled bottle of golden liquid was circulating in the dressing room. The familiar faces of the actors had been transformed with makeup for the first time, and, while that long edgy wait dragged on downstairs, they became their characters. From the curtain, word came back; it was a full house, with standing room only. People were standing all along the aisles and around the back wall. About thirty children were pressed right up against the front of the stage. Mort, the festival's organizer and long-time guiding light came backstage: "The hall is packed, could ye ever go on a half-hour early?"

We could, and did.

The curtain swung back and a whispering murmur arose as from the back of the hall Chris brought up the lights and the set was seen for the first time. The actors moved onto the stage. Another murmur from the crowd. The first comic lines were said, and the thirty children at the front led the place in laughter. They liked it, they liked it! Nods and smiles circled the backstage. We were off to a good start. At the end of the first act, in a performance which had far surpassed anything I had seen from the players during all those rehearsals, the curtain closed to a thunderous applause. For a moment the actors stood there, transfixed behind the curtain. Then, still hearing the sound of clapping, one of them turned to the others, raised his two hands in fists and shook them. "Come on, Kilmihil!" he roared, and led them like a team to the dressing room.

Acts two and three flew by, impeded only by the furious intermission activity of moving the forge across the stage to become our ruined church, and the remaking of the set with fresh rushes and ivy, straw for the forge floor, a dozen hung pothooks, hammers and tongs and a hundredweight iron anvil. A whole townload of people seemed to bustle about across the stage led by Larry and Paddy while in the buzz of downstairs the players prepared for the next act.

There were no hitches. The performance was excellent. At the end of the evening the hotly packed hall rang out with cheers and the players left the stage beaming. There was a feeling of terrific elation; it was as if a football championship had been won, and in the giddy laughter and smiles backstage it was easy to forget that this was actually a *drama* festival and the play that had just been performed was not only one of Synge's, but a difficult one at that. The response said much for the people of West Clare as people from Kilmihil poured into the dressing room, offering handshakes and congratulations.

Shortly after, the adjudicator came to the stage and the audience hushed again. She held a white notepad in her hand and read her criticisms in a confident voice: "I think we'll all agree that we have just seen a very, very good production of *The Well of the Saints* from the Kilmihil Players here tonight . . . some outstanding performances . . . sensitive direction . . . very nicely designed and effective set . . ." Bursts of applause and cheers from the hall punctuated each item of praise. Backstage the cast, half in costume, huddled in the shadows, smiling. Then came the final awards of the festival. Trophies and medals were laid out on a green felt table in the middle of the stage. In a section that included the very much larger towns of Ennis and Shannon with their large casts and four-figure budgets, Kilmihil—having put on the play for around fifty pounds—had no chance of winning outright; it was the placement of Kilmihil in relation to the other *West Clare* neighbors that was all-important. It was down to local rivalry.

So, the adjudicator summarized the ten nights of drama for the casts, directors and supporters assembled on the floor of the Doonbeg Community Hall. The cold night outside was forgotten in a hush of intense hot expectation. Months upon months of preparation had been expended for the moment and, suddenly, it was only seconds away. "First place, with eighty-five points, Ennis Players." A burst of applause. "In second place, with eighty-three points, Shannon Drama Group." Another burst. "And in third place, with eighty-two points . . . Kilmihil Drama Group!" A roar went up from every corner of the hall, cheers rang out, and in our corner of the backstage there was an explosion of happiness. And there was more to come, the adjudicator was still speaking. "Medals for Outstanding Performances to . . . Kathleen Devine of Kilmihil and to Noel Conway of Kilmihil!" Paddy punched the air, Larry threw back his head and let off a great laugh and David nodded to me and clapped his hands.

That night there was some celebrating for Kilmihil in the town of Doonbeg. The next day Chris and I felt like champions walking through Kilmihil and taking congratulations from everyone in town.

CHAPTER FOURTEEN

Francie came tearing up the road on his bicycle. He flung it down at the gate and came yelling up the garden path in his Wellingtons. "She's calving, she's calving, come on!" He stood at the front door, drenched with rain and spattered with muck, grinning broadly. In the parlor Chris put down her brushes in a hurry. We pulled on boots and raingear, locked in the hens, and in a moment were trotting down the mucky road behind Francie on his bike. Down at Downes's the children were gathered excitedly about the yard. Michael was calm. "Well, ye're just in time," he said.

Carefully we entered the dimly lit cabin with Joe and Michael. The children stood in a little huddle gazing in from the door. Francie and Peter held a length of rope between them. The cow, a big Friesian with sad-looking eyes, was tied in a corner, waiting. Joe lit a cigarette. We all looked on. Rain was thrumming on the corrugated roof and the air was close. "She could be a while yet, ye know," said Michael. "She could, ye know," said Joe, drawing on his cigarette.

For us the morning was stilled to this, an event in Kiltumper we hadn't yet witnessed, and one in which we would need some practice if we were in fact to buy cows of our own in the late spring. We had been told there was nothing to it. More often than not the cow would calf naturally out in the field without assistance. You just had to keep an eye to her, that was all. And yet, against this, we had heard quiet mention of neighbors being unlucky with cows calving, and horror stories of dead calves. In the end, these things were all part of farming, and no blame or criticism was given concerning things that were deemed the will of God. More often than not, cows were sprinkled with holy water when they arrived at a new farm, and between the forces of luck and God, the Clare farmer did his business to the best of his ability.

We had been watching the cow for half an hour. The youngest of the children had gone back into the house to play. Francie was running the rope through his hands. The rain was still beating down and anxiety began to fill the little cabin. Then, suddenly, the cow moaned. Joe flicked his cigarette away and Peter let out a yell. The very tip of a calf's hoof was beginning to emerge. "She's calving, Crissie, look, she's calving!" shouted Francie.

"I'm afraid she's not quite right," said Michael. "Isn't she?" said Joe. We waited for a little while watching the cow in labor. Then Michael rolled up his shirtsleeve, doused his arm in disinfectant and slowly inserted it into the cow. "Rope, Francie," he said.

Within moments we were all a part of it, part of the cow's difficult labor, and that morning's struggle for the life of a calf. The rain lashed above us and the air in the cabin was suddenly warm with concentration and effort. The rope was tied about the unborn animal's forelegs and Michael and Joe held it taut, pulling with the cow's own push, easing with her ease. Still the calf wouldn't come. Michael told us to join the pull at the end of the rope, and with Crissie and me, Peter and Francie all holding and tugging in rhythm, at last it seemed the animal was about to come. "Easy, easy," said Michael. Sweat ran off us, the cow moaned. Michael's hand was inside the cow feeling for the calf's head. In a gentle pull it came, covered in a gelatine-like mucous as it slid forward, dropping toward the sop of straw on the floor. Only the hip and hindlegs now remained to pass from the mother, and with all our effort we pulled, watching the lifeless calf. There was a sickening sense in my stomach that the animal would be stillborn and I longed for the thing to be over. Chris looked drained with disbelief. Could we have brought bad luck to our first calving? We felt such a part of it all that we felt responsible. As we pulled, the calf hanging from the cow was motionless. He was covered in a dripping slime, his eyes unseeing. Still we pulled him. And as we did, suddenly he came free, clattering down on the straw, dropping us back against the wall.

Michael was on him in a flash. Nobody said a word. The children looked on with blank expressions. I leaned, exhausted, against the wall, part of the rope still in my hands. Michael was poking a rib of straw into the calf's nostrils, freeing them for air. Then, quickly, he lifted the calf by the hindlegs and held him upwards until the lungs started to move. The calf was alive. In a moment he was placed beneath the mother, who turned to him with a quiet, unperturbed expression and slowly began to lick him. "Another bullock!" shouted Francie, running out into the yard to tell the others the good news. Michael stood back with us against the wall and lit a cigarette. This was the last of this year's twenty calves; he had lost none of them, he had a right to feel happy. "That's it now," he said, turning to us with a smile. "No problem really." He winked at me. "Ye'll be able to manage that, do ye think Crissie?"

We looked at him with pale faces. We didn't know what to say. "Come on in," he said, "Pauline'll have the tea made."

March is a hard month. Northeast winds scour the land and the rain that comes with them is bitter cold. Everyone is driven inward when they want most to be out. From the cottage window in the room where Chris paints we look out on the frosty fields and wonder when spring will come. Again and again our talk comes back to the weather. It seems we are continually being taught the same lesson: to live as we have chosen is to move out onto that solitary (though not necessarily lonely) edge where every day's natural composition truly *affects* you, every wind and storm is part of your business. Weather *is* you. Where once perhaps the day first shaped itself with thoughts of that morning's meetings at the office, you wake each morning now with the first look to the window and the eastern sky. It is neither easy nor romantic to feel such daily dependency upon the weather, and although a year ago we might have sat on the morning train and dreamed of walking down the garden in the misting rain, the reality of farm life has made us more cautious and lessened our enthusiasm.

The bitter, hailing days at the beginning of March were enough to break our hearts. Bundled in raincoats we had taken walks back along the western road and Chris had pointed out the first, fresh growth of the impending spring. Deep blue violets and primroses of the palest yellow. We had a sense of good news, of something personal happening in our own place. Days later, when she took me back there, the easterly wind and the frost had burned everything back. We felt this almost personally. In our letters to America, we feared we were failing to capture the change in our lives. When we described the freezing winds that were stunting our spring, maybe we were being interpreted as either quaint or petulant. Crunching our way up across the black frost on Upper and Lower Tumper for a view of the three counties stilled in late winter, I wished for the bigness of voice of a Thoreau or a Wordsworth. Something to announce, proclaim nature in the grand manner with all its lofty magnificence and greatness of soul—while at the same time putting in a word for the small individual losses of the season, the personal history of weather.

A week to go in the farming training course. I had stuck it out, and now, striding with the rest of the class across mucky fields, I felt a new confidence. I had learned more than I had imagined possible, and with my new knowledge of farm and animal I was aware of feeling a new bond with the land. I had scratched away to reveal some of its secrets, and having passed on each day's lessons to Chris, together we began to shape in earnest our plans for the farm in the coming spring.

One week to go. I left the cottage at half-past nine in the morning to drive to Kilrush. Less than two miles away, on the road into Kilmihil, I saw a car coming from the creamery. It was driving entirely on my side of the narrow road and, as if in a bad dream, the closer it came the more certain I felt that the driver hadn't seen me. I blasted the horn, blasted it again, and in one long awful moment saw the driver look up in surprise, try to pull back across the road, and ram into the front of my car.

No one was hurt. Both cars were wrecked. We

stood in the center of the deserted country road looking at them for a minute, and when the first car came
got a lift back as far as Downes's. I went into the house
and picked up the phone to call the garage. Less than
five minutes had passed. "I hear you've been crashing
into your neighbors up there," said the operator
cheerfully.

It was all right, said Michael, the man who had
crashed into me was the most honest man in the
parish. And so he was. But, for the final week of the
course, I went to Kilrush rocking and bumping in
the side seat of a tractor. From the raised position of
the cabin high over the road I felt like a master of
something. I could see into fields for miles above the
hedgerows. Farmers in their tractors get a different
kind of salute from people they pass, I thought. Yes,
there was something about a tractor. More and more I
was coming to understand, as I never had before, the
full measure of difference between the city and the
country person. There was a completely other sense
of pride at work in the West. It was more than pride in
land, more than pride of the survivor, or the pride of
freedom and independence. It was as if there was a
natural and fiery pride in the knowledge of having
been passed a special destiny of poor land and Atlantic
rain. It could never be questioned, but held instead
with a strong grip marked by silence, faith and per-
severance. No matter what, we could never belong
here the way these people did, for it struck me that
they were as much a part of the landscape as any tree,
rock or field. They were the West, and they knew it.
And yet, from time to time—bumping along in the
tractor, barrowing turf out of the bog, living day after
day in the ever-falling softness of the rain—we could
feel a flash of insight and empathy, knowing if only for
a second something of the quality of that pride.

It seemed everything we did was a measure of the
year coming to an end. We were watching for the

spring and counting the days as we had watched and counted the previous year for different reasons. Chris was hurrying to finish a canvas. She was talking of landscapes she would paint this summer as I was pulling on Wellingtons and thinking of cows. At the course in Kilrush they were telling us we were the best class in years. We knew, they said, how to make a proper beginning at farming but, just to make sure, there would be an exam.

When the paper was laid before me, I couldn't help thinking of my old job in Manhattan and the various uses to which I had put my pen during those years. Question one wanted me to write down how many tons of silage would be needed to feed seven cows and three one-year-old bullocks over a one-hundred-and-fifty-day winter. Question two asked the uses of nitrogen and the correct amounts to apply for early grass. Further down the page question eight was all about soil types and drainage. I applied myself to the exam with more energy and concentration than I had ever needed as a copywriter in New York. That morning the exam meant more to me than anything I had done before. It was the final test, the last thing to be passed before Chris and I would feel free to launch ourselves on the next stage of our life here, the farming of the land. To fail would sour our future. We had come to the end of what romance and good will alone could achieve.

As it was, I passed. Everyone passed. On the final morning all our teachers gathered together at the head of the class, and the District Manager of the Agricultural Advisory Board came in to address us. The class having been forewarned wore its best clothes. We were a group now, and after six weeks together had shared schoolday memories of being called up to the blackboard, of cringing with embarrassment, of being asked questions out on farm trips, of tramping together through Kilrush to demand steaming soup at Cecil Sands's. We were the farmers-to-be of West Clare, the Advisory Board's hope for better things in the future, the generation of farmers who might at last make the difficult crossover from the traditional to the modern. There was sadness in the certainty that the old ways would have gone by the time the people in this class were fifty years old. By then there would be few farmers cutting hay, turning it and tramming it, there would be less of the scythe as there was already of the horse. The demands of competition would see machinery everywhere, and even in the knowledge of better lives for everyone, the romantic view of the old West held me in a clutch of sorrow. *Must* we always wish for better?

Our names were called for graduation. I was last on the list and sat nervously watching the others go up to be congratulated. I was as nervous as if I were being called for a doctorate. When I left the room a quarter of an hour later to climb into the tractor for the journey home to Chris, I held it in my hand like a trophy: Niall Williams's Certificate as a Farmer.

With the first hints of spring came the first of this year's visitors from America. We felt like people waking after a thaw as we drove the newly restored Peugeot to Shannon to meet Chris's sister Deirdre and her friend, Larry. We had been for so long in a mood of hibernation and day-to-day survival that the very idea of summer, of visitors, of bright sunny trips to the sea had been like dangerous fantasies. To think on such things could unnerve the enduring heart. Instead, like those around us, our thoughts had turned inward. We looked out on short, rainy, gray days and read the dark nights away. Suddenly, the world was opening up again. The easterly winds had been replaced by moister, softer breezes from the coast and the early mornings were clamorous with birdsong. Deirdre was our most welcome visitor. This was her second visit in a year, and to our neighbors in Kiltumper she was a friend, awaited, spoken of, and missed. Besides the pleasure of her visit, timed to bring us out of winter and into the best of spring, there was all the news from New York of family and friends, of the new movies, the new music, the new everything that would never arrive in Kiltumper. We were told of jobs, friends' salaries, trips to California and Florida, great new restaurants, new babies, and the general news of how people were getting on with their lives. Chris and I sat in the kitchen with cups of strong tea and listened to this talk of things we had surrendered to a different world.

Deirdre saw Kiltumper differently from her previous visit. She took Larry about the cottage and the fields, and showed him the things she had once been shown. They marched up to the bog, drove into Kilmihil for the messages, and went down for tea and scones to Mary and Pauline, experiencing again the marvelous hospitality of the West. But this time there was a slightly different emphasis. Deirdre saw the signs of our struggle. A third of last year's turf was still dripping on the bog, trees had been cut down, lake-like pools remained on some of the fields. It hadn't all been easy.

"I think it's less romantic than I thought it was last year," she said. The mood spread to Larry. In the morning he offered a helping hand when I said I had to barrow dung into the garden for the potatoes. Of those who have visited us here, I can think of no one else who really grasped the whole picture of life in Kiltumper, the richness *and* the poverty in coming to live here. It did us good to be with them.

Then there was the holiday: we were treated to a bed-and-breakfast weekend. In a sudden day of hazy April sunshine we packed the car and headed for West Cork.

The drive took us down through Kerry, past Killarney and the Lakes, and onto the fabulous scenic wonderland of the Kerry mountains. Here was a famous part of the Irish tourist trail, the eastern route of the Ring of Kerry. Each narrow turn spiraling higher opened up deep views of gray rock, lush greenery under clear azure skies, and stirred the heart. There was an air of danger to the beauty, the single-car roadway having been built for horses a hundred years ago. The sharp turns threatened to launch us out over a drop hundreds of feet down. We drove on wanting to stop everywhere. The view carried us ahead of ourselves. It was a bird's journey with a bird's eye view of Kerry. After the first few exclamations, nobody said anything. The road took us on in silence. This was the conjuring side of Ireland, the entrancement of ancient places made awesome by the sea. Nothing here ever changed, the air itself was full of magical softness, cheek-wetting rains, hair-tossing breezes. It was easy to look up at the towering mountains, rivering everywhere with white spring waters, and imagine the race whose greatest mythology was of "*Tir na N-Og*," land of the forever young.

In the middle of the Caha Mountains we crossed into Cork. Still the countryside kept us quiet. Glengarriff, Ballylickey and Bantry—seaside towns that marked the blue circumference of Bantry Bay. From Bantry to Ballydehob, and from there, with quickening excitement, on to Schull.

Pronounced "skull," it was an unlikely-sounding place to come to for a weekend. Recently Schull had begun to establish a name for itself as a West Cork center for pottery, painting and crafts, and its narrow rising main street was a place of bright colors and lively pubs. Down at the harbor a secretive footpath led out along the water where the white sails of a few yachts glided with a summery air. In July and August the bay would be dotted with hundreds of them, sailing out from Schull and the towering craggy backdrop of Mount Gabriel. Schull is a lovely intimate town, its people friendly. We idled among them—Deirdre and Larry shopping for Aran sweaters, Chris and I grateful for the break and treat. It felt strange to be away from Kiltumper, strange and happy to be on holiday. If, a year ago, it was easy for us to feel free to take off for a week or a weekend, now there was a new hesitation, a conscientious feeling and responsibility for land. Of course nothing could happen to the land while we were away, nothing would change, and yet our year in Clare had created a peculiar feeling of attachment between the fields and ourselves, whether we wished it or not. Was it perhaps a trace of that uneasy nervous air you sometimes see in farmers who have gone up to the city for the day? We hoped not, and tried to shake ourselves free of everything, driving west to Crookhaven and on out the pennisula to the awesome isolation and beauty of Mizen Head, the southwestern-most tip of Ireland.

The day turned fine. April, my favorite month, brought a better day than we had had in nine months. We stopped at Barley Cove, a lovely, deserted beach and climbed down the dunes and walked out on the printless sand feeling like latter-day Robinson Crusoes. There was blue sky and ocean and stillness. Giant, peculiar rock forms came gently down to the shore and held all the colors of that afternoon—bronze and blue, gray and green. Reflected sky glittered in little pools no bigger than a man's hand in a hundred secret places.

You can get a feeling in parts of the West of Ireland that you are the first man and first woman anywhere. You come upon places so remote and mystifying, so wind-lashed and sea-tossed, so rocky or so green they overwhelm your senses. Nature fills the silence with the crash and foaming of Atlantic waves, the shrill crying of seabirds, the flapping of different winds meeting amid the mountains. It makes you aware of your littleness, quietening you in a way nothing else can. When you come upon one of these places you never want to leave; and yet you want to leave suddenly, to shout out, to share with the world the place that has become part of you.

Mizen Head is such a place. An end of Ireland where the land meets the sea and rocks emerge when waves surge back, a windy cliff edge and a chasm full of foam. When Deirdre walked down Mizen Head she felt the giddiness of danger springing in her steps. She *had* to go to the end, to that airy swirling place where you could scream as loud as you liked and still make no sound above the endless churning of the waters. The untamed and untameable beauty of an Atlantic Island.

When we got back into the car we were wet-faced and red-cheeked and tingling. We laughed out loud for release. We drove away from Mizen Head in a silent glow, as if returning from another world.

Spring was late, the grass was slow to come. Day after day at the beginning of April we had watched the hill fields at the back of the cottage for the first signs of greening. But the black weather of February and March had set back everything and after the fodder crisis of the bad summer, the late spring was quickly exhausting the last of the hay and silage. Around us all eyes were on the sky and on the land. We needed warmer weather to push up the grass, we needed sunshine.

While we waited for spring we waited to buy our first cows. Newly versed in farm knowledge we were eager to make a beginning and were impatient with the harsh northeast winds blowing hail and rain from Iceland. Never before had either of us ever given any thought to the growing of grass; it was one of Nature's effortless actions, an unspectacular annual event that happened with regular monotony and went largely unnoticed until the mid-summer day when you had to get out the rusting lawn mower and push it into the garden. Suddenly, grass was a crop. It needed supervision, it needed liming, it needed fertilizing, it needed a spring. The more eager we became to buy our cows, the more we walked out onto the rainy fields stamping Wellies to test wet land, stooping to touch the first stray blades of grass.

At last the wind changed, a week of warmer overcast weather blew in and Michael came up the road to tell us we could get our cows now. He had put the word out that we were in the market for cows-in-calf, and had heard that Maguire's back by Cree might have something suitable. Would I go with him that evening?

I drove to Cree in a knot of anxiety. Knowing nothing about something is a comfortless feeling, and being known to know nothing is even worse. Despite the certificate back at the cottage, I couldn't claim that I knew the first thing about buying a cow. Of course Chris and I had looked it up in the book. We had seen pen-and-ink sketches of good formation cows, and had read the description of what to look for. But between the book and the beast lay a mighty chasm, and how was I to manage the swagger and assurance of a buying farmer, stepping into the pen, groping the udder, squeezing the teats, fingering through the breathy mucous of the mouth? On the short journey to Cree Michael read my worries and offered to do the whole business for me. I would be a spectator, free to decide whether to buy the animal or not, but he would do the talking. I breathed a little easier, but still felt foolish holding the checkbook in my hand.

We pulled up into an open farmyard and heard the familiar sound of milking machines at work. Inside the dairy a woman was at work and she looked out at us at first with a wary expression. We were strangers to her: We must be there on men's business—which farming is in the West. "Is the boss around?" said Michael. Jim Maguire was in among his cows in the next cabin; he slapped six of them out of the milking parlor as we walked in. As is almost always the case in the West, no surprise is expressed at a visit by a stranger. The talk moves immediately into weather and cattle. I stood adding nods and yesses for a quarter of an hour before Michael, like a master-dealer, gradually approached the subject. "Do ye have a bit of a heifer for us to look at?" he said. "I do." "It's for this man here," said Michael, indicating me with a turn of his head. "I don't know this man at all," said Jim, quite cheerfully, coming forward to be introduced. "He's very well-dressed anyway," he laughed, and Michael laughed, and I laughed too.

To Chris and me she was to be Bridget, a small, stocky Simmental cow with a mostly white bullock calf. She was our first cow. She clattered out of the animal trailer and into the cabin that we had scrubbed clean for her. When Michael had gone we sneaked out and stood for ages looking in the door at her. She was a study of peace, and stood looking at us with big brown eyes of quiet contentment while her calf sucked and sucked at her udder to draw milk. Everything about her was new to us, and personal. Looking in at her, checking her before we went to sleep at night, rising early to bring her a bucket of water and a sop of hay, we felt for her the way we hadn't about any of the various cows we had seen coming up and down the road in front of the house every day. Everything Bridget did we watched and reported to each other in case something was in some way significant. But for Chris the calf was most exciting. She quickly named him Lemon-Drop and held out her hand to him whenever she could, half-scared the calf with no teeth would bite it off. But the little calf came up to her and accepted her head rubs in wide-eyed silence.

For two days Bridget stayed in the cabin while we went to buy companions for her. A deal had already been done to buy one of Michael's older cows and the two bullock calves she was suckling. Gerty, as we called her, would join the herd as soon as it was ready for her. In the meantime, we watched the grass slowly coming and set off for the Cattle Mart in Kilrush.

At the Mart there is an urgent mood of business. Men lean over the pens and poke with sticks at the cattle. They smoke slow cigarettes and study the animals on offer with narrow eyes. They move about casually, as if in their own place, nodding and shaking hands like people at a convention. This is where farm business is done. In the grayish half-light of the corrugated-roofed yard some of the farmers in their long coats and low caps look like desperados making their deals. The place seems full of showdowns, rivalries, and judgment. Men hop over the pen gates when no one is looking and handle the backsides of beasts they might bid on. Nobody wants to give away his hand before the animals go into the ring.

Once Michael had shown me the two cows and their calves that he thought we should try to buy, I couldn't help but stand around looking in at them with an air of proprietorship. I eyed the others who came around their pen and fussed for them to go away and leave my cows to me. For two hours the cows stood in the pen while bullocks were brought up to the ring. Michael went away among the dealers. I wished for the thing to be over, for the cows to be bought, for our little herd to be let out into the Big Meadow at the back of the house. The time passed slowly. In the rainy light I grew suspicious of the fifty-year-old, weather-faced men who passed around the pen and looked steadily over at me. Did they know already who I was, what I was there to buy, how much I had to spend? I felt certain they did, but in a recklessly stubborn mood decided to buy the cows no matter what the asking price. I wasn't there to outdeal others. I had none of the canny cool-mindedness of the dealer about me. I was there to buy two cows, the same as if they were two pairs of socks. I, as yet, knew nothing of all the nods and winks, the small signals, the feigned disinterest, the ambling, circuitous walk, the studied avoidance of mentioning price, the various handshakes and the "Lucky Penny," in short, the traditions of buying and selling animals in the West. Nobody, as far as I could figure out, ever approached the thing by saying, "How much is that cow?"

An announcement was made; cows were being brought to the ring. Michael reappeared. We made our way to the tiered auction ring, climbing down to the barrier opposite the auctioneer in his white coat. As the first cows came in, the voice boomed figures over a fuzzy loud speaker system. I could make out the hundreds but no more, and as the figures seemed to escalate rapidly in less than a minute, animals came and left before I had any clear idea of how much they had gone for. As well as this, I couldn't quite discover who in fact was doing the bidding. Miniscule signals were being passed from behind the barrier. The hammer fell and I heard the word "sold" flash briefly past, before the gates swung open, a cow came in and the humming of figures started tumbling through the system again.

"Well, we got her anyway, Niall," said Michael. I looked at him in amazement. "Did we?" I said. "We did then," he said, and gave a broad, knowing grin.

Bridget, Gerty, Susie and Phoebe: our four cows. When Chris's father, Joe, consented to foot the bill for the cows he did so under one condition: that we adorn them with the names of Gertrude, Bridget, and Suzanne. The fourth we could name ourselves. They had very distinguishable and separate personalities, and grew into their names the longer we had them. Solid Bridget, Bossy Gerty, Big Susie, Flighty Phoebe. Four of the five calves remained nameless, as we knew that by November we would be selling them. Only the cows would be with us through the winter. Among the battles of the coming year would be the harvesting of hay for them and their servicing by Hector the local bull. Everything from now on would be new to us.

The day we let our little herd out into the Big Meadow at the back of the house, Mary and Joe came up to see them. In the sudden freedom of a new place on a spring-like day the calves took off, they frolicked out into the field with little kicks and leaps, galloping away across the land followed madly by the swaying udders and ladylike quicksteps of their doting mothers. Here was a new, true dimension to land: animals. Feelings of new responsibility welled up in us. Here were cows under Chris's care in the very field where, for over two hundred years, her ancestors had raised cattle. The idea of the thing seized us with force. It seemed right; it seemed risky. We were duly afraid of what we had taken on, of what only years of experience could actually teach us. We feared we appeared to be dilettantes, unprofessional, foolish and reckless—as the whole scheme of leaving America had so often seemed to us. But our cows *looked* happy, Chris said.

As we moved out into the field among them they weren't startled. They looked at us with careful steady eyes, as if to measure us up. Mary had brought her Holy Water and edged close enough to spray it out over them in blessing. "How are they, Mary?" asked Chris, nervously. "Oh they're fine animals, Crissie,

God bless them," said Mary, "May they be lucky with ye now."

Cow-patrols. Morning, noon and night watches. Singly and together we marched out across the land in the constant rains of April and May to check on our herd. When we couldn't see them from the back wall of the Big Meadow, we went forward with a quickening heart, searching all the dips until we came upon them standing in mesmerized tranquillity, their hides running with rain. It was a comforting feeling to come upon them, a pastoral of connectives between man and nature, a serenity, even when the cattle broke loose, or the cold came inside our clothes. For the first time, we were figures in a landscape. Even the drowsing rain seemed a part of it. Last thing at night, sticks in hand, we went out among them, brushing through the mists like drovers, hearing the last sounds of night and the gathering winds in the trees. In the morning we got up earlier than we had in a year and stepped out again, wading through the hush, printing wet prints across the morning grass.

Charlie, an old friend, had come for the weekend. He had flown from New York on a Thursday evening, rented a car, and driven the winding wet roads to Kiltumper with a bounty of American magazines in his suitcase. Like anyone arriving here fresh from the other side of the Atlantic, he was at once charmed and surprised by the cottage, the fields and the animals. For our part we were caught between embarrassment and pride. Did the garden look messy? Did Charlie recognize that that mass of greenery was not weeds but potato stalks? We looked at everything through his eyes and felt a rush of pleasure when he stood in the parlor and praised Chris's new paintings. "She has really come along a lot in a year," he said, and only when he said it did we believe it. "Come on", said Charlie, "I'm going to take you two to lunch." For a moment we forgot where we were; for a moment we were back in Westchester or coming out of our offices in Manhattan and heading for a French or Italian restaurant. *Where* was Charlie going to take us?

We drove west to Carraigaholt, a small pretty fishing town on the Shannon estuary. Carraigaholt is a lovely place in the summer season, but it was April and three o'clock on a Friday afternoon. Carraigaholt was closed. Charlie was baffled. We headed back towards Kilkee and the Horseshoe Bay. "Jesus, what sort of country is this, you guys," Charlie teased, "you can't even buy lunch!" We smiled at his innocence; if he only knew some of the strange secrets and odd ways of the country as we had come to know them. The windshield wipers came on, rain began to sweep down over us.

In Kilkee we found a place, the Krazy Kraut's. It is a new, tastefully furnished cafe overlooking the bay owned by a marvelously Krazy Kraut, Klaus Meya. While we sat for sandwiches and coffee, Klaus explained that at the grand opening of the Krazy Kraut's he was going to have an art exhibition of West Clare artists. Charlie pressed into the conversation "Chris, here, is a terrific artist and right now she's living only ten or twelve miles from here." We looked at Charlie in amazement; Klaus looked at Chris with a smile: would she bring some paintings, landscapes, for him to see next week?

After the wet summer and late spring, she only had one finished landscape, and so, back at the cottage, in a fit of sudden inspiration she reworked a half-started painting of Mary's bank of turf. She hated it, she said, wasn't it horrible? Wasn't it cheating to finish a landscape sitting in the parlor and only because of the possibility of selling it? I disagreed with her on both accounts; with all our savings now spent and little income anticipated, we were at the limits of our romanticism. Need and poverty narrowed our sights now. While Chris painted I reworked three Kiltumper poems and sent them to the *Irish Press*.

With two paintings, Kathleen's Place and Mary's Bank, lying still wet on the back seat, we drove to Kilkee. It was raining heavily. The landscape was a colorless wash of grays, the sea heavy and churning. Klaus was still smiling. "It is going to be good this year, ya, you see," he said, "sunshine from June to September." We sat together at a table and the waitress brought marvelous strong coffees while Klaus held up the paintings. There was a pause. A painfully long pause. Then, "I like your pictures," he said, "I like them very much, I will buy one of them myself." Chris looked at me across the table. "I will need three more of your pictures like these for the café," said Klaus.

It was like a holiday, driving back from Kilkee that day. It was Chris's first sale to a total stranger and the kind of stroke of sudden encouragement that has so often come for us at the very moment when the whole thing has seemed hopeless. As we drove away we were imagining the work ahead of us; Chris was wondering how in the world she would manage the three more landscapes in the next few weeks. She managed. And two months later, when a massive silver Mercedes full of German tourists drove down our little road looking for her "gallery," I delayed them in the garden while she scurried around inside, readying her paintings in the parlor. They came in and sat down for coffee. One of them was the owner of a small gallery in Germany, and before they left again there was a check, in deutschmarks, on the kitchen table.

In our first week of farming, the weather turned its back on spring. The wind from the east was thickened with hail. The youngest of our five calves moped melancholy across the field and lay down under the gorse for shelter. Chris was worried about him. He had sad puppy eyes in the rain. When the cows moved, grazing over the field, he stayed behind, lying alone. For two days we watched him, not quite knowing what to do. I looked up the pamphlets from the farming course but could only find a leaflet saying calf mortalities cost the country thirty million pounds a year. I didn't want to be an alarmist but Chris wouldn't wait. She called Michael in the evening and asked him to come up and have a look.

In the darkening evening in the misting rain the three of us went up across the fields and converged around the calf. He was lying down and looked up without moving. Chris patted his hide gently, Michael poked him into standing. "He's for the cabin, I'm afraid, Crissie", he said. "He's caught some old cold or something." Out of the field, where only a week earlier we had watched the animals run and play, we drove the mother and calf. It was the saddest sight, separating them from the herd and walking them down the narrow road. We felt like failed farmers, doomed by our own inexperience. It was a sickening night. In the cabin the animals looked morose and imprisoned; we had no proper bucket for water— Chris stole the bright yellow dirty linen tub from the bathroom. We had no suitable litter for the calf to sleep on—we drove hurriedly up to Dooley's. Michael Dooley *always* has hay. We stuffed the trunk of the car with it. If anything could be done we would do it. Word had quickly gone out around the neighborhood: they have a sick calf back at the old house, and up the road in the rain came Mary with a small bottle of Holy Water and the Miraculous Medal that Chris's great-grand-uncle, Big John, had used to great effect for the curing of sick animals. Mary saw the worry on Chris's face and gave her the medal; she told stories of other sick animals years ago, of animals given up for dead and yet cured. We mustn't think it was our fault, she said. We nodded, made tea and sat by the fire in an age-old and comfortless silence.

It was to be a long night. We were useless to do anything. The calf worsened. By morning Michael diagnosed diptheria and I went inside and called the operator to get the vet. "Ye're not in trouble already, are ye?" asked the operator.

It seemed like forever before he came. We walked among the other cows and their calves half expecting them to be sick. We watched the road into Kilmihil for signs of traffic. When the postman came he brought a gushing airmail letter from a new mother at forty telling us how children were the stuff of life, they were what Life was all about. We went back out to the cabin and peered in at the calf. We were a million miles from New York that day. We had gone deeply into another world, for only a year ago we ourselves would have reasoned about the loss of the calf: what was it worth, a hundred dollars? That wasn't so much, it was dinner for two and a show. But here we had crossed over into a different frame of reference, a place of God and of good luck, a place where money was less important than pride, and animals were in your trust as much as in your possession. That day we were one with our neighbors.

The calf had sores around his mouth, his dung was a bright yellow dripping that sometimes wouldn't stop. The rain on the corrugated cabin roof beat like a headache. Breda called on the phone from Dooley's; "Any news of yer calf, Crissie?" We moved between the cabin and the house with buckets of water, forks of hay, wondering if one of our animals was to die. Our minds rattled with unanswered questions as we waited for the vet. There was a further question: what ever would we do with a dead calf? I had horrors of Chris's upset, of writing the news to America, of going down into Kilmihil where everyone would know. In the house Chris looked up "the book" and showed me the page where it said calf diptheria was very often fatal.

At last the vet came. His car drove up in the rain and our neighbors down the road knew that he had arrived. In the semi-darkness of the cabin he held the calf against the wall and felt for his breathing. It was diptheria all right, he said, and shook his head. We stood around the door looking in. Mary arrived in her raincoat to hear the news. The vet was rummaging in his bag for medicine when Chris went over and asked him, "Is the calf going to die?"

He looked down at the bottle in his hand, then up at the hopelessness of her face. "No," he said, "I hope not. You'll give him a shot of this every day for a week and let him off then and he should be right as rain."

Right as rain. Ahead of us there was a week of nursing, of buckets of water, of cleaning out the creamy-yellow calf dung, of feeding hay and standing by the cabin door for hours to watch the calf, wondering if he seemed livelier that day, if his cough was clearing, if his sores were smaller. During the week the cold weather began to shift and at last some signs of true spring drew greenness over the fields like a felt blanket. Our neighbors met us on the road or down in the village and inquired after the calf with smiles on their faces, knowing he was improving. He was let off with his mother on the Saturday, galloping up the fields ahead of us to join the others, bellowing out to them and kicking out his two hind legs with a kind of joyous giddy freedom that made Chris turn to me with a laugh. Standing there on top of Tumper in the drizzling rain, she put her arm around me. We were happy. Our Wellingtons leaked and our coats were soaked through, but still we stayed there, watching our little herd. Our potatoes stalks were a foot high,

Chris had just sold another painting, another of the Tumper poems had been accepted, there was a fine column of turf smoke blowing from our chimney below. And across in the West were the first blooming signs of real summer.

Epilogue

Together in Kiltumper we sit and see ourselves as we were when we arrived with our fragile dreams and expectations. How has it been, after all?

Just two years ago we set out to map the geography of a dream and discover the truth about a country that lay in a place somewhere between imagination and memory. How well do we know it now, this Ireland, this "Irish feeling" that we had thought we knew so well in America?

There is no simple answer, of course. What we *have* come to know is a West of Ireland on the very point of change. Even the way of life we have chronicled here is slowly changing. The West is a traditional place but there is poverty everywhere. What had seemed like the romance of ancient ways, is no longer "quaint" when the experience, at first hand, is one of hardship. We know of an elderly woman who walks daily along the road to a place where she can draw water for her needs.

Our small village went "automatic" and now a new, ugly mustard-colored, push-button telephone sits on our kitchen table, but we are seconds from connection to anywhere in the world. Yet gone is the once-valued opportunity of leaving a message with Gregory the operator, that we would be at Blakes' for the evening and if anyone called could he ring Galvin's (who would run next door to Blakes' to get you since the Blakes didn't have a phone.) Gone are all those days of turning the little winder to crank the post office; our old black upside down telephone hangs on the wall, waiting to be collected and sent into retirement.

More and more people are buying coal, Polish or American coal, because dry turf is scarce, and people are losing the knack of cutting it themselves.

The Christmas box from the shopkeepers down in

the village was done away with this year and replaced with a ten percent discount on Christmas shopping.

Fewer seed potatoes are being sold because people don't plan to grow their own and risk loss and wasted labor. Rather, "new" potatoes are arriving from Cyprus, and Irish growers suffer because of the EEC competition.

As for the rest of the country, it is no secret that the Irish economy is at an all-time low with Ireland's taxes the highest in Europe and foreign debt three times higher than Mexico's. Emigration is a national crisis and a great "brain drain" is crippling the future. When the new immigration law passed in the United States recently, 3000 visas were made available to 36 countries. Ireland, alone, had applications from 200,000 people. Unemployment is very high and welfare recipients have tripled in the past six years. Recently, the Minister for Finance in the new government led by Prime Minister Charlie Haughey launched the strictest budget in decades. Perhaps, there is hope for Ireland's young people. Europeans look to Irish produce and meat, unpolluted and uncontaminated, with envy. Despite the economy, Ireland remains one of the last remote, rural, beautiful places in Europe. There are a thousand secret, isolated spots of beauty here and it is still the home of many writers and poets. It *is* a lovely place to visit.

And what of ourselves and the farm? Our second summer proved as bad as the first. The rains of April, May, June and July brought us to St. Swithin's Day once again, and once again, unbelievably, gray skies of the second of worst-ever summers materialized about us. Once again Chris went gardening in the floods. But our calves grew to fine, healthy cattle, and we slotted into the pattern of the farming community, rising early on dark, frosty mornings to feed silage to our expectant cows.

In the community-at-large, too, we have found a

place. Chris's get-fit classes resumed on demand and she was asked to paint the walls of the playschool room in the community hall in the village, which she did, with scenes from a children's book she is working on. I was asked to coach the parish's under-fourteens Gaelic football team. And the Kilmihil Drama Group? Well, with Larry and Paddy and Martin bustling about, we took a one-act farce on the festival circuit—and won three festivals, two best producer's awards, and one best set award. The group was well launched. By December, our tiny group had become the single representative from County Clare to be invited to compete in the All-Ireland Finals. And on St. Patrick's night, exactly one year after presenting *The Well of the Saints*, we took Brian Friel's farce, *The Communication Cord*, to Doonbeg, and won. Three silver cups on the mantlepiece, a feature in the *Clare Champion* and the group is now set to take the play to the Three-Act All-Ireland Finals—an honor usually reserved for city groups. Kilmihil is on the map at last.

Chris has sold more paintings. Her first short story, sent to the *Irish Press*, was accepted for publication and is under consideration for the Hennessey Literary Prize for the best short story of the year. Meanwhile, the Kiltumper poems are still appearing, and a new novel is halfway written.

These things, then, are the measures of our life here. And if, at times, upon quiet, rainy days when no one comes or goes upon our narrow botharin, we lose track of the spirit that brought us here from Manhattan, it is these things that bring it all back. In the tremendous peace of Kiltumper, Chris and I work on; for a time the outside world disappears. Then, quite cheerily, a typewritten letter arrives from a distant cousin in Connecticut. I walk up the garden path with it to where Chris is stooped over, weeding.

"Dear Chris and Niall", I read aloud to her, "How

is it all going?" And "P.S. How is the pig farming coming along?!"

"Pigs!" Chris laughs. "That's all we need."

She looks up at me and I see her expression change from amusement to speculation.

Why not?

STAYIN' ALIVE

Stayin' Alive

Armed and Female

In an Unsafe World

By Paxton Quigley

MERRIL PRESS
Bellevue, Washington

Stayin' Alive: Armed and Female in an Unsafe World is published by Merril Press, P.O. Box 1682, Bellevue, WA 98009. Additional copies of this book may be ordered from Merril Press at $15.00 each. Phone: 425-454-7009. Cover Photo by Boxer Productions and Cover Design by Tiffany Lindsay.

FIRST EDITION

Library of Congress Cataloging-in-Publication Data

Quigley, Paxton.
  Stayin' alive: armed and female in an unsafe world / by Paxton
  Quigley.-- 1st ed. p. cm.
  Includes bibliographical references
  ISBN 0-936783-43-5
    1. Self-defense for women--United States. 2. Firearms owners--
  United States. I. Title.

GV1111.5Q87 2005
613.6'6082--dc22

2005041509

PRINTED IN THE UNITED STATES OF AMERICA

According to the Department of Justice (1998) 27% of American Women keep a gun in the house and 37.6 million females either own or have rapid access to guns.

IN MEMORY
TO MY DEAR FRIEND, AUTHOR JOHN SACK,
WHO BROUGHT ME GREAT JOY AND HELPED ME
THROUGHOUT MOST OF MY LIFE
1930- 2004

ACKNOWLEDGMENTS

No book is written by one person. Over the years, I have met so many women and men who have given me their knowledge about self-defense and the use of handguns. Although the numbers of individuals who have contributed number in the hundreds, I want to thank certain people who have been paramount in my life. First and foremost, I would like to acknowledge my terrific friends and assistants, Phyliss and Fred Cook, who helped me to train thousands of women in Los Angeles. Others who have worked with me "on the line," who I would like to thank include Nancy Moran Sanchez, Adolph Visconti, Stan Weisleder, Andrew Cooper and all of the other men and women who generously gave their time to help my students on gun ranges in all areas of the country.

I want to especially thank Bob Scott, president, Smith & Wesson, Ken Jorgenson, former public relations director, Smith & Wesson (currently with Ruger) and their associates, who gave me the rare opportunity of being a spokesperson for Smith & Wesson for eleven years and also providing me with Smith & Wesson guns for my seminars.

Also, thanks go to the generosity and friendship of Laura Roberts Niner and Marten Niner, at Pantheon Chemical Company; Jan Lebourel, who gave me the chance to write a "Personal Protection" column for *Handguns* magazine; Don Kates Esq., Mark Benenson, Esq., Helmut Julinot, BJ Julinot, Larry Wilson, Robert Waters, Johann Opitz, John Lott, Alan Gottlieb of the Second Amendment Foundation, the wonderful women at *Women & Guns* magazine, including Peggy Tartaro, Lyn Bates, Karen MacNutt and Gila Hayes. Also, my continued appreciation to Martha Braunig at Executive Security International, Aspen, Colorado and thanks to Jeff Boxer, who photographed the cover of the book.

Additionally, my appreciation to friends, Jeff Mannix, Richard Rosenthal, David Columbia, Max Ramberg, Larry Patterson, Barbara Cohn, Marie Yates, Mel Klein, Allen Baron, Terry and Paul Lichtman, Judy and Arnie Fishman, Mark and Kay Bloom, Allyson Gottfried and her family, Adam, Alan and Marge, and love, to my sons, David and Jonathan and my parents, Hy and Lillian.

Los Angeles, California
2004

REFACE

Intruder dies at hands of armed East Sider
By Vincent T. Davis San Antonio Express-News Web Posted: 11/03/2003 12:00 AM

A 21-year-old man was shot and killed late Saturday on the East Side when he broke through a woman's front window at the Morningview Oaks Apartments.

According to a police report, Ernest Flores III broke through Judy Abram's living room window as she played dominoes with her sisters.

Abram yelled at Flores to leave, but he kept advancing. She ran to her bedroom, grabbed a pistol, and told him she had a gun. When he continued to enter the room, Abram, 55, fired two times while screaming, "Can't you see I have a gun? Get out of here!"

The police report said Flores continued to break through the window as Abram fired the remaining four bullets at him. She dashed to her bedroom to reload, but when she returned, Flores was gone.

Staggering next door, Flores crashed through a neighbor's front window and fell face down on a table where police found him with one gunshot wound to the upper chest.

Police said Abram acted in self-defense and no charges are expected to be filed.

The police report said that prior to the break-in, Flores left a neighbor's house across the street rambling that someone was after him. The neighbor said the last time she saw Flores he was crawling across the street and breaking through Abram's window.

By Sunday afternoon, a maintenance man had replaced the bullet-riddled blinds and two broken windows, but talk of the break-in buzzed on the street. Several children poked their heads into a television news van parked at the location, while residents milled around and compared notes on the incident.
Cont.

Neighbor John W. Prince didn't join those in the street.

The 79-year-old spent Sunday afternoon listening to 1960s soul music with wife Gwenderlyn, 69, in their house on the corner of BookerTee and Morning View.

When asked about the shooting, Prince said when he heard the gunshots he did what he had learned during the Korean War — he automatically hit the floor.

"I can't stand it. It bothers me," Prince said of hearing gunfire.

The 13-year Army veteran and his wife have lived on the corner since the early 1990s, and both said their neighborhood is usually quiet.

"Somebody showed up at the wrong place," he said. "And that's going on around the city."

vtdavis@express-news.net

http://news.mysanantonio.com/
story.cfm?xla=saen&xlb=310&xlc=1078777&xld=310
11/03/2003

TABLE OF CONTENTS

INTRODUCTION

*The illiterate of the 21st century will not be those who cannot read and
write, but those who cannot learn, unlearn, and relearn.*
— Alvin Toffler

If you worry about your safety, you're not alone. A recent Gallup poll reported that six out of ten women in America are afraid to walk in their own neighborhoods or go out alone at night. For these women, the feeling of an ever-present threat of violence or harm effectively denies them the basic guarantees of life and liberty. And the feeling is more than a perception. It is based on a strong dose of reality; not just what nay-sayers would call a neurotic obsession with danger. The fact is, many women in America really are at constant risk. They are victims of society's disquieting inability to protect women from violence and harm inside or outside their own homes.

The female fear factor is doubly destructive because it makes women not only victims of their attackers, but of their own fear-oriented thinking as well.

Ironically, most women are just too afraid to take responsibility and prepare themselves against a possible life-threatening situation. They shrink from learning how to protect themselves even when they are given the chance. Over the years, I have spoken about self-defense gun training with no end of women who rejected it, who came up with a variety of lame excuses as to why they didn't want to learn. Excuses often echo messages in the media spawned by influential organizations, such as the American Public Health Association, the American Academy of Pediatrics, the Harvard School of Public Health, the Centers for Disease Control and Protection, and the American Medical Association. Well-meaning as these groups may be, they issue skewed, half-digested statistics that twist the facts and increase the chances of further female victimization. Sadly, the messages from these prominent groups are all-too-often accepted by the media and the unsuspecting as gospel.

I've seen the problem from a different perspective. I've been in the unique position of teaching nearly 7,000 women in over ten years in more than 20 states how to shoot a handgun for self-defense. As a result, I have had a chance to witness powerful attitude changes from most of these newly-trained women.

Whether they're 20 or 50 years old, they usually come to my seminars with enormous psychological trepidation, a sense that guns are somehow evil, a tool of the devil. I always applaud them for breaking through a gigantic mental barrier to learn how to use a piece of equipment— that's all it is—that has long been an instrument of power excluded to women, until now.

When a woman first grips a loaded gun, her palms sweat and her heart races. When she fires that first shot into a paper silhouette target at a distance of seven feet, her startle reflex is activated by the gun's blast and its "kick," but soon she realizes after firing round after round that <u>she</u> <u>controls</u> the tool—the handgun doesn't control her. She's in charge and sometimes, it's for the first time in her life that she's in charge! Some women are so excited they hoot and yell, "You go, girl. Don't mess with us!"

That's what the 50 women at Mount Holyoke College, an Ivy League women's institution, pronounced implicitly when they started the first college chapter of the Second Amendment Sisters, a national pro-gun women's organiza- tion, in March 2002. The group motivated impassioned exchanges in the student newspaper and on e-mail chat groups.

"You can't achieve power by using guns," exclaimed Jean Grossholtz, an emeritus professor at the college and chair of the women's studies program. "When women can take their rightful place in the world as who they are, not as little make-believe men, that's women's liberation."

Their presence caused the college president, Beverly Daniel Tatum, to issue a special statement reassuring alumnae that members of the woman's group don't carry

guns on campus. That, of course, would violate state law.

They attracted considerable national media attention. *The New York Times'* columnist, Nicholas Kirstoff grumbled that college girls were now shooting guns and blamed it on the 9/11/01 attacks, rather than taking into account that women have every right to protect themselves and know how to shoot a gun. Although he himself had been brought up with guns in Oregon and was "comfortable" with them, his comfort level didn't apparently extend to women and he insinuated that more people would be killed.

Mr. Kristoff would today acknowledge that he overreacted. He was however, right that September 11 provoked many people, and particularly women, to reconsider their position on the gun issue. According to the National Shooting Sports Foundation, there's been a 25% surge in gun sales since that fatal day and women have accounted for roughly 60% of the increase!

Lt. Police Officer Margot Hill, the commander of Boston's domestic-violence unit, said she wasn't surprised to hear more women seemed to be interested in having a gun for protection after September 11. "It was a wake-up call to everyone. People felt that the government couldn't protect them."

Most of these new women gun-owners aren't politically motivated, but propelled by the most basic of female instincts—the urge to protect their own, their families and themselves against harm from those who threaten them. After years of just being scared, awakening to the reality of the dangers faced today as Americans, and as women, women have produced a compelling desire to take action and try to do something about it. Women living alone, working late, or raising children are beginning to look at guns in an entirely different light. They're getting over the blind fear and terror of guns and the media's wholesale demonization of gun-owners, and beginning to realize that the subject is not so black and white, good or bad as it's painted by antigun activists. Despite the nay-sayers skepti-

cism and scorn, women are also seeing that there may be more than a little truth to the maxim that it's not the gun itself, but the person holding it who matters—who controls how the gun is used or misused.

With the specter of homicide bombers in our midst no longer just a remote fantasy, women may actually be able to take a role in American homeland defense. Crazy, you say? Hardly. In Israel, where the government has issued more than 60,000 gun permits so ordinary citizens can help stop attackers who try to set off bombs, an Israeli housewife in 2002 saved countless lives when she shot dead a terrorist about to set off an explosive device in an Efrat supermarket. The terrorist died. How many innocent men, women and children would have died if this woman had not been trained in how to use a gun?

This is a book about women finally coming to the awareness that they must free themselves from years of foolish, naïve, fatalistic illusions of incompetence and invulnerability and use the tools that have been available to men. Millions of maverick women have learned how to free themselves, and millions more need to do it. It's high time women took aim at their outdated behavior and realized they can seize the initiative and play a strong role in protecting themselves and their loved ones in an increasingly dangerous world.

Nonetheless, this is not an anti-male book. It would be wrong of me to say that all women are innocent or are victims. Crimes against people, as well as domestic violence is not just a male's "privilege." Unfortunately, women do perpetrate crime out on the streets and particularly, in their homes. Recent studies sponsored by the National Institutes of Health (2003) have found that many women can be the aggressors and "hit first" against their partner or spouse.

The research said they did not blame women. "We are not saying anybody is at fault," said Miriam Ehrensaft of

Columbia University. "But new data is emerging that says women are also involved in aggression. If we do not tell women that, we put them at risk."

The studies' researchers called for a re-evaluation of treatment programs nationwide. One of the researchers, Deobrah Capaldi of the Oregon Social Learning Center said, "Prevention and treatment should focus on managing conflict and aggression for both young men and women. Each needs to understand the role both play while still putting a 'special responsibility' on the man, who can inflict greater injury."

Nevertheless, women continue to be the primary victims in these domestic violence cases. I hope that as our society becomes more open to the causes of domestic violence and deals with the issue, women will not be prone to victim-hood.

Fortunately, new state laws are being passed to help battered women and more governors are granting clemency to imprisoned women, who have killed their husbands or boyfriends. California has enacted a unique law (SB 1385) in 2004 that states that if battered women can prove their abusers coerced them into committing violent crimes (other than killing their abusers), they will have a chance to win release under this legislation. (The new law also applies to men.) It also allows those who killed their spouses between 1992, when California passed its initial battered defense law, and August 29, 1996, when the state Supreme Court ratified it, to seek new trials.

All women should encourage their state officials to grant more of these clemency decisions and to enact laws similar to California's new legislation. In the interim, women need to take care of themselves and learn to be responsible for their safety and the safety of their loved ones.

CHAPTER ONE
WHY GUNS FOR WOMEN?

"Nothing more simple, I assure you…But I'll tell you what. You must have your mind, your nerve, and everything in harmony. Don't look at your gun, simply follow the object with the end of it, as if the tip of the barrel was the point of your finger."
- Annie Oakley

A recent rash of neighborhood burglaries and assaults had Barbara and her friends unnerved and quietly admitting to themselves that they were scared. The consensus was that they hated feeling so vulnerable, and a fed-up few had actually resolved to take the bull by the horns and do something "real" about it.

A single parent, too, Barbara investigated the possibility of getting a home alarm system, but decided against it when she was told that "alarms are just alarms," and should be viewed as warning devices. Barbara thought about joining her neighbors in purchasing a handgun for self-protection, but with three kids in the house, she held back. Except what if whoever had broken into her garage three times over the past few months decided to go further? Sure, they'd only swiped bicycles and toys at first, but just a few weeks ago she'd come home to find they'd taken the time to clean out the whole freezer.

"My intuition told me whoever was doing this was very comfortable, very confident about how and when we come and go, " Barbara explained, "and that freaked me out."

She finally overcame her doubts and ventured forth to a Chicago area gun store where she bought a shiny new snub-nosed Rossi .38 special caliber, along with a red plastic trigger lock that the salesman showed her how to brace behind and in front of the trigger so the gun wouldn't fire accidentally if by some chance, the kids managed to get a hold of it.

On the way home, Barbara smiled to herself. She'd done the right thing. Now at least, she'd be prepared for

that horrible, unthinkable *I-hope-and-pray-it-never-happens-but-just-in-case* moment. For security and easy access, she decided she'd keep her new purchase safely tucked under her mattress.

Months later, Barbara lay in bed nursing a cold, 2-year-old Kendall at her side. Her teenage daughter had made it off to school, but son, Eric had also felt under the weather and was still home. Around 8 am., Barbara heard the doorbell ring.

"Mama!" Eric yelled. "There's a man at the door. He's saying something about some keys."

Barbara got up from the bed, adjusted her ankle-length nightshirt and went downstairs. She didn't open the door, but peered through the top window glass and saw a big man in jeans and a flannel shirt.

"Your daughter has my car keys from my son," the man said, telling of a friendship between her daughter and a boy Barbara had never heard of.

"I dunno," Barbara said. "My daughter is only 15 and she's at school right now. I'll talk to her when she gets home."

The man nodded, and Barbara watched him turn and leave the front yard. A few hours later, the doorbell rang again.

"Mama," Eric called. "That man is here again." Barbara got out of bed. This time, little Kendall toddled after her.

"We found the keys," the man said. "But I think there's something you need to see," as he pulled out a folded paper from his pocket. "This letter that your daughter wrote to my son," he said, holding the folded paper up against the glass.

Curious, Barbara unlocked the door and opened it just far enough to push the latch on the screen door and take the offered letter. She pulled the screen door closed but left the wooden inner door open - just a crack.

"Uh, this isn't my daughter's..." was all Barbara could say before the man was coming down on her with a 6-inch

rusty blade, jabbing it into her flesh. He held the knife, now bloody, over her. "I'm going to kill you," he breathed, thrusting it again and again as she fell to the floor.

Eleven-year-old Eric jumped on the man's back, locking his thin arms around the man's neck. The assailant bit his hand as they wrestled. The boy howled, but somehow managed to hang on while little Kendall just screamed.

Suddenly, Barbara remembered the gun. Slipping and stumbling in her own blood, she ran off toward the bedroom, slammed the door and locked it behind her. She got to the bed, reached under and grabbed the gun in her now bloody hands. Desperately, she tried pulling the lock off and realized she needed the key which she'd stashed under an exercise machine next to the bed. After several attempts, the key rotated in the cylinder, popping the plastic lock free.

"I'm going to stop this mother fucker right now!" she said to herself running downstairs.

"Get away from my children!" she screamed, mopping the blood from her face with her sleeve.

Spying the object in her hand, the attacker turned, ran through the dining room to the window and drew back his elbow to smash it through just as Barbara pulled the trigger.

Bam! Bam! Bam! The man's body spun as she kept firing until she'd emptied the chamber. He slowly slid to the floor in a heap as she ran to the phone and called 911 bringing an ambulance and the police in a matter of minutes.

The man, Johnny Jones was 37 when he'd attacked Barbara and her sons. Twenty years earlier, he'd been locked up for raping two women but had somehow been released after only four years served for "good behavior." Out only a few months, he was again arrested, convicted of aggravated battery and rape, and sentenced to 26 years in prison. There, he confessed to a couple of murders for which he was sentenced to another 27 years by a judge who unaccountably ordered that the murder sentence be served concurrently with the rape term. Fourteen years later, Johnny Jones was paroled, and not long thereafter showed

up at Barbara's door ready to kill again.

When the judge finally sentenced Jones to spend the rest of his natural life in prison, declaring him "a menace, a career criminal, an urban predator..." Barbara could only think, "better late than never." Except the gun she'd used to save herself and her family was now gone, tucked away on a shelf somewhere in a plastic bag labeled "evidence."

Undeterred by her initial experience, Barbara went right out and purchased a new gun because "the world we live in is just too darn dangerous not to be as prepared as we can."

While we like to think of America as a civilized country and ourselves as a civilized people, the fact is crime and violence remain rampant producing tens of millions of innocent victims each and every year. No matter how many laws are passed, there will always be those for whom they have no meaning and serve as no deterrent. Those who believe otherwise have their heads dangerously in the clouds.

Jaquie Creazzo, 31, was a recently divorced mother of three, living in a small town outside Boulder, Colorado when she left home at 5:30 one cold, icy February morning to pick up her father. Nearing an off-ramp on the Boulder Turnpike, she saw two cars stopped up ahead, emergency flashers blinking and two figures standing there.

"The woman suddenly bolted from the man and started running downhill towards me," recalled Jaquie. "She wasn't screaming, but she had such a look of dread on her face I instantly knew she needed help."

Jaquie slowed and the woman jumped in the passenger seat shouting hysterically that a man with a gun was trying to kill her.

The woman, Rhonda Maloney, a 25-year-old cocktail waitress at a Denver casino had worked until 2 AM, gotten into her car and started home to her husband when she was

bumped by another car and forced off the road. At first the other driver, Robert Harlan, had offered to help, but then raped her and held her captive for hours.

Seeing Harlan now jump in his car and head off after them, Jaquie decided to make for the police station just two exits away. The cars raced along for a while until Harlan pulled even on the driver's side, pointed a gun and started shooting. Jaquie floored it but Harlan came up on her again and kept firing repeatedly at the women.

Unaware at the time that bullets had slammed into her mouth, knee and spine, adrenaline pumping, Jaquie reached the police station and careened up on the lawn about a half-block from the front door. Then she passed out. She didn't see Harlan pull Rhonda out of the car and throw her to the ground but came to long enough to see him return again to grab Rhonda's purse and vest.

"I got a real good look at him and he looked at me. This was the face that I thought was going to kill me so it was burned into my head,"

For the next 45 minutes, Jaquie faded in and out of consciousness until a police officer reporting for duty finally noticed her car and she was able to tell what had happened.

Two days later, the police found and arrested Robert Harlan. A week later, Rhonda's body was discovered under a bridge, the victim of repeated blows to the head and several gunshot wounds.

Jaquie was not expected to survive, but surprised everyone. A bullet had entered her mouth and knocked out her teeth, but far worse was the one lodged in her 5th lumbar vertebra that paralyzed her from mid-chest down and would force her to spend the rest of her life in a wheelchair.

After many agonizing months in a rehab hospital and multiple surgeries, Jaquie was finally able to return home to her three young daughters.

Robert Harlan was a 29-year-old telephone operator at US West where for the prior seven years, dozens of female

employees had claimed they were stalked, intimidated, sexually abused and harassed by him. Although he had earlier been convicted of three sex-related offenses, a prior arrest for rape led to a mistrial when the victim refused to testify. After the Rhonda Maloney incident, Harlan became the #1 suspect in the beating death of a co-worker at US West.

As the prime witness against Harlan at his trial for the murder of Rhonda Maloney, Jaquie feared his friends might try to stop her from testifying or seek retribution later on. Aware the police could only do so much and would not be able to assure her safety, Jaquie considered all of her options and finally decided she had no real choice but to buy a handgun and learn how to use it.

Today, in a fanny pack strapped to Jaquie's wheelchair is a loaded gun. At night, the chair, fanny pack and its contents sit at the ready, next to her bed. While she hopes never to have to use it, knowing she's not entirely vulnerable and can defend herself if necessary is a bittersweet comfort for Jaquie.

Generally speaking, aside from sports shooting, women own and use a gun almost exclusively for self- defense. Of the 26,000 homicides in U.S. in 2000, more than 90% were committed by males. Each year, some 4,000 American women are murdered, mostly by men.

While overall violent crimes have decreased slightly over the last few years, lo and behold, the number of reported rapes has actually increased! The FBI said in its annual Uniform Crime Report that crime nationwide fell 0.2% in 2002, but rape went up 4.0% with the Northeast leading the nation by a 6.2% increase.

In 2000, the Justice Department's National Crime Victimization Survey claims there were only 261,000 *reported* victims of sexual assault, attempted or completed rape. Except the FBI says only 35% of rapes are ever reported and estimates something like 1.2 million rapes

were committed in the U.S. in 2000, which averages out to more than 3,300 every day of the year.

Experts do agree that approximately one out of every six American women have been or will be the victim of an attempted or completed rape during their lifetimes.

What's extra horrifying is that if 2/3's of all rapes and sexual assaults are **not** reported, all those bad guys are still out there, emboldened by their successes and ready for more.

Why do so many rapes go unreported? According to the 2000 National Crime Victimization Survey, most victims just fear retribution from the assailant or his family and friends! And even when they do initially report an assault to the police, they often don't follow through because they're too frightened to testify and their cases are dropped.

One such casualty is Michelle Robinson who ended up in an Indianapolis jail cell while her rapist was released without even having to post bail. Yes, you read that correctly

Robertson, 34, a mother of a grade-school child was attacked by a knife-wielding two-time sex-crime felon, who came through her bedroom window at night. For months afterwards, she had nightmares reliving the attack.

Too scared to testify in open court, she had missed three prior appointments to give her statement in the presence of the defense attorney, so Judge Patricia Gifford issued a warrant for her arrest for failing to appear as a material witness.

"Nobody wants to make a victim into a victim twice," the judge said, "but unfortunately, within our system of justice, to make it all work, you need to come to court to testify. By not appearing, the case becomes impossible. And as a result of her not appearing, the defendant had to be released, which I don't think anyone thought should happen."

Beth Gelhausen, director of the Prevail Victim Assistance Program was shocked and said trials are "incredibly trau-

matic" for sex-assault victims. "I can picture this woman being dressed, ready to go and not being able to walk out of her bathroom. I've seen victims become physically ill and not be able to do this."

"I've never been in jail before" said Michelle. "I was in a big cell with about 20 other women. It's a black hole – hard metal beds, no pillows or mats. They don't care if you sleep on the floor."

The moment of truth came when she finally got out of jail the next day, was brought into court and had to walk right past her attacker. "I looked over at him," Michelle confided. "And then I knew I could do it." Soon after, her rapist was found guilty and is currently in prison.

Many other women are not victims of chance circumstances but of ongoing violent relationships, from which escape is difficult or seemingly impossible.

One such example occurred in Chicago on Wednesday, May 3, 2002, just before midnight, when Ronyale White's estranged husband threatened to kill her. She called 911 at 11:40 p.m. screaming that he was outside the house and that she had a restraining order that was supposed to be given "Priority 1A" status by the police department.

After the operator told her the police were on their way, Ronyale locked her bedroom door and activated a tape recorder. Five minutes later, she called again saying her husband had a gun and was warning her she was going to die.

In her third and last call at 11:50 p.m., she pleaded for the police to arrive as a helpless operator heard a man's voice threatening death, followed by a loud noise, like a door being kicked in. Seconds later, two shots were heard and the phone went dead. Police arrived at Ronyale's house at 11:57 p.m. - almost 17 minutes after the initial call - and found Ronyale dead on the floor.

Would Ronyale be alive today if she had a gun and

knew how to use it? Probably. She had time to lock her bedroom door and turn on a tape recorder, so she would have had the opportunity to load her gun and be ready when her enraged husband started threatening her before he kicked the door in.

Sharlotte Pearson, a domestic violence victim, was prepared. After taking the police department's advice, Sharlotte moved to Forest Park, Florida from Pensacola to escape her former husband, Marvin Pearson, who had beaten her repeatedly both before and after their marriage. But, he soon found her. On a cool late fall evening, she returned from work and her niece told her that Marvin and her niece's boyfriend, Wallace, had gone to the store for food. "I felt I was in great trouble," explained Sharlotte, so she decided to get her gun from the attic, loaded it, and put it in her bedroom drawer.

When the two men returned, things appeared peaceful until Marvin took her into the bedroom where they began arguing and then fighting. He hit her and bit her on the lip after telling her not to scream. He continued to beat her even after waking up their youngest son who was on the bed asleep in the same room.

Sharlotte shouted to Wallace to call the police. When Marvin ran to stop Wallace from making the call, she got her gun. The two men briefly fought and Marvin ran into the bedroom. Determined to stop him, Sharlotte shot and killed him.

She was arrested and charged with murder. At her trial on May 23, 2002, her lawyer said, "this trial is about a bully, a bully who had beat on her and beat on her and beat on her some more. Sharlotte Pearson said don't tread on me, leave me alone."

After hearing a day and a half of evidence, the jury took just 30 minutes to find Sharlotte not guilty. "Now I can raise my boys," Sharlotte happily declared just before calling her mother to tell her the news.

"What I had to do had nothing to do with shooting or murder; what I did had to be done for my safety and the safety of my kids," said Sharlotte, smiling for the first time after her grueling time in court. She has returned her gun to the attic, but as she said, "it's there for me if God forbid, I need it."

A gun can also be a great deterrent and there are many stories of mavericks—women, who have stopped attacks without having to shoot their weapons. One man learned the hard way to never to cross his mother-in-law, especially if she has a permit to carry a gun.

One Saturday afternoon on January 7, 2003, in Atlanta, Georgia, Jim Halston, 41, dragged his estranged wife, Denny, from her mother's car. While she kicked and screamed, he carried her into his house where he punched her on the right side of her head. Denny's mother pulled out her handgun from her purse and ran into the unlocked house where she ordered Halston to sit on the floor until the police arrived.

Halston was arraigned on charges of simple assault, harassment and a charge of indirect criminal contempt, which stemmed from a "protection from abuse order" signed 10 days prior to the altercation, which ordered Hill not to have any contact with his wife.

After Denny received medical care, she said that she knew that her mother was carrying a gun, but she never thought that her mother would be her "savior." "I've been beat up so much by him," she explained, "that I thought this may be the time when he would kill me, but my mom knew what to do."   .

According to the U.S. Department of Justice (1998) 27% of American women keep a gun in the house and 37.6 million females either own or have rapid access to guns. That's a lot of women, but the majority of women

don't have guns.

Over the years, women have asked me, "What can I do if I don't want a gun?" I explain that there are other options, but in the end the smartest way to protect oneself is with a gun. It is by far the most powerful weapon a woman can have for self protection. Of course, I understand that even if you have a gun, you may not be able to use it or you may hot have it in your possession, so it is crucial to have other alternatives.

The following chapter offers options that can be effective for preventing an assault.

CHAPTER TWO
OTHER SELF DEFENSE OPTIONS

"Live as brave men (women);
and if fortune is adverse,
front its blows with brave hearts."
    - Cicero

A gun is not an all-purpose self defense device. A gun should only be used for particular, life-threatening situations, which includes the possibility of rape.

Furthermore, even if you have your gun on you or near you, you may not be able to use it for a variety of reasons, including the risk of wounding or even killing others.

That's why I recommend that all women take self defense classes that teach the basics of learning how to fight using their bodies. Years ago, it was difficult to find these types of classes, but now practically every city offers a myriad of programs. I always advise that the earlier in life you've taken a course, the better chance you have of not being a criminal target. If nothing else, you learn to become an aware individual, which is half the battle of not being victimized. If you're a mother with children as young as five years old, I suggest that you find a class for both your sons and daughters. They'll have a good time and they'll learn the meaning and feeling of personal empowerment.

PEPPER SPRAY

A student of mine, Elana Solera, was accosted one early morning in a hospital parking structure. "I had to go to the Long Beach Hospital at about 1 a.m. because my sister was having a baby. I wasn't particularly nervous, but I parked as near as possible to the entrance to the door, and still had to walk about 100 feet," she explained. "Without even thinking, I always carry my pepper spray on my key chain for that just-in-case situation. That night was one of those situations. I must have taken about ten steps when this

13

guy came out in front of a car. He yelled at me and started toward me."

Elana doesn't remember how long it took him to get to her, but she raised the small canister and squeezed the button squirting a stream that hit the guy's eyes. He started moaning and wiping his hands on his face, and then he collapsed. Elana ran into the hospital screaming for help and a security officer ran to her. "We went out to the parking structure and the guy was still down on the ground! I always knew it was powerful stuff, and I saw it in action," said Elana, who bought a fresh canister the next day, hoping never to use it again.

Pepper spray (or pepper foam) is considered to be a nonlethal weapon and is designed to incapacitate an attacker <u>instantly</u> without after-affects. The product goes under various brand names and different formulas. Some are made by reliable companies, others aren't. Pepper spray contains an oleoresin capsicum solution, an all-natural substance, better known as cayenne pepper, which is derived from various hot red pepper plants. When sprayed properly—whether in stream, cone-of-mist, or burst units—it has a devastating short-term effect on humans, regardless of their intoxicated or emotional condition. The pepper causes the membranes to swell, producing instant eye closure, uncontrollable coughing, gagging and the sensation of intense burning to the skin. Also, it contracts the diaphragm causing the attacker to double over, often halting him in mid-stride.

I've spoken to police officers, who've been pepper-sprayed as part of their training, and they all report that the pain was so intense that they never wanted to be sprayed again! Fred Cook, a Los Angeles area police officer says, "getting hit with pepper, is like putting your hand on a hot stove and not being able to take it off. The pain keeps intensifying."

It's important to spray to the attacker's face. The ideal range of spraying is within four to six feet of an attacker.

Spraying the canister at distances of <u>less</u> than two feet can cause incomplete evaporation of the spray and can retard the full effect of the active agent for as long as 30 seconds—much too long of a time when being assaulted.

Unfortunately, it has its limitations. If it's raining, snowing or very windy, the spray may be ineffective and not hit the target or if the wind is blowing in your direction, you, rather than the attacker, may be affected by the spray. And indoors, the spray may disable everyone!

A number of years ago, I was giving a seminar for 300 employees in the ballroom of a large hotel in Waikiki, Hawaii, when one of the attendees pulled out a small pepper spray canister to show the woman sitting next to her and she accidentally pushed the canister's button squirting the pepper spray into the air. Within a minute, people started choking and coughing, including me while I stood on the stage at least sixty feet away from the spray's burst! Everyone had to evacuate the room and returned about 15 minutes later after the air conditioning was put on full blast.

If a training class is available in your community in the usage of pepper spray, do take it. Even though you'll use spray canisters filled with an inert liquid, you'll develop a sense of how accurately you can spray an attacker, and at what distance. One squirt of spray may not knock down your assailant. Know that you may need to continue spraying before the attacker is down.

If there isn't a class, check out the various pepper spray companies online and purchase an inert canister. It allows you to rehearse scenarios with a friend, who can attack you from different positions, including from behind. Practice pulling the canister out of your pocket, purse or key-chain. Get to know the feel of the canister so you know which way the spray nozzle is pointed. It's a good way to ascertain how quickly you react in a crisis situation. Practice spraying numerous times.

I do recommend that you make it a habit while walking to carry your small canister in your strong hand in a ready

position. As soon as you perceive a threat, place your thumb on the spray's actuator, so you'll be ready to spray. If you're fighting with the attacker, it may be extremely difficult to get your canister out of your purse or pocket.

What do you do after you've sprayed the attacker? Does he fall into a heap moaning and crying while you watch? Not necessarily so. He could react in a deranged and violent way. Self-defense expert Massad Ayoob, who trains police officers in the use of sprays, recommends that you simulate the worst-case scenario during your training and practice moving backward or sideway and spraying again to the attacker's face. After that, Ayoob advises that you divert your movement so that if the attacker carries on his assault he most probably will strike toward the position where last he saw you.

You can carry pepper spray canisters across most state-lines. Unfortunately, you can't take these products on planes, even in checked luggage. Changing air pressures at high altitudes can cause the canisters to leak and could destroy your clothes and cosmetics. Buy a canister at your destination point and when you leave, give it to someone. If you discard it, don't be careless, since you don't want a child to find it and use it. And that reminds me, if you do have young children, you must be careful to keep it away from them. If your children are curious or unruly, I suggest you think twice about acquiring a spray product.

If you or one of your children is accidentally sprayed, the symptoms can be relieved by flushing the eyes with cool water, going outside for fresh air, and washing the entire body and hair with soap and cold water. Left untreated, the symptoms should stop in 15 to 45 minutes. If not, call a doctor. If the spray has been discharged indoors normal ventilation will remove the spray in 45 minutes. Clothing that's been sprayed should be washed or cleaned.

Canisters are available in different sizes and can be purchased through catalogues, hardware stores, drug stores or at gun stores. There are more than 100 sprays on the

market, so be careful what you buy. There should be a minimum of 10 seconds' total continuous discharge of spray and a ten percent content of oleoresin capsicum with a 2 million or more SHU rating. This information should be stated on the manufacturer's instructions.

Most states allow pepper spray. However, in Michigan, the law states that pepper spray can be no stronger than 2% OC, which makes it ineffective. In Wisconsin, a UV dye is not allowed and citizens can buy only one state-approved brand, PepperGuard Pepper Spray. In New York, pepper spray can only be purchased from a state licensed firearms dealer or pharmacist and in Massachusetts, a purchaser can only buy from a licensed firearms dealer and must acquire a Firearms Identification card (FID).

STUN GUNS

I've talked to a number of women who carry stun guns and I've warned them that a stun gun doesn't offer "distance defense," like pepper spray does, since you can only use it once the attacker is next to you.

It's not easy to use. A stun gun, which sends out a charge of electricity, only works if the victim manages to firmly hold it while pushing the button and digging the small electrodes into the attacker's body for up to four seconds. Frankly, I don't of know any assailant who will allow his victim to do that, although I have heard of stories where the attackers were immune to the bolts of electricity because they were previously electrocuted. Most probably, he will grab the stun.

What does a stun gun do? It is designed to scramble the nervous system. The resulting energy loss makes it difficult for the attacker to move. It must make contact with the skin or body. Touching an attacker with the two metal prongs on the stun gun quickly causes temporary loss of balance and mental confusion. The longer the unit maintains contact with the attacker's body, the more effective the device is in repelling the attacker. For 1-2 seconds will cause muscle

spasms and a dazed mental state. For 3-5 seconds will cause loss of balance and muscle control, total mental confusion and disorientation leaving him dazed for up to fifteen minutes giving the victim a chance to run away. Rarely does it cause cardiac arrest. You cannot suffer a charge-back to your own body—that means you can feel safe when using the device even if the assailant is touching y o u .

Even if a child were to use the device and apply it to themselves, their muscles would go limp in 1/1000th of a second, causing them to immediately drop it. Stun guns are not toys, and like guns, should be stored away from children.

Rather than using it as a weapon, I think it's more useful as a deterrent. Let's say you're in an underground parking lot and you feel threatened by someone coming toward you, you could warn him to stay away while you hold up the stun gun at eye level, push the button which fires the crackling, bright blue bolts of electricity across the electrodes. You and your stun gun could stop the person from coming any closer to you and giving you a chance to get away.

Available in assorted sizes and different amounts of voltage from 25,000 to 100,000 volts, stun guns can be purchased in gun stores. They are not legal in all states, so check with your local police department before purchasing a stun gun.

MINI-BATONS

I always carry a black mini-baton (also known as the Kubotan) in my purse and use it for my keys. It's a solid plastic ribbed dowel three and a half inches long and three-eighths in diameter with a key-chain on one end (but, you shouldn't keep your small pepper spray canister on it). Designed by a leading master martial arts instructor, Shihan Tahuyuki Kubota, the mini-baton is used by police, prison guards, other law enforcement personnel and savvy

women.

To use it defensively, you need to be trained. I was fortunate to meet and be taught by Kubota in his Glendale, California, studio where he taught me various wrist-take downs and neck-lock take-downs, as well as how to use the baton as a handle to slash across an attacker's face and eyes. But, I must admit that I didn't feel secure executing the techniques after the four-hour personal training. It would have taken me many weeks if not months of practice with another person to master the defensive moves.

I recommend that women use the mini-baton as a deterrent rather than as a fighting device. Whenever I don't feel particularly safe whether walking on the streets or in parking lots, malls, and other public places, including elevators, I carry it in my strong hand with the six keys dangling down. The mini-baton certainly makes a statement. I've noticed many people, especially men, cautiously eyeing it when I carry it.

A few years ago, I entered an elevator in New York's Flatiron office building holding my mini-baton in my left hand and a man followed me. As we ascended, he looked at the baton and asked me, "Are you a police officer?" I said no and focused my attention on the elevator panel. There was a long pause. Then, he said, "ma'am, don't worry. I'm in law enforcement. I know what it is," as he gestured toward the baton. "You're smart to carry one in New York."

Many of my students have reported similar stories. Besides functioning as a deterrent, the mini-baton can be a symbol to its owner. One of my students told me that when she holds the mini-baton it prompts her to be aware of her surroundings.

Since the mini-baton plus the keys is rather weighty, I don't use it in the car ignition, nor do I leave it with a car attendant. I always use another set of car keys for my car. And by the way, because the mini-baton is large, I never have a problem finding my keys in my purse!

Plastic mini-batons are legal to carry in the U.S. and I've never had a problem taking mine through airport security; however, I've heard that metal mini-batons have been confiscated.

You can purchase mini-batons for under $10 at gun stores and through mail order. They come in most colors, but black is most intimidating.

DOGS

If you don't already have a dog, consider owning one. Studies indicate that houses with dogs are less likely to be burglarized than homes without them.

Also, the chances of being car-jacked are lessened if you take your dog in your car. Most criminals will pass up an auto with a snarling German Shepherd in the back-seat. Additionally, the likelihood of you being attacked is diminished when you're walking with a large dog. I recommend that real estate agents, traveling saleswomen, and women who work in unsafe areas take their big dogs with them.

There are two categories of dogs I'm talking about. A **watchdog** requires the least training. It can be big or small. This dog barks insistently when an entry is attempted and lets the intruder know that he's been detected, and if you're home it usually goes to the entry point to alert you where the break-in is occurring. By giving warning of an intruder's presence, a watchdog allows you the time to take protective or defensive measures.

One of the easiest ways to train a watchdog, is to chain it to a tree when it's about six months of age. If possible, ask a stranger to invade the dog's territory and then run away. Then, praise the dog excessively. Do this drill a few times a day for a week and soon it will know to bark when a stranger comes near your house, yard or car.

For the great majority of people, a protection-trained dog is quite adequate. A **protection dog** has advanced training. On your command, it barks and lunges at an aggressor. Depending on the training it may or may not

actually bite. Also, upon your command, it immediately sits and is silent.

According to Kent, Washington dog trainer and self defense instructor Timothy Maynard, a protection trained dog is "not a "toy" to be shown and displayed as a source of authority. Keep it to yourself and use it only for emergencies. People tend to develop attitudes and as soon as a local jogger or child gets bitten by an unidentified pooch, it will suddenly start to look 'just like your dog'!"

"A protection dog is not an asset without the knowledge required to maintain the training," says Maynard. "A protection dog must be maintained or the asset of protection becomes a liability for your home owner's insurance."

"A protection trained dog is not a cure all for personal security. This does not give you cause to go to "crack infested" areas and peddle Tupperware, or increase your mountain bike workout. The fact that you have a protection trained dog is no different than a handgun. I tell all my students that this (gun or dog) is an excuse to STAY out of trouble. Common sense rules here friends, without that all the guns, knives, ninjas and protection dogs in the world can't help you!"

Don't expect a small dog to be an effective protection dog. They're best for warning of danger. You want a dog that weighs at least 50 pounds. I recommend buying from a reputable breeder a Doberman, a Rottweiller, a German Shepherd, Great Dane, an Akita or a Rhodesian Ridgeback for protection training. Expect to spend $500 to $5,000. If you can't afford these prices, large mixed breeds are just as good and many are more emotionally stable than the larger registered dogs.

One of the best dog training available is Schutzhund, which was begun in Germany and has chapters worldwide. If your dog is exceptionally good in terms of temperament, you and your dog can get involved in various levels of Schutzhund competition, which can be especially rewarding and fun. (Click-on: www.germanshepherddog.com or for

all breeds, www.dvgamerica.com)

The trained and maintained protection dog is an asset when compared to the untrained dog. Most dogs have a natural instinct to protect, but in today's environment teaching the dog to trust when and when not to protect is imperative. Protection dogs provide a physical first line of defense, allowing you time to get away, phone 911, or even to round up family members to get them into a safe room until the police arrive, or to respond with lethal force if needed.

According to Maynard, "the security dog in the home requires some forethought. All entry doors and gates must be posted "Beware of Dog" and a warning given if you have a chance. 'If you don't get away/out of my house/ away from my car my dog WILL protect me'. A warning effort will go over well in court. The signs show a willingness to warn bad guys. The vicious dog signs WILL be used against you, as the defendant's lawyer will say you knew you had a mean dog and refer to a picture of the sign."

For other dog training schools, consult your phone directory.

KNIVES AND DAGGERS

Forget about using knives and daggers unless you've taken a special course. If you're not well-trained, the attacker can take a knife away from you and use it against you. Federal, state, and local laws prohibit carrying really effective weapons, so those interested in carrying knives for self-defense must settle for something less.

IMPROVISED WEAPONS

Almost everything in your environment is a possible weapon. Don't be afraid to grab and smash with glasses, bottles, hammers, clipboards, staplers, pots, lamps, chairs, tables, pool cues, flashlights, golf clubs and baseball bats.

You can toss at your attacker your coat, paper clips,

coins, ash tray, sand, dirt, and plates of food, drinks, salt or pepper. A pen, pencil, fork, spoon, ruler, knitting needle, umbrella tip and screwdriver can be pushed into soft areas of an attacker's body. Go for the face with the edge of a credit card, key, knife, comb, box cutter, CD, or fingernail clipper. To gain distance, consider taking off your belt and swinging at your attacker in a figure eight pattern.

YOUR CHECKS

The next time you order checks have only your initials (instead of first name) and last name put on them

If someone takes your check book they will not know if you sign your checks with just your initials or your first name, but your bank will know how you sign your checks.

When you are writing checks to pay on your credit card accounts, DO NOT put the complete account number on the "For" line. Instead, just put the last four numbers. The credit card company knows the rest of the number and anyone who might be handling your check as it passes through all the check processing channels won't have access to it.

Put your work phone number on your checks instead of your home phone. If you have a PO Box use that instead of your home address. If you do not have a PO Box use your work address.

Never print your Social Security number on your checks

Place the contents of your wallet on a photocopy machine, do both sides of each license, credit card, etc. You will know what you had in your wallet and all of the account numbers and phone numbers to call and cancel.

Keep the photocopy in a safe place. Carry a photocopy of your passport when you travel in either the US or abroad.

WALLET STOLEN? HERE'S WHAT TO DO IF YOU LOSE YOUR PURSE OR WALLET

We've all heard horror stories about fraud that's committed using your name, address, SSN, credit card numbers, etc. Identity theft is the fastest-growing crime in America, striking some 700,000 people from all walks of life. Many of us don't know what to do when this dreadful act occurs. I have first hand knowledge: Unfortunately, my friend's wallet was stolen while she was shopping at a department store and within a week the thief/thieves had ordered an expensive monthly cell phone package, applied for a VISA credit card package, had a credit line approved to buy a Dell computer, received a PIN number from the DMV to change her driver's license and personal record information online! Ouch, that hurts!

Here's some critical information to limit the damage in case this happens to you or someone you know:

Everyone always advises, cancel your credit cards immediately, but the key is having the toll free numbers and your card numbers handy so you know who to call. Keep the list where you can find them easily (having to hunt for them is additional stress you WON'T need at that point!). And, you might want to consider exchanging this information with a trusted friend or relative so if you're on the road you can access the information.

File a police report immediately in the jurisdiction where it was stolen. This proves to your credit providers that you were diligent, and is a first step toward an investigation (if there ever is one). Also, get a copy of the report as proof.

But here's what is perhaps most important: Call the three national credit-reporting organizations immediately to place a fraud alert on your name and social security number. Additionally, order credit reports. I had never heard of doing that until advised by a bank that called to talk with me because an application for credit was made over the Internet in my name.

The national credit-reporting organizations' numbers are: Equifax :1-800 525-6285; Experian (formerly TRW): 1-800-301-7195; TransUnion: 1-800-680-7289; Social Security Administration also has a fraud line at 1-800-269-0271.

The alert means any company that checks your credit knows instantly that your information was stolen and they have to contact you by phone to authorize any new credit. By the time my friend did it - almost two weeks after the theft - all the damage had been done (there are records of all the credit checks initiated by the thieves' purchases, none of which she knew about before placing the alert). Since then, no additional damage has been done, and the thieves threw her Gucci wallet away and someone then turned it in to the police. It seems to have stopped the thieves in their tracks.

CHAPTER THREE
DISPELLING GUN MYTHS

"Courage is contagious
When a brave person takes a stand,
The spines of others
Are often Stiffened"
- Rev. Billy Graham

You may not be sure whether you want to learn how to shoot a gun, let alone buy one, because you've heard so many stories and statistics that illustrate how guns can be detrimental to you. Many of these so-called facts that are bandied around the media and discussed at cocktail parties are truly false, but are considered accurate, especially by people who are against guns. Myths about weapons can endanger women's safety by scaring them and stopping them from using a highly effective way to protect themselves.

To help you get a broader understanding of the gun issue, the following are the most common myths:

"You're more likely to shoot yourself or a family member than an attacker..."

When Los Angeles real estate broker Donna Foster, who was worried about her personal safety, first heard about my women's gun self-defense seminar, she wildly reacted, "It's a fact, I probably would be shot by my own gun. I heard on TV that a gun owner is 43 times more likely to kill a family member than an intruder. So, why would I want a gun?" This fallacious stance, which has crept into our popular culture is almost certainly one of the most common reasons given why women shy away from learning how to shoot a gun.

Who started this false piece of information and why has it gained so much authenticity? These oft-repeated figures derive from an initial study, "Protection or Peril? An Analysis

27

of Firearms-Related Deaths in the Home," published in a 1966 *New England Journal of Medicine* by Dr. Arthur Kellermann and his colleagues, followed by another two studies, "Suicide in the Home in Relationship to Gun Ownership" (1992) and "Gun Ownership as a Risk Factor in the Home," (1993) and which were bank-rolled by the antigun National Center for Policy Analysis (NPIC), Centers for Disease Control (CDC).

The latter study centered on gun-related deaths in the homes in King County (Seattle), Washington. It was limited to fatalities in the home involving a gun which belonged in the home, and found 1.3 accidental deaths, 4.6 criminal homicides and 37 suicides involving firearms. The authors originally warned that the study was of a single nonrepresentative county. To say the least! Both the case studies and control groups in this study had exceptionally high incidences of social dysfunction and instability, including a high incidence of financial instability. For example, 52.7% of case subjects had a history of a household member being arrested; 24.8% had alcohol-related problems; 31.3% had a household history of illegal drug abuse; 31.8% had a household member hit or hurt in a family fight, and 17.3% had a family member hurt so severely in a family fight that medical attention was required.

The authors freely used the "43" as if it were definitive and national even though the case and control groups did not even represent the diversity of the counties studied, let alone a "normal" American family. Also, the researchers acknowledged no attempt was made to count "cases in which burglars or intruders are wounded or frightened away" by defensive gun use, yet concluded that "the advisability of keeping firearms in the home for protection must be questioned."

Furthermore, to prove their hypothesis, Kellermann and his associates assumed that the victim of the crime and the victim of the homicide were the same person. Actually, the deceased may have been the attacker. Indeed, Kellermann

says, "Fifteen victims were killed under legally excusable circumstances. Four were shot by police acting in the line of duty."

According to author and attorney Don Kates, "The data presented does not show that even one homicide victim was killed with a gun ordinarily kept in that household. Indeed, the indirect evidence indicates that most of the homicide victims in the study were killed using guns not kept in the victim's home."

Ultimately, it was shown that no more than 4% of the gun deaths in the study could be attributed to the homeowner's gun.

Through the years, peer-reviewers, medical doctors and scholars asked the CDC and Kellermann for the research to evaluate the conclusions. Kellermann steadfastly refused to divulge the raw data for scientific inquiry, which is routinely expected of honest researchers. That naturally raised the question of the validity of any and all of Kellermann's data. Complaints were issued to both the CDC and to members of Congress. In any event, the media continued to spout the spurious "43" implanting it deeper into culture as "scientific proof."

In Spring, 1966, Congressional subcommittee hearings on CDC funding were held and naturally, Kellermann's work was discussed and the CDC's long neglected duties of scientifically scrutinizing his study. One of those who gave testimony during the hearing was Dr. Miguel Faria, Jr., a consultant neurosurgeon and the editor-in-chief of *The Medical Sentinel*—the official publication of the Association of American Physicians and Surgeons. Faria condemned the CDC's abandonment of integrity in research and said, "…when it comes to the NCIPC, we don't have science… You don't go about in science to make a statement and then find corroborative evidence to support that statement…You go the other way around. You gather facts, you test those facts, and then you make a generalization."

Kellermann's study was considered so flawed, the CDC

was forced, finally, to rein in Kellermann. And so, in the summer of 1996, the U.S. House of Representatives voted to shift $2.6 million away from the NCIP of the CDC, earmarking "gun funds" for other health research.

But, Kellermann didn't leave the government dole. Almost immediately after leaving the CDC umbrella, he was picked up by the U.S. Department of Justice's National Institute for Justice (NIJ). It publishes a series of monographs available to the public and the new title of the June 1996 issue was "Understanding and Preventing Violence: A Public Health Perspective," which was a reiteration of Kellermann's past discredited research.

The truth is that 2 million people a year use a gun for self-defense and that 98% of the time the gun is merely brandished to stop a crime. In less than 1% of the cases is a gun actually fired at the attacker. These statistics, researched by John Lott in his seminal book, *More Guns, Less Crime: Understanding Crime and Gun Control Law,* (University of Chicago Press, 2000), received far less media attention and the research was actually derided by critics, who continued to utilize Kellermann's study as the bible of gun facts.

"Why should I own a gun since friends, acquaintances and relatives are the most likely killers."
There is really no broad definition of "acquaintance" used in the FBI's Uniform Crime Reports, and most victims are indeed classified by the FBI as knowing their killer. According to Guy Smith in *Gun Facts,* what's not made clear is that acquaintance murder primarily includes drug buyers killing pushers, cabdrivers killed by their clients, gang members killing other gang members, etc. Only one U.S. city, Chicago, reports a precise breakdown on the nature of acquaintance killings, and the statistics give a very different impression: between 1990 and 1995, just 17% of murder victims were either family members, friends, neighbors or roommates of their killers. The rest

were people with criminal records, killed by other criminals.

"Guns are not effective in preventing crime against women."

Of the 2.5 million annual self defense cases using guns,
more than 7.7% (192,500) are by women defending
themselves against sexual abuse. According to the U.S.
Department of Justice (1998), the probability of serious
injury from an attack is 2.5 times greater for women offering no resistance than with a gun. As mentioned earlier,
the governmental agency also reports that 27% of women
keep a gun in the house and 37.6 million females either
own or have rapid access to guns.

"I don't want a gun in the house. More children are hurt with guns than any other method."

Women are naturally very worried about guns in the
home, and although some women would consider having a
gun, they tend to be adamant about not having one because they're fearful their children would get a hold of it.
Most people don't realize that very few children are involved in gun deaths.

The National Safety Council (1997) reports that 0.1% of
all deaths for children in the U.S. between 0-14 are from
firearms. The rate of "children" 0-24 years old is 0.4%. In
another study, the National Center for Health Statistics,
National Vital Statistics Report (1997) says that children are
12 times more likely to die in a car accident than from gun-
related homicides or legal interventions (being shot by a
police officer, for example) if they are aged 0-14. For the
group 0-24 years old (which bends the definition of "child")
the rate is still 8.6 times higher for cars.

"Guns are safer when they're locked up."

It's usually assumed that safe storage gun laws reduce
accidental gun deaths and total suicides. According to a

study, *Safe-Storage Gun Laws: Accidental Deaths, Suicide and Crime*, which analyzed both state and county data spanning nearly twenty years, the researchers found no support that these laws reduce either juvenile accidental gun deaths or suicides. "Instead," according to John R. Lott, Jr., the study's lead author, "these storage requirements appear to impair people's ability to use guns defensively. During the first five full years after the passage of the safe storage laws, the group of fifteen states that adopted these laws faced an annual average increase of over 300 more murders, 3,860 more rapes, 24,650 more robberies, and over 25,000 more aggravated assaults."

Lott cites the example of a Merced, California family, whose guns were put away because of the state's safe storage law. The father, John Carpenter, who lost two children in an attack in 2000, said a gun would have stopped the man who broke into his home with a pitchfork. "If a gun had been here, today I'd have at least a daughter alive," Carpenter said.

Although I am not opposed to securing guns, I think it's important to assess your family situation especially if you have children at home and make a determination whether you can educate and trust your children about not handling a gun. In the next chapter, I discuss the issue of children and guns in the home.

"The U.S. has the highest homicide rate in the world because Americans own so many guns."

The Swiss, Finns and New Zealanders have a high gun ownership rate. Switzerland has extremely lenient gun control (more so than U.S.) and has the third lowest homicide rate of the top nine major European countries and the same per capita rate as England and Wales. New Zealand has a lower rate than Australia where guns have been banned. Finland and Sweden have very different gun ownership rates, but very similar homicide rates. Israel, with a higher gun ownership rate than America, has a murder

rate 40% lower than Canada. Ironically, many of the countries with the strictest gun control have the highest rates of violent crime. Australia and England which have virtually banned gun ownership have the highest rates of sexual assault, robbery, and assault with force of the top 17 industrialized countries.

In fact, as recently as July, 2002, the British Home Office reported that the true level of crime in England is as much as 40% higher than official figures show. Surveys of crime levels by several police forces show that up to 6,000 more crimes are being committed every day than the current official national figures suggest. Previously the police have recorded only incidents that were actively pursued. Home Secretary, David Blunket, who according to *The Daily Telegraph,* was shocked with the new figures, ordered the police to record every crime reported so that figures were more accurate. In the past, many minor crimes were overlooked if there were a more serious incident to be dealt with: for instance, a theft following a murder would rarely be counted! *The Daily Telegraph* reported that "some crimes have also not been recorded because the victim withdraws a statement or complaint or because officers thought the offence too trivial to pursue."

"If all law-abiding citizens are allowed to carry concealed handguns, people will end up shooting each other."

Millions of Americans currently hold concealed handgun permits and only one permit holder has ever used a concealed handgun after a traffic accident, and that case was ruled as self-defense. Most violations that lead to permits being revoked involve accidentally carrying a gun into restricted areas, like airports or schools.

"In case something horrible happens I can call 911. The police can protect me and people don't need guns."

The courts have continuously ruled that the police do not

have an obligation to protect **individuals.** In *Warren v. District of Columbia Metropolitan Police Department 444A.2d1* (District of Columbia app. 1981), the court states, "Courts have without exception concluded that when a municipality or other government entity undertakes to furnish police services, it assumes a duty only to the public at large and not to individual members of the community."

Currently, approximately 150,000 police officers are **on duty** at any one time. This includes desk clerks, command sergeants, etc. Since there are about 271,933,702 people in the U.S., there is only one **on duty** cop for every 1,813 people. According to *U.S. News & World Report* (July 17, 1998), 95% of the time the police arrive too late to prevent a crime or arrest the suspect. If you call from a cell phone you are even less likely to get help. In over 90% of cities, technology doesn't give police dispatchers the location of the cell phone caller, making police protection less likely for travelers.

Numerous other gun myths circulate through American society and the media, including the constitutional argument regarding the Second Amendment. You can read further by exploring:

www.americanselfdefense.com/gunfacts3.pdf

Chapter Four
GUNS, FAMILY PROTECTION AND KIDS

"Courage is resistance to fear, mastery of fear - not absence of fear."
- Mark Twain

"I'm not sure why I'm here learning how to shoot. I've got two kids at home. I am afraid of an intruder breaking in, but I'm also afraid of a gun in the house—that the kids will get hold of it—yet I want to be able to protect them. It's such a terrible conflict," said Sandra, during my seminar for members and their daughters of a local Junior League.

"Yeah, I feel the same way," chimed in Diana, "my husband wants a gun but I'm not sure I can handle one in the house. How do I know that I'll be able to pull the trigger? I've got a four- year-old son who's into everything. There must be a way to keep a gun safe!"

"Safe guns? Hey, I don't even want my five-year-old playing with toy guns," said Alice.

To be sure, there's lots to think about when you have kids and are also thinking about having a gun in the house for protection. More than half of the seven thousand or so people who've attended my personal safety seminars have been mothers, many whose husbands are frequently away, or single parents in charge of their family's safety. Women are nurturers and care-givers, yet the thought of taking responsibility for having a gun in a house with children or grandchildren is frequently too much for some of them to handle.

I certainly understand their anxiety. But in actuality, their fear and apprehension is often more complex than meets the eye. Not infrequently, it stems from doubt and uncertainty as to their own capacity to act, should the need to use a weapon arise. The "courage quotient," I call it.

The critical question to ask yourself: Do I have what it takes to use a gun if that's the most effective way of protecting my family? Coming up with an answer isn't so easy

because the state of mental and emotional preparedness that it takes to actually pull a trigger isn't something any of us, male or female, are born with. Nor does courage mean the absence of fear. Some of the bravest women I know didn't start out that way. They <u>learned</u> to be brave by studying and practicing what do to in emergencies. In most cultures, as we discussed in an earlier chapter, bravery and courage are considered testosterone traits, male qualities: "he's got the guts of a lion," "the courage of a bull," or "that takes balls." Not too often (if ever) do we hear: "now that took ovaries!"

But real courage at its roots, is of course, gender-blind. Not an exclusively male prerogative, it's simply doing what you have to do, in the face of real and sometimes paralyzing fear. And, as with most things in life, happily, it's something you can learn. If you want. It's been my experience that anyone so motivated can develop the **courage** to use a gun to protect themselves and their loved ones from harm. How? Through education and training.

The famed Green Berets, Navy Seals and other distinguished combat operatives didn't just pop out of the womb combat ready. They got that way only through rigorous, disciplined training and education so when it's time to be brave and courageous, they know what to do. They're ready! And you can be ready, too! And the closer the crisis is to what you've been trained for, the more courageous (read: prepared) you will be.

Ask yourself the following questions:
> Have I ever been in a situation with my children when I felt threatened and vulnerable?
> Was I fearful?
> What action did I take?
> Was I successful?
> Did I feel good about what I did or didn't do?
> How did my children react?

If the answers you come up with aren't entirely satisfying, consider the difference if you'd been better prepared and known in advance what action to take to best safeguard yourself and your children from whatever harm you had to confront.

The following is a true story of a maverick woman who was prepared:

Jeanine, a St. Louis mother of two sons, a 13-year-old and eight-year-old, had to confront an intruder alone at 4 a.m. while her husband was away on business. The first sign of trouble was the loud noise that awakened Jeanine, who got out of bed to investigate and found a young man in his early 20's, a total stranger, sitting on the roof of her patio storage cabinet and privacy wall three floors above ground level.

She later recalled, "I realized immediately that he was under the influence of drugs by his incoherent mumbling, glassy eyes and bizarre behavior." She ordered him to leave, told him she was calling the police, then slammed and locked the patio door. She yelled to her kids to lock their bedroom door, and then went directly to her bedroom and called the police and the dispatcher assured her a car was on the way.

Aware of the drugged condition of the tall, husky man, who was over six feet tall and weighed 175 pounds (Jeanine is five-foot-two and weighs 125 pounds), she got her gun. Just as she finished loading her gun, Jeanine heard a crash as the intruder forced open the patio door and entered the living room. She knew the police were on the way, but the crisis had not waited for them to arrive.

She moved down the hall toward the living room.

"I knew I was violating the training doctrine which says to stay put, take up a defensive position, and let the intruder come to you," she explained later. "But I felt compelled to put as much distance between the danger and my kids as I could. I didn't know what was about to hap-

pen, but I wanted it to be as far away from them as it could be."

Entering the front room, she faced the man at close range - six to eight feet. "I knew instantly he was already too close! I knew that if I had to fire, it would be necessary to shoot him in the head to be sure of stopping him."

She chambered the first round in her pistol. She flicked the safety off, her finger found the trigger, and she leveled the sights right between the man's eyes.

Jeanine did not say a word; her actions spoke for themselves, with great conviction and persuasion. The man looked at her and the pistol pointed at his head and shouted, "Oh shit!" then turned and fled through the door he had forced open, vaulted over the six foot patio privacy wall, and raced down the stairs.

Jeanine ran to the front door, pistol in hand, watching the man's direction of escape. She provided this additional information and a detailed description of the intruder and his clothing to responding police when they arrived several minutes later. Soon after, the suspect was arrested.

This potentially lethal confrontation came to a happy conclusion. No shots were fired; no one was injured. Incidentally, he was out on bond for a previous offense at the time he committed this crime—another all too common story.

I asked her how she managed to do everything right in the face of such danger, terror, and stress. She said, "It seems like I was on automatic pilot. I knew what to do. In time of emergency you seem to do what you are trained to do without thinking about it. I was never conscious of thinking about what I was doing or intended to do next - I just did it. I was prepared to defend my kids, prepared to shoot if necessary; he could not mistake my resolve. That made it his next move. Fortunately for both of us, he made the right choice - he turned and ran."

I asked if she would recommend every family having a gun. She thought for a moment and said, "No, no, you

should only have a gun if you have training and you gotta know that you would pull that trigger. Also, if you've got kids, it's got to be put away so they can't get to it."

Of course, there's always a risk in owning a gun when you have children, just as there is a calculated danger in having sharp knives, cleaning fluids, a medicine chest and even a swimming pool. Any sane, serious, responsible person <u>must</u>, in my opinion, be <u>very</u> concerned about having a gun in the house.

Easy to say, I know, but, as a mother, not so simple to do. Having a gun around for personal protection, sports or hunting is one thing. Keeping it **secure** from inquisitive hands is another. The safest gun, child-wise, is, of course, an unloaded one locked in a safe, which also makes it perfectly useless if you need it in a hurry.

If you've got children around and are considering having a gun for that "just-in-case situation," the fact is, you'll probably need to make some basic changes in your home and life style. But if you're a reasonably responsible adult, the task shouldn't be all that daunting or time-consuming. We're not talking rocket science. The biggest question in most people's minds, and rightfully so, is: "should the gun be loaded or unloaded?" The answer can only be arrived at after a thorough, searching appraisal of all the risks and advantages involved.

From years of thinking about the subject, here is what I've learned:

First, make no mistake— loading a handgun in the face of danger, adrenaline pumping, is no Texas Two-Step. According to police authorities and shooting experts, fear and panic render hands and fingers, not to mention arms and legs, and brain, a lot less dependable.

Doubtful? Place an unloaded gun on a table, and put brass (do <u>not</u> use live ammunition) on the other side of the table. Have a friend give you the go-ahead to load and time you. This will in no way simulate the stress of a real crisis, but you will clearly see how clumsy you can become

from the mere pressure of being timed. (If you have a revolver, using a speed-loader can help, but only if you become adept at loading in the dark, under extreme pressure).

Considering these adrenaline-induced constraints that usually create the need to use a gun for self-protection, I've concluded that if you're reasonably confident that you can <u>safely</u> <u>secure</u> your loaded handgun from coming into the wrong hands, you're a whole lot better prepared by keeping it loaded rather than unloaded.

What, you say? Keeping a loaded gun around? How politically incorrect, at the very least! But my function here is to deal with reality, not fantasy, and reality requires candor.

Years ago, while writing *Armed & Female*, I felt differently and said, "Your gun should be loaded only when you are at home, and if, for example, you come home at night and load your gun and then decide to leave, you should unload it and safely secure it again."

I've changed my opinion. I came to realize that most people simply won't take the time to unload and load their guns. It's too much to expect as a practical matter. Even from responsible people. The best way, as I mentioned before, is to keep it loaded, but secured in a portable safe.

I have not changed my mind about unloading a gun and safely securing it if you're going to be away for an extended period of time and not taking it with you. You wouldn't want your Beretta in the hands of a burglar, who more than likely would sell it on the black market to only God knows who.

You may be surprised to learn that 51 percent of all American households possess at least one firearm, so it's reasonable to assume that many children in this country have been taught gun safety and are coexisting comfortably with the risks and benefits of gun ownership. You may argue that you've heard there are a lot of kids getting killed with their parents' guns, so let's talk about statistics.

According to the Centers for Disease Control and

Prevention (CDC), (whose rabid anti-gun bias although well documented is little known by the general public) overall firearm mortality <u>declined</u> 11 percent between 1993 and 1995, while auto fatalities rose 22 percent. The National Safety Council estimates that in 1995 among children under 5, accidental deaths from guns (including rifles and shotguns) numbered 50. That's right, not 500 or 5,000. Fifty. Among all children under age 15 the number was 200, and a majority were gang-related deaths. While accidental gun deaths are always sad and tragic by comparison, 2,900 children died in motor vehicle crashes, 220 children died from choking, 1,000 died from fires and burns, and 950 from drowning. Hundreds more children die in bicycle accidents each year than die from all types of firearm accidents. They just don't make the Six o'clock News.

Child firearms deaths are usually, but certainly not always, the fault of careless adults. It's people just not giving enough attention to securing their guns. According to a 1993 Los Angeles Times poll, 4 in 10 gun owners don't keep their guns locked up. Many hide their guns in

---

Home Is Not The Safest Place For A Child To Be

According to two U.S. studies published in May, 2003, a home is not the safest place for a child to be and it's not because of guns!

The studies done at Cincinnati Children's Hospital Medical Center found that home injuries, though continuing to fall, remain a leading cause of death in children and teens, especially African Americans.

The good news was that the annual rate of accidental deaths in the home fell by 25 percent between 1985 and 1997. But the researchers who used government statistics found that dangers still abounded.

The two research teams found that 2,800 children die each year from unintentional injuries in the home. Between 1985 and 1997, 69 percent of deaths in children and adolescents under the age of 20 were the result of such injuries.

Twice as many black children as white children died accidentally in the home — 7 per 100,000 for blacks as compared to 3.3 per 100,000 for whites.

Children younger than 5 and boys were the most likely to be injured, the studies found. The most common causes of injuries and deaths were fires or burns, drowning or suffocation, poisoning and falls. Falls were the leading cause of injury, accounting for 1.5 million visits to emergency rooms.

inappropriate places.

One woman I know stashes her .38 at the bottom of a laundry basket in the bedroom closet. Another hides hers at the back of a top shelf in the kitchen. Other "secret" hiding places include: inside a boot in a closet, inside a vase, a heating vent, a shoe-box and of course, the ubiquitous under-the-mattress. Then there's the old hollowed-out-book trick. During the day, it's mixed in with other books yet immediately available in an emergency. At night, you can keep it near your bed. The problem is, while some of these "hiding places" might at first glance appear inaccessible to an inquisitive child, don't you believe it! Most kids have a unique knack for finding things in the most-out-of-the-way places.

A few of my students feel comfortable storing their guns in locked night-stands during the day and taking them out at night. One drawback is the possibility of misplacing the key, unless it's always kept in the same place—hidden from everyone. Another problem is that night-stand locks are usually not all that secure and can be easily compromised by a burglar or an inventive child. As to having a loaded gun out on the night-stand, unless, you're on the run or rehearsing for a TV episode of "The Sopranos," I don't recommend it.

There are a plethora of trigger locks on the market. I don't recommend them because they can be taken off rather easily and in an emergency, you need to use your gun immediately. However, if you prefer a trigger lock, only use it on an UNLOADED gun. A trigger lock on a loaded gun is totally unsafe.

Smith & Wesson, for example, provides a Master Lock trigger lock with every gun that's sold. The keyed-lock must be placed behind the trigger so the trigger can't be pulled. The manufacturer expressly warns that the gun should not be loaded while locked. The downside is losing or misplacing the key, or worse, your child getting a hold of it.

So, what's the best way to secure a gun? In my opinion,

storing it <u>loaded</u> in a safe along with other guns, jewelry, valuables, etc. As Lyn Bates, contributing editor of *Women & Guns* magazine says, "The consequences of a poorly designed (or wrongly used) security system can have devastating consequences when the gun is loaded, including your gun may be stolen; you may not be able to get to your gun in time when you need it; you may have an unintentional discharge when locking your gun up; a child may get to the loaded gun, an intruder may get to the loaded gun or you may have difficult accessing it."

If you have only one gun, I recommend a small portable safe (also called "lockboxes," "small gun safes," "minisafes," etc.) especially designed for a gun. There are many available on the market and my favorite is the "GunVault," by GunVault, Inc., which comes in many different sizes. This battery-operated durable safe is made of 16-gauge steel housing and looks very presentable. To open, you slide your fingers among the contoured grooves, locate the correct buttons using the braille-like dots and enter your private security code.

Never use the combination that came from the manufacturer. Select a combination that is simple for you to remember and long enough so that someone won't find it by accident. Also, write it down and hide it somewhere. If your child (or an unauthorized adult) gives it a try, the built-in computer will block access after five wrong attempts.

Another feature is audio feedback as you push the combination or it can be disabled if you want to open it without anyone knowing. The lock also has a "Security Sleep Mode," which will become unresponsive after 5 minutes if someone is "playing" with the key pad. A low battery warning tells you when it's time to replace the batteries. I recommend that you get new batteries every six months. (It can also be powered externally if you don't like to use batteries.)

The safe mounts vertically or upside-down, so you can

have it under your bed for easy access without the lid popping open and the gun falling out. Also, all of the GunVaults can be fitted with an optional steel security cable, so that it can be attached to anything around your home, office, car, RV, etc. List prices range from $190 to $240.

Mossberg InstantAccess has a lighted numeric keypad on top. It has two batteries—a main 9 volt one outside the safe, and a backup 9 volt one inside the safe. Either battery will power the lock and a audible signal tells you when either is low. It can be mounted or carried around and comes with a carrying case that doesn't look like a lockbox. List price is $219 and $229 for a marbleized finish.

There are many other lockboxes including one of the first ever made, the Cannon Safe Quicksafe, as well as the PistolPal, the HANDGUN BOX and the V-Line.

When it comes to child gun safety laws, more than a dozen states have enacted Child Access Prevention Laws, (CAP), a.k.a. "safe storage" laws, that require adults to either store loaded guns in a place that is reasonably inaccessible to children, or use a device to lock the gun. If a child obtains an improperly stored, loaded gun, the adult owner is criminally liable. Some states require gun stores to provide purchasers with a written notice about the law, and to place a warning sign at the counter.

Chicago was the first city to <u>mandate</u> the use of trigger locks and the police can now go house to house and arrest

States with CAP Laws:
California
Connecticut
Delaware
Florida
Hawaii
Iowa
Maryland
Massachusetts
Minnesota
Nevada
New Jersey
North Carolina
Rhode Island
Texas
Virginia
Wisconsin

Some cities have made it a crime to leave a loaded firearm where children can access it:
Elgin and Aurora, Illinois
Houston, Texas
Baltimore, Maryland

owners who don't have them on their guns and confiscate their firearms!

Massachusetts was the first state to require that all guns sold in the state come equipped with a lock. It's unclear how the state will enforce the regulation. Will they also go house to house with search warrants? It seems that there are a number of show-boating politicians out there getting ready for the next election. Federal legislators are also looking into adopting similar requirements.

Regrettably, safety rules don't always increase safety. Take the example of "child-resistant" medicine bottle caps. Harvard University economist W. Kip Viscusi claims that these caps result each year in "3,500 <u>additional</u> poisonings of children under age 5 from (aspirin-related drugs). . .(as) consumers have been lulled into a less-safety conscious mode of behavior by the existence of safety caps."

As we discussed before in Chapter 2, guns clearly deter criminals. Polls by the *Los Angeles Times*, Gallup and Peter Hart Research Associates show that there as few as 760,000, and as many as 3.6 million, defensive uses of guns occur each year.

The defensive nature of guns is further revealed in the different rates of so-called "hot burglaries," those where a victim is at home when a burglar strikes. In Canada and Britain which both have tough very restrictive gun-control laws, almost half of all burglaries are "hot." In America, where greater gun ownership is permissible, only 13% of burglaries are "hot." Criminals don't behave differently simply by chance. U.S. felons admit in surveys that when committing crimes they are much more worried about encountering an armed victim than about the police.

In my opinion, it makes more sense to support the prosecution of those adults whose careless behavior results in an avoidable death or serious injury than to limit the rights of law abiding citizens to protect and defend them-selves against criminal invasions.

A FAMILY CODE SYSTEM

If you're planning to have a gun in your home and family members from time to time come home at night after you've gone to bed, I strongly recommend that you establish a code system so you will **never, ever** mistake your child or significant other for an intruder. Let's say that your teenager returns home at midnight. Rather than being quiet and tiptoeing in when entering, they should be instructed to awaken you and call out a code word or phrase you've agreed upon in advance. Following this simple procedure can help avoid confusion when you're awakened by footsteps or noise.

SHOOTING AND PREGNANCY: DO THEY MIX?

Over the years, I've received many calls from pregnant women asking if the sounds of gunfire can be transmitted into the uterus and hurt the fetus's hearing? Should prospective mothers take precautions against exposure to lead fumes? Also, is it safe for a pregnant woman to clean a gun?

According to obstetrician and gynecologist, Dr. Curtis Vickers, fetal ear development begins between the 8th and 10th weeks of pregnancy. He says the womb environment is cushioned against exterior influences. "Some sound waves will transmit through," he explains in *Women & Guns* magazine, (August, 1995) "It's simple physics that sound transmits best through solids, second-best through liquids. Sound's worst transmission is through air. Wherever you have an interface you lose some of that transmission. So sounds traveling through air and then hitting skin—which is considered a fluid medium—and then all the body's layers to the fetus, it's doubtful that the sound waves generated by most guns would cause any problems."

And what about lead exposure from discharged rounds? There haven't been any definitive studies on pregnancy and exposure to lead at an indoor gun range. However, many studies describe the amount of lead exposure in numerous

range settings and consequences of the amount of lead exposure to the fetus during pregnancy. We know that developing fetuses are extraordinarily sensitive to lead— more so than children and far more so than adults.

According to Dr. John M. Latz, "In children, blood lead levels as low as 10 micrograms/deciliter of blood causes damage. In adults, lead levels must reach 4—50 micrograms/deciliter to produce symptoms. Therefore, the danger is that while the adult may feel fine at a level of 10, 20 or 30 micrograms/deciliters, the developing fetus may be irreparably harmed given that children experience damage at 10 micrograms/deciliter. Remember, also, that lead does cross the placenta into the fetus's circulation and also is found in breast milk."

Does this all mean no shooting while pregnant? Dr. Latz contends that if you do shoot, adequate range ventilation is necessary and you should monitor your blood levels. He advises that you consult with your physician. My attitude about pregnancy and shooting? Why take the chance. If you want to practice, "dry-fire" (that means no bullets!) at home.

TOY GUNS

What about toy guns? Should you allow your kids to play with them? It's a matter of personal choice. When my sons were tots, I never gave them toy guns, but when they turned seven and eight, my husband, returning after a long business felt a necessity to buy them plastic rifles. I protested, but they were already playing with them.

Today, I see very obvious ill effects from kids playing with toy guns. To me, guns are tools, not toys. In my mind, a **toy gun** is an oxymoron. In today's violence-filled world, children see guns grievously misused and mishandled daily on T.V., in video games, and in far too many instances, in real life. Such exposures coupled with allowing play with toy guns just further confuses children as to guns, their function and the harm they can do. In 1997, Toys 'R' Us

took toy guns off their shelves. (Management claimed they were not selling well). As far as I'm concerned, taking toy guns off the market would be a very effective means of helping dispel the confusion. Without toy guns, whenever a kid saw a gun, they'd know it is real. And nothing to be played around with.

GUN-PROOFING YOUR CHILDREN

Having safely locked your gun away, can you now sit back secure in the knowledge that you've done everything possible to avert an accident? The answer is no. There is no way to 100% child-proof your guns, unless you also gun-proof your children. What am I talking about? And just how and when do you undertake the task?

There is certainly no possibility of a baby in a crib finding a loaded gun, so you've got maybe a year to think about it. According to the National Safety Council, the number of infants killed, accidentally or criminally (usually child abuse!) with firearms is on the order of only 10 out of nearly 40,000 such gun deaths. They don't call it the *terrible twos* for nothing, because between the ages of two and four, nothing is safe in the house from those curious little hands.

So as soon as there is comprehension, start making it clear to your youngsters that they are NEVER, EVER, NEVER to touch, handle or remain in the presence of a gun, at home or anywhere else, unless you are personally there with them. If they're at a friend's house and a gun is present, they should leave the house immediately and tell you about it when they get home.

After you're certain that message has been communicated loud and clear, as and when the child is old enough and interested, you can advance the child-proofing process by incorporating all the do's and don't's of safe and responsible gun handling as a positive parent-child bonding activity.

The ideal strategy is to show a child how your gun

operates while you're cleaning it, and then, later, to take them to a range and show them what really happens when the trigger is pulled. Once a child understands how a gun operates, has heard the sound and fury of a gunshot, up close, and witnessed the damage a gun can do, he or she will have a vastly different view of a gun along with a newfound sense of respect and caution.

At what age should children be educated about guns? There is really no hard and fast rule, but one good barometer may be evidenced in the care of the family pet. A child mature enough to responsibly handle the feeding, medication, and cleaning chores of a household pet is generally old enough to be taught how to be trustworthy with guns. Of course, there are some children (as well as some adults), who, no matter how old, are emotionally unstable and should never handle a gun.

When you believe your child is mature enough to see what really happens when a gun is shot, take them to an outdoor range or other outdoor safe area and try the following exercise, which in my opinion, graphically and dramatically gets the point across.

After making certain your child is comfortably equipped with appropriate eye and ear protection, set a cantaloupe or other melon on a box about seven yards away. Then stand back with the child and have them watch as you fire a round (preferably a hollow point, because it is more damaging) into the melon exploding it off the mark! With your child, examine the incredible destruction and locate where the bullet entered and exited. Since a melon is quite similar in size to a human head, you can easily explain the kind of damage that would occur if a person were shot with just one bullet. I cannot emphasize enough how critical this lesson is to your child's true understanding of guns. Most kids think a bullet only makes a small hole in the body, like the thousand or more they see every year on T.V. Your youngster may be frightened after this exercise, but if it takes a little fear to gain respect for a gun, it is well worth

the effort.

If and when you think your children are ready to shoot, your next step is some kind of proper instruction. You can, of course, do your own teaching. You might also consider contacting a local NRA club that offers firearms familiarization programs. Also, give them the NRA's "Eddie Eagle" training about firearms. Their message is "if you see a gun, don't touch it, leave the area immediately, tell an adult." Junior Rifle courses afford nonathletic kids an excellent way to learn the meaning of teamwork and the excitement of competition.

Your kids don't necessarily have to be target shooters in order for you to gun-proof them. What they need to know, through your own gun-safety practice and instruction, is that guns are <u>dangerous</u> and must be treated with great respect. If they learn that, your concern will not be that your child may take your gun, but that your son or daughter may be in another child's home and that an irresponsible child may take the family gun our of a drawer or a closet.

KIDS & GUN SELF DEFENSE

I also recommend that at a certain age your daughters and sons join a martial arts or kick boxing class, but they should also take a gun self-defense course. I remember one mother, Barbara, a Ketchum, Idaho mother of three daughters, took my seminar, and called me that evening saying she wanted to enroll her three daughters in my next seminar that following weekend. She said she was so excited about her new feeling of empowerment, she wanted to pass on that experience to her daughters. "My youngest is eleven," she explained, "and I especially want her to know that she has control over her body, in fact, her life, and that she can defend herself."

I'll never forget that Sunday when all three sisters were on the shooting line having the time of their lives. And guess who shot the best? The youngest who was eleven years old! She was a better marks-woman than any of the

adults. When I asked her how she felt, she said in her eleven year-old style, "this is very cool."

KIDS & COMPETITIVE SHOOTING

According to the National Shooting Sports Foundation (NSSF) spokesman Gary Mehalik, more and more kids are seeking an alternative to traditional after-school sports and turning to competitive shotgun shooting with NSSF's Scholastic Clay Target Program (ages 6-12) for an experience they claim "unmatched on any playing field." Even the Brady Campaign to Prevent Gun spokesperson Nancy Hwa says, "We don't have a problem with target shooting and sport shooting. But we do think that parents have to be very careful about the maturity level of their children, about how the guns are being handled."

Accident prevention is the top priority. No training is conducted on school grounds. Once the kids have demonstrated their "maturity and sense of responsibility," they start their competitive training at their local firing range. Competitive shooters who show outstanding marksmanship are invited to participate in NSSF's Junior Olympic Training Development Camp in Colorado Springs, CO, which provides an opportunity for young women and men to hone their skills with top Olympic shotgun coaches as well as a place to display their talents for future consideration on the U.S. team. (See Chapter 8 for more information).

Whatever decision you make in regards to having a gun at home, remember, as a responsible adult, make absolutely certain that your gun is safely secured so your children and their friends will not handle them unless you want them to. As far as your children are concerned, gun safety is <u>your</u> responsibility!

Chapter Five
WHAT GUN SHOULD I BUY?

Baton Rouge, LA, July 31, 2002 – Police in the Louisiana capital were searching for a suspected serial killer on Wednesday after DNA tests linked one man to the brutal murders of three women in the past 10 months. Local authorities warned women to take precautions, but had little information to offer them about the killer or what he looked like. Louisiana Governor Mike Foster reminded women Thursday that they can pack a gun to protect them from a serial killer. "You have the right to get a gun permit," Foster said, "Learn to use it."

First of all, you can't buy a handgun on the internet! Even on *Ebay* it's off limits. You can purchase a gun at a gun store, a gun show or from another person. But, every state has different laws regarding purchasing a gun, so learn the rules by going online to the National Rifle Association website.

If you want to buy a gun for self defense, don't purchase one until you've taken a gun safety and training course. First, you need to feel comfortable shooting a gun and most importantly, you need to know that you could shoot someone who is attacking you or a loved one. I have met a number of women who clearly said they could not shoot anyone even if he was a bad person, intending grave physical harm to them or their children. I've always replied, "then, you shouldn't own a gun."

Brandishing a gun at someone doesn't always stop him. The truth is if you point a gun at an attacker and don't intend to shoot him and you hesitate, he'll sense it and come after you. He could easily grab the gun away from you and kill you.

Once you've taken some classes, you'll begin to understand who you are in terms of your fears, personal convictions, mental readiness and physical abilities. In my Empowerment Seminars, after my introductory remarks, each woman briefly tells the class why she's there. All of them voice their concerns about crime and their personal safety

and want to know how to take care of themselves. But nearly all are scared about learning how to shoot a gun and some are nervous about having one in the house.

I remember a woman named Alana, a 32 year old spirited, high-powered advertising agency executive, who was quite candid about guns. "I don't want to be here. I don't like guns and I'm frightened of guns. My husband owns lots of guns and they're in the house and I won't touch them. He wants me to learn how to use them just in case he's not home," explained Alana. "He drove me here and literally pushed me through the door," joked Alana, laughing at herself.

Although Alana is a large-boned woman with big hands and could easily hold a .357 Magnum, she insisted that she learn on a "small gun." She was so terrified of guns that the thought of handling a large-framed gun was too scary for her. Even holding an unloaded snubbed-nosed .38 special in the classroom made her anxious. She remarked to everyone that she was sure that she would "shoot her toes off."

Alana was also worried about the gun's recoil. She called it "the kick," and heard that she could be knocked off her feet by "the kick." Like so many of my students, Alana was a real challenge to me. Frankly, while I instructed her in the classroom with my marvelous friends and assistants, Phyliss and Fred Cook, I was concerned that she wouldn't be able to do live-fire shooting on the range. She seemed so confused and had a hard time remembering how to unload the revolver. To help her, my assistant, Phyllis, took her aside and worked with her for about 15 minutes until she finally was at ease with the mechanics of holding a gun. (I'll tell you later what happened to her once she started shooting).

Her dread of the gun plus her apprehension that she couldn't control a handgun is typical of many first-time shooters. Control is a major issue for women because they believe that they won't be able to safely handle a firearm.

As a gun instructor, I have to reassure the students that they are all capable of handling and shooting a gun.

Over the last 11 years, I have taught seminars in rural, suburban and urban areas throughout the US and I continually hear women's stories of why they a fear gun, often to the point of being phobic. But, at least the women who take my all-day course have made some commitment and are open to conquering their fears.

Based on my experience, I have found it much simpler to teach beginning shooters how to shoot revolvers rather than semiautomatic (also called auto-loaders) pistols. It's not that I'm against semi-autos (I own a few and I enjoy shooting them), but they are more complicated to operate than "wheel guns." A novice shooter finds it difficult to load a magazine, especially if she has long manicured fingernails or has arthritis. Because women are usually not as strong as men, a woman often has difficulty thrusting the magazine forcefully enough into the magazine well to ensure a good seating. Often, too, she may have trouble pulling back the slide and then releasing it smoothly.

Also, it's far easier to see if a revolver is loaded or unloaded. With a pistol, to visually verify if a cartridge is in the firing chamber, you need to do a pinch-check. Again, this is not a simple task for a first-time shooter.

If the semi-auto has a de-cocking lever or a safety, learning how to manipulate it quickly and successfully is not easy for a beginner. I have frequently watched a novice shooter forget to release the safety before shooting. Her inability to recover immediately often leaves her feeling anxious that she can't control the firearm. She then believes the firearm controls her.

Furthermore, if a semi-auto malfunctions, it isn't an effortless procedure to clear the stoppage. It takes practice—a lot of practice! (I can't tell you how many times, I've practiced clearing a "double-feed" and a "stove-pipe"). A number of lightning-fast steps have to be completed in just the right order to fire a cartridge, eject the empty case, re-

cock the hammer, and chamber a new round. Also, when I've explained to a beginner that her pistol may malfunction, often, she panics, and loses confidence that she can't control the gun.

In a semiautomatic pistol class that I taught in Spokane, Washington, I heard a student cry out, "Malfunction! Is it going to blow up in my face?" "No," I said, but it wasn't easy to convince her that it wouldn't happen.

Another factor that can't be ignored is that it's simpler to clean and dismantle a revolver, and everyone should know that after you've shot your gun you need to clean it. Even though a semiautomatic will come with instructions in the manufacturer's box showing how to break down the gun, it's not easy to follow the instructions. Disassembling a semi-auto requires some dexterity and strength, especially when replacing the slide. The best way to learn is to have someone show you how to do it and then practice over and over again.

Finally, and unfortunately, many gun owners—female or male—don't target practice. They simply put their guns away in a safe, in a drawer, or underneath their pillow. And when they finally go out to practice, some people don't

---

CLEANING YOUR GUN

There are many different gun cleaners on the market, but my favorite is M-Pro 7, which is non-toxic, biodegradable and odorless. Users include the U.S. Air Force, Army, and Marine Corps, the Los Angeles County Sheriff's Department, Missouri Police Department, Canadian Military, Japanese Military, etc.

Before you clean your gun with M-Pro 7, always make sure the revolver or semi-auto is unloaded and disassembled according to manufacturers' instructions. Spray the cleaner on the entire firearm and brush with a nylon brush to remove exterior carbon deposits. Wipe down with a dry cloth (use cotton swabs for hard to reach areas) and re-oil to protect the finish.

Bore: To clean the bore, swab with a patch thoroughly soaked with gun cleaner. Wait 1-5 minutes and then run a bore brush through the full length of the barrel 2 or 3 times. Run a dry cleaning patch down the bore. Continue applying patches soaked with gun cleaner followed by dry cleaning patches until the patches are white.

remember how to safely handle a gun. At least when they own a revolver it's less complicated to load, shoot and unload it.

Couple all of the above considerations with a novice shooter's "fear factor," and it makes sense for a woman (and for that matter, a man) to learn how to shoot a revolver rather than a semi-auto. Of course, once you feel competent with a revolver, and if you want to learn how to shoot a semi-auto, you'll find that since you've gained confidence around a revolver, it will be easier to learn how to shoot a 9mm, a .45 or .40 semiautomatic.

Those who have learned on a revolver and are interested in a semiautomatic may want to try the Smith & Wesson Model 3953, a 9mm double-action-only pistol with no de-cocking lever. This is a good choice for those transitioning from a revolver to a pistol. The double-action-only function requires the trigger be pulled through the complete firing cycle, which is similar to a revolver being shot in double action.

POSTSCRIPT

You may have wondered how Alana fared in shooting that day. Well, she quickly moved up to a .357 Magnum, with a 4-inch barrel. And, she was the best and the fastest shooter in the class! At the end of the day when we returned to the classroom for graduation, Alana, who was all pumped up, announced to everyone that she lost her fear.

"I love shooting! I love the gun I used! I want to take it up as a sport! I can't wait to show my husband my target," Alana gleefully said.

The entire class broke into applause and cheered her.

Soon after, Alana and her husband decided to do competition shooting and joined an IPSC (International Practical Shooting Confederation) club, which involves shooting a number of scenarios, that use targets that are about the size of the head and upper torso of a person.

IPSC trains you to reload quickly, to run safely from one

place to another with a gun in your hand, and to shoot at targets that are moving or partially hidden.

The last I heard from Alana she was beginning to place first, beating her husband!

AMMUNITION

Ammunition manufactured in the United States is among the best in the world. For self-defense use, select ammunition produced by the most widely recognized manufacturers. These include Cor-Bon, Federal, Remington and Winchester. I don't recommend ammunition that is hand loaded, re-loaded, or of foreign manufacture for **defensive** rounds.

Ammunition is expensive, especially for the larger calibers such as a .45-caliber. So, when you're **practicing**, purchase "target loads" or reloads and have high-quality ammo in your gun when you are at home or traveling. Target loads are usually called wadcutters or semi-wadcutters. The bullet is square in front.

In the past, most ballistic experts recommended hollow-point bullets for self defense. Hollow-point bullets are hollow from the leading edge of the bullet back almost to where the brass case encloses it. The hollow-point bullet is designed to spread and more than double its size after it enters the human body. It has excellent stopping power because it wreaks such enormous damage, and is less likely to pass through your target and endanger someone else. Hollow-points tend to ricochet less than standard bullets, which minimizes the likelihood of wounding an innocent bystander who may be within range.

Bullet selection for an autoloader is much more critical than for a revolver because autoloaders are designed to use smooth, round bullets so they won't get snagged on the way to the chamber. For the autoloader, hollow-points have been designed with a metal jacket surrounding the hollow-point bullet.

Also, there's a new type of ammo called "frangible" ammunition, which is revolutionary and is available to citizens through Bismuth Cartridge, Hevi-Shot, Longbow, Precision Ammunition and PMC. It is **lead-free so it's environmentally safe** and it comes in all calibers except .22 ammo. "Frangible" means fragile, breakable and capable of fracturing into tiny fragments when it hits a surface that is harder than it is. That means there are no ricochets or back splatter. Nontheless, since it is "round-nosed," it will go through the walls of a typical home or apartment and could hit a family member or a neighbor. You can use this ammo for practice on all ranges—indoor and outside. It's expensive, but the benefit to your health, the environment and the safety of innocent people is immeasurable.

MY FAVORITE GUNS:

I've always thought of a gun as analogous to a shoe: what fits me and is comfortable for me, may not be the same for someone else. After saying this, I do have some favorite handguns that you may want to rent and shoot before deciding what to purchase.

Favorite Revolvers:

My all-around favorite revolver for home self-defense is the stainless steel Smith & Wesson Model 65, four inch barrel, chambered for the .357 Magnum, although I practice with .38 loads.

For carrying concealed, I like a Smith & Wesson Model 64 with its concealed hammer, which lessens the chances of it snagging on something.

Favorite Semi-Automatics:

My favorite 9mm semi-automatic is a P26 Sig Sauer; it has never malfunctioned on me! I also like the classic .45 caliber, 1911 light-weight Colt Commander.

For carrying concealed, I prefer a .380 Sig Sauer, Model P230. It, too, has never jammed on me.

Another 9mm semi-automatic that I like is a Beretta Cougar, Model 8000L; it's short, but not too short!

Another good semi-auto for carrying concealed is the .380 caliber Beretta Model 86FS Cheetah. The barrel can be tipped up by flipping a lever, allowing it to be immediately loaded one round at a time in an emergency and allows a user to load the pistol without having to retract the slide.

Paxton Quigley's
Photograph Section

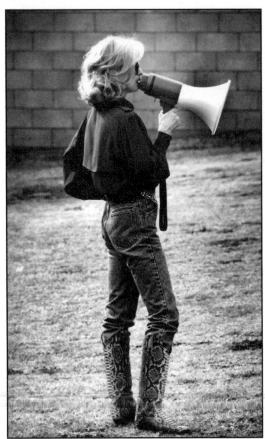

Left:
Paxton teaching at Long Beach Shooting Range (Long Beach, California.)

Below:
Students at Orange County Shooting and Training Center (Tustin, California)

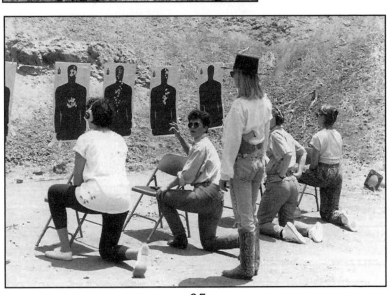

Right:
Paxton on the set of Walker Texas Ranger with Chuck Norris

Bottom:
At a Smith & Wesson event at Sports Unlimited (Louisville, Kentucky)

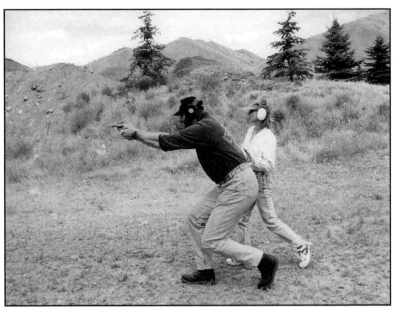

Top:
Paxton teaching a student (Ketchum, Idaho)

Left:
Photo Flier for Paxton's Seminar (Tucson, Arizona)

You Are Invited To Attend A Woman's Seminar

Women's Empowerment In The 90's

Presented By
PAXTON QUIGLEY

"Twelve million women are gun owners, and they're joining a guru named Paxton Quigley. Her message is being heard."
Tom Brokaw, "NBC Nightly News"

Paxton Quigley (Left) is the author of ARMED & FEMALE and NOT AN EASY TARGET. She has taught thousands of women personal safety strategies. She has appeared on more than 300 radio & t.v. shows and has been widely quoted in major newspapers and women's magazines, including THE WALL STREET JOURNAL, GLAMOUR MAGAZINE, TODAY SHOW and 60 MINUTES.

THE PERSONAL SAFETY & AWARENESS STRATEGIES SEMINAR WILL TEACH YOU:

Awareness Techniques: Most Attacks Can Be Avoided.
Psychological Profiles of Attackers: Who Do They Look For? Are You A Target?
How To Avoid: Follow-Homes, Street Robberies, Car Hi-Jackings, and Other Daylight Attacks.
Security Tips In The Home, Verbal & Physical Self-Defense, Non-Lethal Sprays & Other Self-Defense Weapons.
Handguns: Gun Safe Handling, Rules & Laws, Legal, Moral & Ethical Responsibilities.
Overcoming Women's Culturally Conditioned Fear Of Guns.
Shooting Proficiency: Classroom Training & Range Target Exercise, Including: Prone Shooting,
Point Shooting, One-Handed Shooting & Moving & Shooting.

JENSEN'S, 5146 Pima, Tucson

BEGINNER SEMINAR: SUNDAY, OCTOBER, 19TH, 10-4pm

SEMINAR TUITION: $150 RANGE FEE (paid that day): $24

For Information & Reservations: Diane, 520-325-3346

Make checks For $150 Payable To: Paxton Quigley Enterprises, Inc.

Top:
Paxton teaching students how to yell in Atlanta, Georgia.
Bottom:
Shooting from a prone position, Long Beach Firing Range,
Long beach, California.

Top:
Paxton teaching students at LAX Firing Range in Los Angeles, California.

Bottom:
Paxton teaching a student how to clean a gun.

CHAPTER SIX
YOU AND YOUR GUN

"If someone comes to kill you, arise quickly and <u>kill</u> him."
- The Talmud, Tractate Sanhedrin. 1994. The Schottenstein Edition. New York: Mesorah Publications. Vol. 2, 72a.

One of the most common questions I'm asked is "what gun do I recommend for a woman?" Unfortunately, there's no easy answer. Often, finding the right gun for yourself takes trial and error and you probably should rent (by the way, renting is not an option in New York) many different models at gun ranges before purchasing one. I always explain that a gun is like a shoe; what's "comfortable" for me may not be "comfortable" for you. A comfortable gun is one that fits your hand and you can shoot it as accurately as possible. Also, knowing how to clean it and fix the gun, if it malfunctions is part of your comfort level. You should never fear your gun. It should become one of your best friends in case you need it for self-protection. Additionally, if you like to sport-shoot and you're single, you've got a built-in hobby where you could meet your soul-mate—remember girls, a lot of guys—doctors, lawyers, teachers, professionals, businessmen, you name it—enjoy going to the shooting range.

And as I said before, probably the most important issue is could you shoot your attacker? I've spoken to a number of women who have told me that even if their lives were in danger, they could not shoot anyone. My reply to them is simple: don't think of it as shooting the assailant, but rather **stopping** him from inflicting harm against you. It is not to kill or wound him.

THE PSYCHOLOGY OF STOPPING YOUR ATTACKER OR ATTACKERS

To survive on the street or in your home, you want to prevent a potential aggressor from assaulting you or get him

to stop the attack. For some people to get to that step is difficult either for religious reasons, political affiliation, psychological upbringing, media information, or a combination of all of them. It also means getting over "the fear factor."

A number of self defense experts have written magazine articles about being psychologically prepared to stop an attacker. A common recommendation is getting training so that you can be psychologically ready to achieve that "Stopping" state of mind. And it turns out, **trained** individuals are far more successful in an actual self defense experience than those who are untrained. Prepared people usually survive.

While reviewing the book, *True Stories of Americans Defending Their Lives With Firearms,* Paul Markel, in *Combat Handguns,* (September 2003), observes that "throughout the ("book") we see that those persons with prior training and experience fared far better and received little or no injury compared to the defender who merely owned a gun."

I have attended the following courses and highly recommend them:

The American Pistol Institute, Jeff Cooper, Paulden, Arizona; Chapman Academy of Practical Shooting, Ray Chapman, Hallsville, Missouri; Lethal Force Institute, Masaad Ayoob, Concord New Hampshire; Defensive Training , Inc., John and Vicky Farnam, Niwot, Colorado; Smith & Wesson Academy, Springfield, Mass. and Executive Security International, Bob Duggan, Rifle, Colorado. (I have also taken courses from Mike Dalton and Mickey Fowler, American Shootist Institute, California, when they worked together and additionally attended the short-lived but terrific, G. Gordon Liddy Academy, G. Gordon Liddy). Although non-gun oriented, I strongly recommend IMPACT, which has the reputation of quickly ridding oneself of the "the fear factor," and has training centers throughout the country. (Classes are for women, children and men).

RESISTING AN ATTACKER

Data from the 1979-1985 installments of the Justice Department's Annual National Crime Victim Survey show that when a woman resists a stranger rape with a gun, the probability of completion was 0.1 percent and of victim injury 0.0 percent, compared to 31 percent and 40 percent, respectively, for all stranger rapes (Kleck, *Social Problems*, 1990).

A paper (Southwick, *Journal of Criminal Justice*, 2000) analyzed victim resistance to violent crimes generally, with robbery, aggravated assault and rape considered together. Women who resisted with a gun were 2.5 times more likely to escape without injury than those who did not resist and 4 times more likely to escape uninjured than those who resisted with any means other than a gun. Similarly, their property losses in a robbery were reduced more than six-fold and almost three-fold, respectively, compared to the other categories of resistance strategy.

Two studies in the last 20 years directly address the outcomes of women who resist attempted rape with a weapon. (Lizotte, *Journal of Quantitative Criminology*, 1986; Kleck, Social Problems, 1990.) The former concludes, "Further, women who resist rape with a gun or knife dramatically decrease their probability of completion." (Lizotte did not analyze victim injuries apart from the rape itself.) The latter concludes that "resistance with a gun or knife is the most effective form of resistance for preventing completion of a rape"; this is accomplished

DOES YOUR GUN FIT YOUR HAND?

Although most of us learn how to shoot a handgun with two hands, in a gun battle hands and arms usually take the first hits. This could leave you with only one hand to shoot your gun, so when selecting your gun, practice shooting it with your dominant hand, as well as your weaker one. Many of the gun manufacturers, such as Smith & Wesson and Beretta are now making guns fit the human hand.

As I mentioned in *Armed & Female*, "The difficulty in selecting a suitable handgun comes in deciding first upon either an autoloader or a revolver, then upon a caliber that will suit your needs, then upon a size of handgun, than upon a grip or stock that can be gripped comfortably and will allow your <u>trigger finger to touch the trigger at the proper place.</u> Fitting these four requirements into one gun is quite a job. *If your gun does not fit you in any of these*

*areas, you will not shoot it well, and that is nearly the same
as not having a gun at all."*

Remember, that the longer the barrel, the more accurate the gun will be over seven yards (although most self-
defense actions occur within seven yards), and the heavier
the gun will be. A heavy handgun is only a detriment if you
plan to conceal it in a purse, fanny pack, holster, or will be
carrying it in the car.

Also, If you have a tough time reacting to a gun's recoil,
find another gun that you can manage. I remember my
first revolver, a snub-nosed five-shot revolver, with a recoil
that left the "webbing" between my left thumb and second
finger (yes, I'm a southpaw!) a bloody, painful mess that
needed iodine and a big band-aid. It didn't take me long
to sell that gun! One of the best ways to familiarize yourself
with your gun is to dry-fire it, although you won't feel the
recoil.

When you first learn to shoot or if you only get to the
range twice a year, I suggest to my students that they spend
at least one half hour a day for two weeks just handling the
unloaded gun. Again, make sure that your gun is unloaded
each time you pick it up. In *Armed & Female,* I recommend that while you are watching television, get to know
your gun. "Aim at the TV or at lamps around the room and
pull the trigger; pull the slide back and lock it back, if your
gun has that feature, then unlock it and slide it forward
again—slowly. Never let the slide snap and always let it
snap forcefully forward... Switch hands, aim using your
sites and fire at the television. Handle your gun as much as
you can for the first few days, until it feels like part of your
hand and at least one spot on your hand is sore from the
unaccustomed contract with the strange piece of metal."

If you plan to legally carry your weapon in a purse,
fannypack, holster, etc., first spend time carrying it unloaded in your home, so that you can get the "feel" of the
gun. Then at home, practice drawing the unloaded gun
from its concealment. As Jeff Cooper, the legendary gun

instructor, said to me while I attended his class, "In a gun battle, who ever shoots first has the best chance of winning the fight." Knowing this, drawing the weapon quickly becomes paramount and is often overlooked by the practicing novice shooter.

Also, I recommend that you take a class in handgun retention. As Duane Thomas succinctly explains in *Handguns For Sport & Defense* magazine (October 1992, page 43), "...When you face a violent criminal across your gun's sights, whether he has his own handgun or not, there's always one gun present with which he can kill you if he can get his hands on it—your own!"

Since 1991, Massad Ayoob of the Lethal Force Institute (1-800-624-9049) has been presenting weapon retention training to his entry-level students. (By the way, I highly recommend Ayoob's entertaining, yet serious handgun courses). Another gun self defense school, the Firearms Academy of Seattle (1-800-327-2666), is the only other school in the country that teaches a highly effective weapon retention class to civilians based on the Lindell Method, which was developed in 1975 by James Lindell, an instructor in Defensive Tactics for the Kansas City Regional Police Academy. Many of his maneuvers are based on his background in judo and other martial arts.

WHEN PRACTICING WITH A CARDBOARD SILHOUETTE, WHERE DO YOU SHOOT?

In most beginner classes, you will learn to shoot to the center of mass. In intermediate and expert levels, you will be shooting both to the torso and to the face.

Why to the face? Recently, more "bad guys" are wearing body armor and the only way to stop them is to shoot their face, since the torso is safely covered. It is certainly difficult to shoot to the face because when we think of a face, we can think of it in a spiritual way as well as a physical way. As part of your survival skills, practice and become confident in the head shot for that just in case situation.

SHOULD YOU CARRY A CONCEALED WEAPON?

"I must not fear. Fear is the mind-killer. Fear is the little-death that brings total obliteration. I will face my fear. I will permit it to pass over me and through me. And when it has gone past I will turn the inner eye to see its path. Where the fear has gone there will be nothing. Only I will remain."
- excerpt from "Dune," by Frank Herbert, 1965.

Brenda Barnett, 47, who lives in Hailey, Idaho, a town adjacent to the world famous ski resort, Sun Valley, commutes to Boise for business at least once a week. The three hour trip, mostly on a two-lane highway is almost deserted certain times of the year and is usually a dull drive except Brenda livens it up by listening to "Books on Tape." Halfway through a trip one grey October morning, Brenda looked up at the rear view mirror and saw a fast approaching red pickup truck. As it drew closer to her, she noticed two young men in the vehicle. Thinking nothing of it, she slowed down so the truck could pass her.

"As the truck came alongside me, the guy in the passenger side made some lewd gestures at me, and all of a sudden, the truck bumped the side of my car," Brenda recalled. "I started going faster, but the truck hit me again and I realized they were trying to force me off the road. No one was on the highway and I was scared."

But not scared enough. Brenda picked up her .357 four-inch barrel Taurus which she always keeps on the passenger seat and held it up in the air. "Those guys took one look at that big gun," Brenda laughed, "and they were off like greased lightning."

Brenda has a license to carry a concealed weapon in the state of Idaho and even though the crime rate in Idaho is low compared to other states, she always has her gun in her car or concealed in a purse, ready if something potentially

dangerous befalls her.

To many people's surprise, numerous American women not only own their own guns but also legally carry them. For example, in Arizona, out of 67,000 people who legally carry handguns, 6,200 of them are women. Of course, a woman (or a man) should be trained in carrying a gun and shooting from the origin of concealment whether it's a fanny pack, purse, briefcase, jacket pocket, etc.

Antigun critics state that women get a false sense of security when they carry a gun. I disagree; when i have carried a gun I have felt more in control of my surroundings and certainly far safer. I have spoken to countless women, who legally carry concealed guns and echo my feelings. I rarely find that women who carry are fearful about their safety, unless, of course, they are being stalked. I urge women who keep a gun at home to also think about legally carrying one, especially when they're out alone, either walking, riding public transportations or in a car. Regrettably, I've met a number of people, who would not have been raped if they were carrying a gun. But fortunately, I know women who saved themselves because they defended themselves with a gun.

Carrying a concealed weapon is a big responsibility. I do not recommend it for everyone. First, you need to decide how you will conceal your gun so that others don't know you're carrying it and get "freaked out" if they happen to see your Glock or Smith & Wesson peaking out of your jacket pocket. Gun stores sell a number of different purses, fanny packs and even briefcases. Another alternative is to holster your gun and one of the best holsters is a "pancake" holster, which is looped through your belt and "sits" in the small of your back. Try out the various alternatives in the store for functionality as well as fashion design, and you may want to purchase a variety of concealing modes depending on when and where you will be carrying a concealed weapon.

One of the most common questions asked in my classes

is whether the gun should be loaded or unloaded when carrying. A defense gun must be ready to be fired at any moment and therefore it must be loaded when carrying it. If you use a semiautomatic, there should be a round in the chamber.

As Lyn Bates, contributing editor of *Women & Guns* magazine explains, "You can't count on having enough time, in an emergency, to safely draw, then safely rack the slide to chamber a round, then aim and fire if necessary. Modern revolvers are safe to carry fully loaded; if yours is so that that its only safe condition is hammer down on an empty chamber, it is time to get a new carry gun."

In all situations, gun safety is paramount:

1) Keep the gun pointed in a safe direction. Be particularly vigilant when taking out your gun and putting it in its concealed mode;

2) Be aware of all situations. There may be a time that if you're attacked or feel that your life is in jeopardy that you may not be able to shoot in self-defense because you could injure or kill innocent bystanders;

3) In a self defense situation, always keep your finger off the trigger while you bring the gun up and aim it, unless you need to shoot immediately. In some situations, you may need to draw your weapon as a deterrent, but won't need to shoot it;

4) If you're in a gun fight and if you have the opportunity, take cover. Most tactical gun experts contend that if a crime victim takes cover as soon as possible in the face of gunfire, she will survive at an exponential rate. Cover can conceal you and potentially stop a bullet from hitting you. A bush, for example, is not cover, but it can be concealment.

5) Use judgment; Lyn Bates, says that people always ask, "will I be making the right decision?" Bates explains, "Just the fact that you formulate that question, and worry about it, shows that you are a responsible person who is concerned about doing the right thing."

If you're planning on carrying a concealed weapon, you need advanced instruction oriented toward defensive training. I teach an advanced class where you learn how to draw from concealment safely and quickly. It also includes exercises in taking cover so that you are as little exposed as possible in an outdoor gunfight situation. After taking advanced instruction, do continue to practice on an outdoor range going through various scenarios that you've been taught so that you can keep your muscle memory. You can also do the same at home without loading your gun. Always make sure prior to practicing at home that your gun is unloaded. Remember that one of the most important safety rules is never assume a gun is unloaded. Always think it's loaded. Again, before handling a gun, check to see that it is unloaded.

Every state, as well as local jurisdictions within each state, has specific gun laws. Know your state's gun laws. Although there are 38 states that have "shall issue laws," each area has different regulations for carrying a concealed weapon. "Shall issue" statutes require licensing authorities to issue CCW licenses to citizens if they meet specific requirements: background checks, fingerprinting;

Armed & Famous in New York

As of 2003, among the more than 3,600 privileged New Yorkers allowed to legally carry a loaded weapon are actors Robert De Niro and Harvey Keitel, shock-jocks Howard Stern and Don Imus, developer Donald Trump, record executive Tommy Mottola and Channel 5 TV anchor John Roland. Also on the list are ex-Seagrams CEO Edgar M. Bronfman, defense lawyer Barry Slotnick, state Senate Majority Leader Joseph Bruno, Daily News co-publisher Fred Drasner, Manhattan Judge Leslie Crocker Snyder, Arkansas Lt. Gov. Winthrop P. Rockefeller and Assistant state Attorney General Steven Pagones. Ex-top cop Howard Safir and Simon & Schuster publishing czar and author Michael Korda have gun licenses, but they can't legally carry them since they don't have "carry" permits. Their "premise" permit allows them to keep a gun in their homes and demands that when they travel with their weapons, the guns must be unloaded and locked in a safety box, with the ammunition kept separate.   Source: Levine Breaking News

clean mental health and criminal records, and in a number of states, mandatory training requirements, which may include passing a proficiency test.

By law, there are places where you can't carry a gun. In Texas, for example, a concealed handgun can't be carried into a school, college, hospital, nursing home, church, court, racetrack, sporting event, polling place, or amusement park. Also, some businesses, local government buildings and public transit authorities may display signs barring the carrying of guns. Employers may also stop their employees from carrying a gun while working and some businesses actually have locked individual storage lockers to secure a gun.

There are some states which have "discretionary" licensing, which means a state can deny an individual on arbitrary grounds usually requiring proof of need. New York state, which has "discretionary licensing," varies from jurisdiction to jurisdiction in its licensing requirements, processing time and "need" requirement. New York City is the worst city in terms of law-abiding citizens getting a CCW permit, let alone having a gun in the house!

Fortunately, some states are changing their laws. Recently, Colorado was a discretionary licensing state until its legislature passed "Shall Issue" in March, 2003.

If you don't want to carry your gun in a purse, fanny pack or holster, but want your gun to be handy, it's legal to keep it in the car in some states. Common places to conceal a weapon are in the glove box, but it's not that accessible, in the console between the front seats or under the driver's seat. Another favorite place is on the passenger seat under a jacket or newspaper, but if you stop suddenly the gun can slide off the seat onto the floor making it difficult to retrieve it, if needed. Once you leave the car and you're not taking your gun with you, make sure it's in a secure place and your car windows are shut and the doors are locked!

A few states have reciprocity with other states. If you're lucky and live in South Dakota, for example, the state has agreements with Alaska, Florida (including non-resident permits), Georgia, Indiana, Kentucky, Michigan, Montana, North Dakota, Utah, Missouri, Ohio, (limited to 60 consecutive days) and Wyoming.

Many times a woman, who legally carries a gun can help a loved one and thwart an attack. In September, 2002, in Dallas, Texas, the following story almost seems like it was a scene from a movie. Dr. David Avery and his wife, Patricia, were returning home one afternoon. As Avery backed his GMC truck into his driveway, a green Honda pulled in front of him. A man wearing a mask and brandishing an AK-47 jumped from the vehicle and ordered the 70-year old man to get on the ground. Avery didn't know what would happen to him or his wife as he lay face down on his driveway.

Patricia, who always carries a .38 revolver, without being seen by the assailant, quickly got out of the car and positioned herself behind the passenger side door and squeezed off five shots. Fleeing toward the green car, the masked man returned fire, striking the couple's truck several times, and drove away. The next day, the police recovered the car with what appeared to be a bullet hole in the rear window.

Neither Avery nor Patricia was injured, but police said she might have wounded the gunman. Avery said, "If it wasn't for her being so cool-headed, we would've been in trouble. I told her she was a hero."

Traditionally, men have legally carried a concealed gun and it is only recently that more women are carrying in their purses, pockets or fanny packs. In some respects, the "concealed carry movement" is a women's issue. In fact, according to author and research director of the Independence Institute, Gary Koppel, "about a quarter of those who apply for and receive carry permits are women." When Alaska governor Walter Hickel signed concealed

carry legislation in 1993, he said that the constituents he found most compelling were "the women who called and said they worked late and had to cross dark parking lots, and why couldn't they carry a concealed gun?"

Some years ago, I taught two weekend seminars in Anchorage, Alaska, and I was astounded and delighted that the majority of the students had concealed-carry permits and were extremely comfortable toting their guns. I almost had the feeling that everyone carried! One of the women told me during the class that there's an Alaska saying, "If you're a liberal, you carry a .38 and if you're a conservative you carry a .357 magnum!"

Leading women advocates for concealed-carry laws include Texas Sate Representative Suzanna Gratia Hupp, whose parents were murdered a number of years ago in a mass killing in a restaurant in Killeen, Texas; Rebecca John Wyatt, the founder of Safety for Women and Responsible Motherhood; and Marion Hammer, the former president of the National Rifle Association and activist in the Florida concealed-carry debate. Hammer once brandished her handgun to stop a gang of assailants.

A comprehensive study by University of Chicago law professor John Lott, with graduate student David Mustard (*More Guns, Less Crime*, University of Chicago Press) examined crime data for 3,054 counties, and found that while concealed carry reform had little effect in rural counties, in urban counties, it resulted in a substantial reduction in homicide and other violent crimes such as robbery. Additionally, there was a statistically significant rise in no confrontational property crimes, such as larceny and car theft. According to the authors they hypothesized that many criminals decided that the risks of encountering a victim who could fight back had become too high!

Lott and Mustard estimated that if all states that did not have concealed carry laws in 1992 adopted such laws, **there would be approximately 1,800 fewer murders and 3,000 fewer rapes annually. Also, they said that the**

biggest beneficiaries of concealed-carry reform were women, even if they didn't carry guns. Many authorities in the gun movement think that the adoption or improvement of concealed carry laws in more than a dozen states since 1992 may be one of several causes for the decline in murder rates in the nineties.

In fact, in October, 2003, the Associated Press reported, "A sweeping federal review (Centers for Disease Control Report) of the nation's gun-control laws - including mandatory waiting periods and bans on certain weapons - found no proof such measures reduce firearm violence." The analysts also noted after their review of 51 gun laws that "firearms-related injuries" in this country have declined since 1993 despite the fact that "approximately 4.5 million new firearms are sold each year."

Numerous cases now exist about females who legally carry concealed guns and stop a crime because they were carrying at the time of the incident.

One of the best stories was reported in the Post Gazette newspaper and was written by staff writer, Lori Shontz. It occurred in Pittsburgh one early morning on October 15, 2002, when a 42 year-old woman found herself in a rather bizarre situation. Charmaine Dunbar, an off-duty security guard at the University of Pittsburgh, was walking her dog when a man approached her from behind, pointed a gun at her telling her to stand there while he shot her.

"He looked like a monster," she said. He didn't seem human."

Charmaine picked up her dog with one hand and held her other hand up in warning; she was carrying a gun, but did not reach for her it. The man said, "Stand there while I shoot you."

Charmaine's fight mechanism tore through her mind as she hysterically pleaded for her life and then started running. Somehow she hoped that she could dodge the bullets. To her surprise, her loud shouts apparently upset her assailant and he fled in the opposite direction. She yelled

out for help and someone called the police. An officer arrived, escorted her home and took a report.

After he left, as Charmaine sat on her sofa reviewing in her head what had just happened to her she began to feel good about her actions. She had survived what she thought was a close call; perhaps she had learned her wily-ness and aggression when she had taken a handgun course so that she could carry a weapon with her for her job. "I just figured, 'Why not start out again?,'" Charmaine said. "Never in my wildest dreams did I imagine that I would see that man again."

While walking, she noticed two men talking on the opposite corner. As she walked up a hill and passed them, soon after one of the men came up behind her. When he caught up with her, Charmaine looked at him and realized he was the man who had threatened to shoot her before.

As nonchalantly as possible, she calmly remarked to the man, "This hill gets to you," and the man agreed. At the top, he was so out of breath, he sat down. Charmaine felt she had a chance to get away and walked more quickly, but then she heard someone running behind her. She turned and saw the man pull a .22-caliber rifle out of his pants and point it at her.

She knew that she needed to fire before he was able to take aim, she steadied her gun and fired twice at his abdomen. He continued to lean over, apparently unaffected, and Charmaine thought, "Oh my God, my bullets didn't work."

Then he stood up, yelled, and fell over. Charmaine ran to her parents' house and returned to the scene with her father. They waited until the police came because she didn't want him to flee.

Charmaine shot a man named Daniel Wesley, 28, who had sexually attacked or tried to attack six women in the previous six weeks. In each of the attacks, the woman was approached from behind, just as Charmaine was. In three of the five incidents, the man mentioned a weapon or the

victim actually saw it. Two of the assaults ended in rape, a third in forcing the woman to perform oral sex. According to police, the attacks had steadily grown more violent since they began on September 25. Several nights that week, undercover officers staked out the 8-10 block area in which Wesley had been active, hoping to catch him.

Some detectives even pulled voluntary overtime shifts to catch the attacker.

Police said Wesley might have gotten wise to the undercover police and shifted to a different part of the city, which led to Charmaine's encounter.

The women ranging in age from 10-33 identified Wesley from photos as their attacker.

According to Police Chief Robert McNeilly, Jr., "there was no indication Charmaine was searching for her attacker and she wouldn't be charged."

Charmaine, who is married, the mother of three and the grandmother of one, said she rarely practices shooting. In the past year, she fired her gun twice, once when visiting relatives in Alabama, and a second time on Sept. 14 when she took a recertification course, as required by law.

She spent three years on active duty in the Army beginning in 1980, and learned to fire an M-16. She didn't get a permit to carry her own gun until 1997, when she took a job as a security guard. Through that agency, she worked on a government job where she was required to provide her own gun.

Ever since Charmaine has owned the handgun, she has kept it in her bedroom in case someone breaks in. She also carries it in her car when she goes out at night and in a holster on her right hip – and under her baggy clothes - when she exercises.

Although Charmaine's story never appeared on TV's *Sixty Minutes* or Fox News, she is a maverick. Charmaine stopped a predator of women.

Unfortunately, very few women, or for that matter men, carry guns. For example, in Florida in 2002, 300,603

people held valid concealed gun license holders. Most of them were in the 36-50 age range and 85 percent of the licensees were men, according to State Division of Licensing statistics. In the U.S. only 1 to 4 percent of the adult population legally carry a gun for protection.

I strongly believe that if more and more women had permits to carry a gun there would be far less crimes against women in the next following years.

My position is based on John Lott's data that clearly demonstrates that in those jurisdictions where citizens can legally carry a concealed weapon, rape significantly declines. Also, there's a remarkable story (see *Armed & Female*, pages 15-17) that occurred in Orlando, Florida in 1967, when more than 6,000 women were trained to shoot a handgun by the police department over a six month period. As a result of that training, while most other crimes escalated or remained steady, rape in Orlando fell from a 1966 level of 36 to only 4 in 1967 and stayed at that low level for a number of years, while rape increased throughout the state and the nation. Experts who analyzed the situation contend that the rape rate decreased because of the media publicity and because the women were armed and trained.

VEHICLE IDENTIFICATION ON YOUR VEHICLE

The vehicle identification number of your vehicle, which can be seen through your windshield, has now become the center of attention for crooks. If the number is copied down, and taken to either a car dealer or lock smith, a duplicate key can be made, and your car can be stolen. It is suggested that while your car is parked, to leave a piece of paper or business card over the VIN plate so it cannot be seen.

SAFETY IN YOUR HOME

In one of my gun defense seminars for women in Los Angeles, one of the students, Melanie Blankstone, a single woman, who lives alone in Beverly Hills, asked me what to do after she purchased a handgun and brought it home. Most importantly, I advised her to put the firearm in a safe place—either a portable gun safe or other kind of safe in her bedroom (since she had a large home, I suggested that she have more than one gun in her home)—and then to take the time to strategize on what she would do if an intruder entered her house. Melanie was terrified at the thought of planning for an attack, but I explained that preplanning is necessary because you will behave in an emergency only what you have been trained to do and if you haven't done anything, you may find yourself in fear and total confusion.

SETTING YOUR PRIORITIES

No material possession, whether it's an expensive computer, a flat-screen television, jewelry, or stereo equipment, etc. is valuable enough to protect with lethal force. However difficult it may be to you, let the intruder carry-off your belongings. You only want to use your gun to protect yourself or your loved ones. You own a gun to STOP a violent criminal attack. Don't assume you can intimidate an attacker by brandishing your weapon. If he sees you waiver or have reservations, he may attempt to take it away from you.

One of the most important rules of home defense is DO NOT "clear" your house, which means that if you think someone has entered your home do not go from room to room looking for the bad guy or guys.

According to John P. McFarland (*Combat Handguns* magazine, March, 2004), "Every ex-military person knows that the tactical advantage is with the defender, not the

attacker. The defender is difficult to detect because he/she is stationary and hiding behind some type of cover or concealment. The attacker is exposed and therefore subject to ambush. If you attempt to clear your house you have become the attacker and the intruder is the defender."

DETECTING AND RECTIFYING YOUR HOME'S VULNERABILITY TO INTRUDERS

First, do a walk-through in your house. Look for weak areas such as inadequately secured doors and windows. On exterior doors, check for deeply set dead-bolt locks with strike plates, plus sturdy, jimmy-proof locks on all windows, as well as secondary locks or wooden or metal dowels to block sliding glass doors and windows. Also, inspect bathroom windows, as well as garages and basements. When replacing items, don't skimp and buy inexpensive products. Remember, your dealing with your life and the lives of your family. Consider buying a home alarm system with motion detectors, but know that the alarm is a warning device and not a protection system as some security companies claim.

Self defense expert Gila Hayes, explains in the November-December, 1999 issue of *Women & Guns* magazine, "Identify hiding places that could conceal an intruder, waiting to attack when you are off guard or asleep. Remember, a motivated criminal can squeeze into small recesses you might overlook. Try to eliminate hiding areas. For example, coat closets near a front door can be blocked by stacking storage boxes in the bottom, making it difficult to stand inside."

DEVELOPING A SAFE ROOM

A few years ago when the movie *Panic Room* opened there was talk among the Hollywood *cognoscenti* regarding the installation of these rooms in their homes. Actually, the rooms are called "Safe Rooms," but to sell tickets to the movie the screenwriter made up the more exciting term "panic room."

Since 9/11, more people are concerned about home safety. According to the *Wall Street Journal* (March 14, 2003), 300,000 Americans have Safe Rooms. Elaborate Safe Rooms with ventilation systems run by generators, batteries or solar power start at $400,000 and are usually built for wealthy people who have art and jewelry worth millions of dollars or who have to deal with the threat of kidnapping and extortion. A mid-range customized Safe Room developed by Maryland builder, Zytech, costs $26,000.

But you don't have to be wealthy to have your own Safe Room to protect yourself against an intruder. Even though you may have an alarm system, one of your best home defense strategies is to make your bedroom into a Safe Room since most rapes occur at night while you're sleeping.

To do so, you need to install a solid-core door and equip it with a Medeco dead-bolt lock. Then purchase two flashlights along with extra bulbs and batteries and put them inside the room in a place where you can easily access them. Install a second phone line that is not part of the regular house phone system or keep your cell phone well charged in your bedroom. Secure your gun or guns and spare ammunition, as well as soft body armor. Finally, buy a first aid kit and a fire extinguisher.

Check if your bedroom has an escape route to the outside. Then ask yourself the following questions:

1. Can I get to a neighbor's house and ask for help?
2. Are my neighbors usually home?
3. If I need to run down an alley, is it safe?

If you live on the second floor, purchase a rope or chain ladder (I recommend Quick Escape Ladder) so you can leave through the window, and practice climbing down the ladder so you know how to do it in case of an emergency.

Now, let's go over what you need to do if an intruder enters your house, other than through your bedroom.

First, retreat to your Safe Room if not already there, dead-bolt the door, make sure your gun is loaded and call the police from your cell phone or separate phone line. Tell the operator that you have a gun and you're prepared to shoot, if necessary. Follow the dispatcher's instructions and stay on the phone until the police come. When the police arrive, **PUT YOUR GUN DOWN!** The police won't know if you're the bad gun or the good guy. To them, you're a person with a gun and they're as fearful as you are and could shoot you! Again, under no circumstances should you leave the Safe Room and look for the intruder in the house. Remember, exiting the Safe Room could put you at a disadvantage. The dangers are tremendous. Best advice: Wait for the police to arrive. You can give a verbal warning to the intruder: "Get out! We are armed (always say "we" even if you're alone)! We've called the police. You won't be hurt if you leave now!"

If you have children, everything changes. Instead of making your room into a Safe Room, it's better to make your youngest child's room into a Safe Room, because it saves time to bring everyone together in one child's room. When your children are mature enough and can understand the concept of home self- defense, you may want them to create their own Safe Rooms and establish their own escape routes. For now, however, the most important thing is to rehearse responses to various scenarios that may occur. Also, teach your baby-sitters your Safe-Room defense strategy.

If you have a large home, you may want to create a second Safe Room near your kitchen. Or if you use your den or home office frequently, make that a Safe Room, too. Remember, any room can be made into a Safe Room—even a closet. I know women who have made their bathrooms into Safe Rooms because they feel vulnerable while bathing.

If you live in a rental and can't afford to purchase a solid-core door and dead-bolt lock, you can improvise by buying a Door Jammer, which easily screws on to the bot-

tom of your door. Once installed, all you have to do is push the Door Jammer's lever down with your foot and the door can't be forced open. An intruder would have to break through it.

Also, consider installing a Safe Room in your office. I recommend that when you're staying after hours, contact the security guard so that it will be known that you're on the premises.

Unfortunately, in our dangerous times, more precautions need to be taken at home, in the office, in the car, and when you're traveling. The saying, "better safe than sorry" holds true.

YOUR HOME FLOOR PLAN

Certainly, you know the layout of your house better than anybody. You can walk through every room in the dark without tripping over

---

Full Metal Auto

Cars are becoming "Mobile Safe Rooms" for some people, especially celebrities and the wealthy. According to *Newsweek* (March 17, 2003), armored cars are becoming popular in the US since September 11th. Ford introduced the $140,000 Lincoln Town Car BPS—for Ballistic Protection Series—which can stop an AK-47 and block a grenade. GM manufactures an armored Cadillac Deville capable of deflecting bullets from a .44 Magnum. Owners of Cadillac Escalades and Hummer H2s are putting full metal jackets on their cars at prices ranging from $30,000 to $350,000 above sticker price! If you're interested in outfitting your present car, contact Secure Car World wide: www.securecarworldwide.com or 866-CAR-1481

---

furniture or knocking over lamps, unless you're a very messy housekeeper. You also know the contents of your house better than any stranger, and you are probably capable of feeling your way through the living room to where you know candles are stored should you have a power failure. But, as I mentioned before, you may be surprised to see how many places a stranger could hide, and how quickly someone could enter your house and move through it behind the cover of furniture or appliance.

It will take only a few minutes to sketch the floor plan of your residence with furniture and fixtures in places, and only

another few minutes to study the layout for places of cover where you would be able to conceal <u>yourself</u> and take aim on an intruder who was entering your place or moving through a room.

Once you have studied the floor plan for each room, note how the furniture aligns and offers concealed angles from which to shoot toward doors, windows, and hallways. Go to those rooms and crouch alongside or behind the barriers to experience first-hand the cover they offer and the angles afforded.

Select a spot in each room that provides the best vantage point for seeing all entries to the room at the farthest distance from each room. This may be difficult to determine, and you may have to move some furniture to construct such a spot. You may think this is outrageous, but without a secure, concealed point of defense you will lose the tactical advantage in your own home. And without tactical advantage, you may be forced to defend against a surprise attack from an unknown direction, so that the attacker may well overwhelm you and cause you to react with panic and recklessness. Luck becomes your weapon at that point.

FINDING COVER AND SHOOTING ANGLES

Find your vantage point in each room of your house. It must provide you with a cover and a shooting angle to every door and window in the room. It must also be a position from which, if you had to shoot, you would not risk the lives of innocent family members or neighbors behind where your target would be moving. As you study and adjust the layout of your rooms, you have the advantage of preplanning the direction in which you might have to shoot. Find a spot for the living-room couch or reading chair such that, when you hide behind it, you will have a view of entrances to the room and angles to shoot from that will not permit a stray bullet to penetrate a wall into a bedroom or family room or possibly go through a window headed

directly for your neighbor's kitchen door. If you cannot find a spot from which every shooting angle would be safe, you must <u>absolutely</u> load your handgun with ammunition which will not penetrate walls.

THINK COVER

According to Paul Markel (*Combat Handguns* magazine, November, 2003), "I was always taught to always 'think cover'. Be 'cover conscious' was the phrase....The question is, what should you do en route to this cover or what if cover is not immediately accessible? Many firearms instructors require their pupils to 'break the plane' after firing only one or two shots. To break the plane the shooters must either move laterally left or right, or they must drop down to a crouch or to a knee. Breaking the plane changes the target picture the bad guy is engaging. Hopefully, this will give you that split second advantage to neutralize the threat. Moving laterally not only takes you out of harm's way for a moment it also allows you to move toward cover."

Practicing lateral movement is not easy since you should do it on an outdoor range with the assistance of an instructor or a friend, who is a shooter. I did lateral movement training at a number of gun training courses, including John Farnam's and Ray Chapman's courses and the Gun Sight school. It's actually fun to do and you come to realize how agile you can be in an emergency situation. Once you've mastered the drill, you can do it at home with an **unloaded gun that you have checked at least twice.** Markel recommends using a solid backdrop, such as a full bookcase for practice.

TACTICAL ADVANTAGE IN YOUR BEDROOM

Locating a position of tactical advantage in your bedroom (and most likely, your Safe Room) is a little more difficult and a lot more critical. More critical because bedrooms are usually arranged in one section of a house,

so the shooting angles from within your bedroom can easily lead to penetration of your children's bedrooms. And more difficult because in a bedroom there is usually a minimum of furniture from which to find concealment.

In most bedrooms the bed will be used for a shooting barricade, and must therefore be positioned in the room to give the tactical advantage from a crouch that will provide concealment from shooting angles to all the doors and windows in the room. And that position of the bed must be such that a shot toward the bedroom doors or windows will not have as a background the walls or doors of other, occupied bedrooms. It may take some research and rearranging, but if you have children or family members in the house you must be absolutely sure that your tactical positions within your residence will not compromise the safety of anyone.

REHEARSE YOUR TACTICS

After you have scrutinized your floor plans and gone into each room to establish your vantage points, take a few more minutes to rehearse getting into position in each room at night, with no light coming except through the windows. You will only have to do this rehearsal once, so make it good. In fact, you may want to run through your home tactics one night with your **unloaded gun** in hand, so you can really see the angles and learn the positions.

Again, you will do in an emergency only what you have been trained to do. Think of this practice as training; take it seriously. The object is to learn tactics, eliminate confusion and reverse the surprise advantage your opponent has. Do it once under simulated conditions and you will not forget it should the time come to defend yourself in your home.

TEAMING UP WITH YOUR SIGNIFICANT OTHER OR HOUSEMATE(S) FOR HOME SELF DEFENSE

I have been describing self defense tactics with the idea that you are alone and defending yourself. What about if

you're partnered or have a roommate? A mistaken identity shooting can occur, so preplanning and coordination is important. What is their role in an overall home defense strategy? Obviously, two people are better than one; two individuals working together as a team is a far more effective opponent.

According to officer Bob Campbell, "Efficiency is not doubled, it goes up exponentially. A second set of eyes and hands is a great aid in a critical incident." In *Women & Guns* magazine, (September-October, 2002), Campbell explains, "There is more than a tactical advantage in having a reliable, effective partner. The mental component is important. Your gear is subject to failure, but not you partner. A partner is like the duality of backup guns. The synergistic effect of a teammate's presence can defuse a critical incident before it 'breaks bad.' "

If you and your partner team-up, my best advice is to find a qualified instructor, who excels in reality-based training that includes tactics, support and coordination. Total familiarity of your gun is crucial. Furthermore, if each of you own different gun models, you both should be proficient with each other's firearms. Since most self defense situations occur in close proximity averaging about seven feet, the teamwork needs to be practiced within those parameters. As Campbell remarks, "two people training is not standing on the line shooting together."

It certainly is an enormous commitment for both of you to engage in team self defense, but if you're serious about each other's safety, you'll be introduced to a field that previously was only available to SWAT teams and other law enforcement groups. And, it can be downright fun!

Although home defense planning does take time and, it is a procedure that you will not regret if an intruder enters your home.

CHAPTER NINE
SPORT SHOOTING AND HUNTING

SPORT SHOOTING

I don't want to ignore other aspects of gun shooting, which include various sports shooting activities. These group activities can provide you with a new social group and if you're single, there's a good chance you could meet a new "significant other."

Competitive Pistol Shooting

Whether they're shooters or not, most women don't know about the sport of competitive pistol shooting, which was started by the U.S. Congress when it established the National Board for the Promotion of Rifle Practice (NBPRP) in 1903. The organization added pistol matches the following year. In 1936, the NRA conducted its first National Championships and is the governing body for precision pistol shooting in the U.S.

Hundreds of matches are held throughout the country and one of the best ways to get started is to attend a match to see if this sport is right for you. (The "Coming Events" section of *Shooting Sports USA* magazine lists all upcoming NRA-sanctioned tournaments). Also, if there is a shooting club in your area make arrangements to go to one of its practice sessions.

A standard course of fire for pistol competition is a "3-gun aggregate." This is fired with .22 caliber rimfire, an unspecified caliber centerfire, and .45 caliber handgun. But, a competitor doesn't need to own three different guns. In most tournaments, people enter and fire only one of more stages of the aggregate. Many competitors entering the complete aggregate bring only .22 and .45 caliber handguns since the .45 caliber may be used for the center-fire stage.

You don't need a lot of expensive equipment to get started in competitive pistol shooting. A .22 caliber-rimfire handgun

(either an autoloader of a revolver) and eye and ear protection is all you need. A 20X to 30X spotting scope is helpful to you so you can see your shots on the target to make sight corrections.

Match grade ammo is available at gun stores, but costs more than standard loads. Many serious competitors handload their own ammunition (excluding .22 rimfire), since the loads can be "customized" for a particular gun.

Another type of competitive handgun shooting is Defensive Pistol Shooting (10,000 members worldwide), which simulates "real world" self defense scenarios that typically require shots from 3 - 20 yards and often requires the shooter to change firing points and shoot from awkward positions. Defensive Pistol matches offer diversity and truly test both accuracy and speed. During my initial training, I competed in a few of these events and really enjoyed the challenge of playing "cops and robbers."

Shooters competing in Defensive Pistol events or Tactical matches are required to use practical autoloaders or revolvers, such as a Beretta, Glock, Sig Sauer or Smith & Wesson, (.9mm/.38 Special or larger caliber) and holsters or fanny packs that are suitable for self-defense use. Practical concealed carry type holsters are necessary. No "competition only" equipment is allowed since the goal is test the skill and ability of an individual, not her equipment or gamesmanship. Defensive Pistol competition is divided into four divisions so all popular pistols and revolvers have a place to compete competitively.

Even people with disabilities have the opportunity to compete. In 1997, the NRA started the National Rifle Association-Beeman Grand Prix Championship, a 12 city championship tour that has been especially attractive to female and minority participants of all ages.

Every event is conducted at a different location (hotel ballrooms, high school gymnasiums, sporting goods stores, rehabilitation hospitals and at a sportsmen's show with over 23,000 spectators) with widely varying range conditions.

Actually, the biggest problem shooters face is traveling to and from the events, especially if they're in wheelchairs. Winning an event title is an incredible feat on many levels. For information, contact the National Rifle Association.

Competitive Shooting For Kids

You may have thought that gun competitions for kids didn't exist, but on the contrary, there are numerous junior competitions throughout the U.S., culminating in the National High Junior Pistol Matches (there are also rifle competitions). And perhaps even more surprising is that in 2001, 2002 and 2003 a female high school student, Teresa Meyer, came in first place beating out the boys! Based on her accomplishments, Teresa was invited to the Olympic Training Center in Denver by the assistant coach for further training and a possible position on the USA Team. What does she offer for other young shooters, especially female juniors? "Try it! Stick with it. It's fun." (Women & Guns, January-February, 2004)

Shooting is excellent training for young people: It's very personal, it challenges the individual and tests personal motivation. Also, shooting hones the senses, sharpens the eye, and focuses concentration, which is often lacking in kids. For more information on competitive shooting for young people, contact your state NRA or the national office in Fairfax, Virginia.

If you're unsure about your children using live fire, consider airgun competition. Since 1965, the Daisy Corporation and the U.S. Jaycees have cosponsored a program that begins with shooting events in local hometowns and ends with an international event. More than 2,000 Jaycee chapters (250,000 kids) throughout the country conduct supervised classes to teach girls and boys ages 10-14 proper gun handling and marksmanship. Kids can go on to compete in state and regional competitions and then those winners compete at the International BB Gun Championship Match, the oldest and largest continuous airgun com-

petition in the world.

Hunting

Although hunting is not a self-defense issue, more and more women are taking up hunting . According to the National Sporting Goods Association (2001), of the 19.2 million active hunters in the United States, 13% or 2.4 million are female. (Hunters were defined by the NSGA through a nationwide survey of persons 7 years old and older who had participated more than once in the past year).

I was given the opportunity to hunt wild boar in Central California, but I never took up the challenge. Was I afraid? Well, frankly I was. People had whispered in my ear that wild boars were extremely aggressive and I better know how to shoot fast and well. That stopped me.

Do I plan to hunt in the future? Yes, I definitely want to try it. But, first I need to practice shooting a rifle and a shot gun. Since I've spent years shooting a handgun and teaching handgun proficiency, I've never made the time to practice long gun shooting. I've shot skeet and trap at various NRA events years ago, but unfortunately, I never mastered either sport.

In general, a majority of women abhor the idea of hunting and get into the "Bambi Syndrome" when they think of hunting deer. Many women don't know that all across the nation, whitetail deer numbers have skyrocketed. Five hundred years ago, the deer population was kept in check by predators — wolves, cougars, bobcats, bears, coyotes, and Indians. But since large scale development and the restraints on hunting, coupled with the decline of natural predators, the national whitetail herd now exceeds 30 million!

According to James Swan, author of *In Defense of Hunting*, "Mushrooming herds are becoming a wildlife-management nightmare. Lyme disease, carried by deer-borne ticks, has been reported in 43 states. Deer can also carry tuberculosis, as well as chronic-wasting disease, the myste-

rious brain-eating illness that belongs to the same family of illnesses as mad-cow disease and Creutzfield-Jacob disease.

"Insurance companies report over 500,000 deer-car collisions annually, resulting in about a hundred human deaths. (Let us not forget that more people are hurt and killed by deer than by any other species of North American wild game.) Several studies place the total number of deer hit by cars at four to six times the number reported. The average insurance claim for a deer-car collision is $2,000. Deer damage to agriculture crops and landscaping costs more than $1 billion a year."

Swan says that hunting is the most economical and effective way to limit the size of herds and control the problems that their explosive growth has caused. Many anti-hunters don't know that most hunters believe it is wrong to kill game that will not be eaten. To waste a game animal like a deer is a sin to them. At the same time, we need to shoot more deer, but what to do with all the venison?

There's a terrific solution that is being implemented, which shouldn't anger anyone who is anti-hunting. Several organizations have been channeling surplus venison and other game meat to the needy. The USDA estimates that in 2,000, 33 million people (22% of all children were living in poverty) didn't have enough food to meet their basic daily needs. One nation-wide Christian faith-based group, Farmers and Hunters Feeding the Hungry, has coordinated and paid for the processing and distribution of over 1,400 tons (12 million servings) of venison for the last seven years. Hunters for the Hungry is another group of venison-donation charters across the U.S. It has collected and donated over 1.5 million pounds of venison since 1991. Safari Club International's Sportsmen Against Hunger focuses on both national and international big-game hunting and estimates that its wild-game meat and other donations help feed some 230 million people a year.

If you've considered taking up hunting, all 50 states

require people to take a hunter-education course to get a hunting license. As Swan says, "(You'll) nourish you soul, (and) be able to continue a very old tradition of sharing wild game with those who need it."

BIBLIOGRAPHY & RESOURCES

Atwood, Margaret, *The Handmaid's Tale*, Random House, 1986

Ayoob, Masad, *In The Gravest Extreme*, Police Bookshelf, 2001

Bates, Lyn, "Murder and the Reasonable Woman," Women & Guns, March-April, 2004: 12-57

Baty, Kathleen, *A Girl's Gotta Do What A Girl's Gotta Do*, Rodale, 2003

Chapman Academy of Practical Shooting, 4350 Academy Rd., Hallsville, MO., 65255, 800-847-0588

Citizens Committee for the Right To Keep and Bear Arms, Liberty Park, 12500 N.E. Tenth Place, Bellevue, WA., 98005, 800-486-6963

Combat Handguns, Harris Publications, 1115 Broadway, NY, NY, 10010

Executive Security International, Gun Barrel Square, 2128 Railroad Ave., Dept. Web, Rifle, CO., 01630, 888-718-3105

Gottlieb, Alan, *The Gun Rights Fact Book*, Merril Press, 1989

Gun Owners of America, 8001 Forbes Place, #102, Springfield, VA, 22151, 703-321-8585

Gun Sight Academy, 2900 W. Gunsite Rd., Paulden, AZ, 86334, 928-636-4565

Gun World, 265 S. Aviation Drive, Orange, CA., 92868

Hayes, Gila, *Effective Defense*, 2nd Printing, The Firearms Academy of Seattle, 2004

Jews for the Preservation of Firearms Ownership, P.O. Box 270143, Hartford, WI, 53027, 262-673-9745

Hoff, Linda, "All in the Name of Hunting," Woman's Outlook, October 2003: 30-66

Impact & Prepare, 800-345-5425

Kasper, Shirl, *Annie Oakley*, Oklahoma Press, 1992

Kates, Don, Polsby, Dan, "Of Genocide and Disarmament,"
    Journal of Criminal Law and Criminology 86, (Fall
    1995): 247-256

Kelly, Caitlin, *Blown Away: American Women and Guns*, Pocket
    Books, 2004

Kleck, Gary, Kates, Don B., *Armed: New Perspectives on Gun
    Control*, Prometheus Books, 2001

Kopel, David B. *The Samurai, the Mountie, and the Cowboy*,
    Prometheus Books, 1992

Korwin, Alan, *Gun Laws of America*, Bloomfield Hills Press,
    2003 Lethal Force Institute, P.O. Box 122, Concord, NH.,
    03302, 800-624-9049

Lott, John R., Jr., *The Bias Against Guns: Why Almost Everything
    You've Heard About Gun Control Is Wrong*, Regnery,
    2003

Lott, John R., Jr., *More Guns Less Crimes: Understanding Crime
    and Gun Control Laws*, University of Chicago Press, 2000

MacNutt, Karen, L. "Bare Arms," Women & Guns, March-April,
    2004: 50-52

National Rifle Association, 11250 Waples Mill Road, Fairfax,
    VA., 22030, www.nra.org

Markel, Paul, "Under Fire-Your Move," Combat Handguns,
    November 2003: 16-95

McFarland, John, P., "Home Defense Alert," Combat Handguns,
    March 2004: 58-59

Quigley, Paxton, *Armed & Female*, St. Martin's Press, 1990

Quigley, Paxton, *Not An Easy Target: Paxton Quigley's Self-
    Protection for Women*, Simon & Schuster, 1995

Rauche, Walt, *Practically Speaking: An Illustrated Guide: The
    Game, Guns and Gear of the International Defensive
    Pistol Association with Real-World Applications*, Raunch
    and Company, 2004

Riley, Glenda, *The Life and Legacy of Annie Oakley*, Oklahoma

Press, 1994

Second Amendment Foundation, 267 Linwood Avenue, P.O. Box 488, Buffalo, NY, 14309

Second Amendment Sisters, 900 R.R. 620 S, Suite C-101, Box 228, Lakeway, TX, 78734

Silk & Steel Foundation, 1770 Bucks Hills Road, Southbury, CT, 06488

Single Action Shooting Society, 877-411-SASS, www.sassnet.com

Stange, Mary Zeiss, ed., *Heart Shots: Women Write About Hunting*, Stackpole Books, 2003

Stange, Mary Zeiss, Oyster Carol K., *Gun Women: Firearms and Feminism In Contemporary America,* New York University Press, 2000

Students for the Second Amendment, 12911 Vidorra Circle, Dept. WG, San Antonio, TX, 78245, www.sf2a.org

Wilson, R.L., *Silk And Steel: Women at Arms,* Random House, 2003

Woman's Outlook, National Rifle Association, P.O. Box 420648, Palm Coast, FL, 32142

Women & Guns, P.O. Box 488, Buffalo, NY., 14209, 716-885-6408

Zelman, Aaron, Stevens Richard W., *Death By "Gun Control:" The Human Cost of Victim Disarmament,* Mazel Freedom Press, Inc., 2001

WOULD YOU LIKE MORE COPIES OF
STAYIN' ALIVE
ARMED & FEMALE IN AN UNSAFE WORLD

JUST MAIL IN OUR SIMPLE-TO-USE FORM HERE TO
ORDER MORE COPIES!

-OR-

CALL (425) 454-7009

DISCOUNT SCHEDULE

1 COPY	$15.00	25 COPIES	$250.00
5 COPIES	$67.00	50 COPIES	$425.00
10 COPIES	$120.00	100 COPIES	$800.00

Merril Press
P.O. Box 1682
Bellevue, WA 98009

Please send me_____copies of Stayin' Alive.
Enclosed is my check or money order in the amount of
$_____.

-OR-

Please charge my: ☐Visa ☐Mastercard ☐AMEX ☐Discover

Number: _____**Expires:** _____

Signature:_____

Print Name:_____

Street:_____

City: _____   **State:** _____

Zip:_____   **Phone:** (_____)_____

111

POLITICALLY CORRECT GUNS...

is a take-no-prisoners invasion of the Gun Control crowd's territory, lobbying humor grenades at their hypocrisy, bombing their misplaces zeal with cleaver vignettes, and surrounding their antigun rhetoric with such pointed parody that even Gun-Banner Bill Clinton will have to laugh at himself.

Alan Gottlieb has done it again-defending our gun rights with wits and facts, this time with some really strange but true stories.

This hilarious parody of gun control is filled with political cartoons and gags, but hitting home a serious point about the individual right to keep and bear arms. It exposes the hypocrisy of the elite who want armed guards for themselves but no weapons for you. **Just mail in our simple-to-use form here to order copies, or call: (425) 454-7009.**

DISCOUNT SCHEDULE

1 COPY	$14.95	25 COPIES	$250.00
5 COPIES	$67.00	50 COPIES	$425.00
10 COPIES	$120.00	100 COPIES	$800.00

Please send me_____copies of *Politically Correct Guns.* Enclosed is my check or money order in the amount of $_____.

Please charge my: ☐Visa ☐Mastercard ☐AMEX ☐Discover

Number: _____**Expires:** _____

Signature:_____

Print Name: _____

Street: _____

City: _____ **State:** _____ **Zip:**_____

Phone: (_____)_____

Mail to: Merril Press, PO Box 1682, Bellevue, WA., 98009

Politically Correct Hunting

An irreverent romp through the world of hunting, poking a little fun at hunters and a lot of fun at their animal rights opponents. Posing as an alphabetical dictionary of

hunting lore, Politically Correct Hunting dispenses jokes, tall tales and homey wisdom.

As Jim Zumbo, Editor of Outdoor Life, says: "Politically Correct Hunting is a fun book that should be on every hunter's night-stand. Ken Jacobson's wit will keep you amused, informed and entertained. This book is loaded with tips, jokes and some downright good philosophy."

Just mail in our simple-to-use form here to order copies, or call: (425) 454-7009. Mail to: Merril Press, PO Box 1682, Bellevue, WA 98009:

THE HANDGUN IN PERSONAL DEFENSE

This new book's author, Robert K. Campbell, grew up with handguns as a way of life. Twenty-three years of police experience gave Campbell practical insight into the handgun's role. With a degree in Criminal Justice, this staunch supporter of citizens' rights was well armed to produce this insightful handbook for owning a handgun. Campbell shares his knowledge in *Handgun,* from information on the top handguns to how to drill for a terrorist raid.

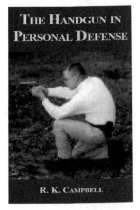

In addition to authoring *The Handgun in Personal Defense*, Campbell is well-published in the firearms, police and outdoors field. Some magazines you might see him in are *SWAT Magazine, Shotgun News, American Gunsmith, Krause's Handguns, Gun Digest* and *Shooters Bible.* Campbell also works as a contributing editor at *Women & Guns* and also *Gun Week*, two of the most important publications in the firearms field.

Just mail in our form here to order, or call: (425) 454-7009.

- -

DISCOUNT SCHEDULE

1 COPY	$15.00	25 COPIES	$250.00
5 COPIES	$67.00	50 COPIES	$425.00
10 COPIES	$120.00	100 COPIES	$800.00

Please send me_____copies of *The Personal Handgun in Self-defense.*

Enclosed is my check or money order in the amount of $_____.

Please charge my: ☐Visa ☐Mastercard ☐AMEX ☐Discover

Number: _____Expires: _____

Signature:_____

Print Name: _____

Street: _____

City: _____ State: _____ Zip:_____

Phone: (_____)_____

PETA FILES
The Dark Side of the Animal Rights
Movement

ights
what
d the
ence,
tens
ople
ad-
an."

"(He
radica
what
are jus
nificar
Radio

d the
n for
eans
sig-
KVI

To o   *our*
simpl   *009.*

Pleas   *Side*
of the
Enclo   f
$_____
Please   er

Num

Sign

Print

Stree

City: _____ State: _____ Zip:_____

Phone: (_____)_____

Mail to: Merril Press, PO Box 1682, Bellevue, WA 98009